INFRASTRUCTURES IN PRACTICE

Infrastructures in Practice shows how infrastructures and daily life shape each other. Power grids, roads and broadband make modern lifestyles possible – at the same time, their design and day-to-day operation depends on what people do at home and at work. This volume investigates the entanglement of supply and demand. It explains how standards and 'normal' ways of living have changed over time and how infrastructures have changed with them. Studies of grid expansion and disruption, heating systems, the internet, urban planning and office standards, smart meters and demand management reveal this dynamic interdependence.

This is the first book to examine the interdependence between infrastructures and the practices of daily life. It offers an analysis of how new technologies, lifestyles and standards become normalised and fall out of use. It brings together diverse disciplines – history, sociology, science studies – to develop social theories and accounts of how infrastructures and practices constitute each other at different scales and over time. It shows how networks and demands are steered and shaped, and how social and political visions are woven into infrastructures, past, present and future.

Original, wide-ranging and theoretically informed, this book puts the many practices of daily life back into the study of infrastructures. The result is a fresh understanding of how resource-intensive forms of consumption and energy demand have come about and what is needed to move towards a more sustainable lower carbon future.

Elizabeth Shove is Professor of Sociology at Lancaster University and Principal Investigator of the DEMAND Centre (Dynamics of Energy, Mobility and Demand), funded by the Research Councils, UK. She has written about the dynamics of social practice, infrastructures, material culture and consumption including: *The Dynamics of Social Practice: Everyday Life and How It Changes* with Mika Pantzar and Matt Watson (Sage, 2012) and *The Nexus of Practices: Connections, Constellations and Practitioners*, edited with Allison Hui and Theodore Schatzki (Routledge, 2017).

Frank Trentmann is Professor of History at Birkbeck College, University of London, and also at the Consumer Society Research Centre, University of Helsinki. He was the Principal Investigator (PI) of the 'Material Cultures of Energy' project funded by the Arts and Humanities Research Council, UK and is also a member of the research centre DEMAND. His latest book is *Empire of Things: How We Became a World of Consumers, from the Fifteenth Century to the Twenty-First* (Penguin, 2016) with several foreign translations.

INFRASTRUCTURES IN PRACTICE

The Dynamics of Demand in Networked Societies

Edited by Elizabeth Shove and Frank Trentmann

Routledge
Taylor & Francis Group

LONDON AND NEW YORK

First published 2019
by Routledge
2 Park Square, Milton Park, Abingdon, Oxon OX14 4RN

and by Routledge
711 Third Avenue, New York, NY 10017

Routledge is an imprint of the Taylor & Francis Group, an informa business

British Library Cataloguing-in-Publication Data
A catalogue record for this book is available from the British Library

Library of Congress Cataloging-in-Publication Data
Names: Shove, Elizabeth, 1959- editor. | Trentmann, Frank, editor.
Title: Infrastructures in practice: the dynamics of demand in networked
societies / edited by Elizabeth Shove and Frank Trentmann.
Description: Abingdon, Oxon; New York, NY: Routledge, 2019.
Identifiers: LCCN 2018025196| ISBN 9781138476042 (hardback) |
ISBN 9781138476165 (pbk.) | ISBN 9781351106177 (ebook)
Subjects: LCSH: Infrastructure (Economics) | Municipal services. |
Sustainable urban development. | City planning–Environmental aspects.
Classification: LCC HC79.C3 I5254 2019 | DDC 363.6–dc23
LC record available at https://lccn.loc.gov/2018025196

ISBN: 978-1-138-47604-2 (hbk)
ISBN: 978-1-138-47616-5 (pbk)
ISBN: 978-1-351-10617-7 (ebk)

Typeset in Bembo
by Deanta Global Publishing Services, Chennai, India

Printed and bound in Great Britain by
TJ International Ltd, Padstow, Cornwall

CONTENTS

FIGURES

TABLES

CONTRIBUTORS

Anna Carlsson-Hyslop was a Research Associate at the Sustainable Consumption Institute of the University of Manchester when writing this chapter. She is a historian of science and technology with expertise on British energy history. Her recent publications include: (2017) 'The evolution of energy demand in Britain: politics, daily life and public housing, 1920s–70s', *Historical Journal*, (with Trentmann, F.); (2016) 'Past management of energy demand: promotion and adoption of electric heating in Britain 1945–1964', *Environment and History*; and (2013) 'Governing transitions: cases and insights from two periods in the history of the UK gas industry', *Energy Policy*, (with Arapostathis, S., Pearson, P. J. G., Thornton, J., Gradillas, M., Laczay, S. and Wallis, S.).

Noel Cass is a Senior Research Associate in the Demand Centre at Lancaster University. He is an environmental sociologist with interests in energy systems (particularly the built environment and mobility). Recent publications include: (2017) 'Energy-related standards and UK speculative office development', *Building Research & Information*; and (2017) 'Satisfying everyday mobility', *Mobilities*, (with Faulconbridge, J.).

Heather Chappells is an Associate Lecturer at the University of British Columbia, Vancouver. She is an interdisciplinary social scientist with expertise on the sustainable dynamics of energy and water systems and practices. Her publications include: (2012) 'Resilience in practice: the 2006 drought in Southeast England', *Society and Natural Resources*, (with Medd, W.); and (2011) 'Disruption and change: drought and the inconspicuous dynamics of garden lives', *Social and Cultural Geography*, (with Shove, E. and Medd, W.) .

John Connaughton is a Professor of Sustainable Construction in the School of Construction Management and Engineering at the University of Reading. He is a chartered surveyor and was formerly a partner of Davis Langdon (now AECOM), a leading construction consultancy. His research interests include the construction professions and professional practice, energy use in buildings and improving the construction process.

Olivier Coutard is a full-time Senior Researcher with the French National Centre for Scientific Research (CNRS) and former Director of LATTS (https://latts.fr/). He is researching the governance of urban infrastructure services (water and energy supply, telecommunications, urban transportation), reforms in those sectors and their social, spatial and environmental implications. He is the editor or co-editor of: *The Governance of Large Technical Systems* (Routledge, 1999); *Sustaining Urban Networks* (with Hanley, R. and Zimmerman, R., Routledge, 2005); (2014) 'Urban energy transitions: places, processes and politics of socio-technical change', *Urban Studies*, (with Rutherford, J.); and *Beyond the Networked City* (with Rutherford, J., Routledge, 2015).

Aude Danieli is a French Ph.D. candidate in sociology at LATTS (Territories, Societies, Techniques – Université Paris-Est and Ecole des Ponts-Paristech). Her research focuses on the recent modernisation of the electricity meter in France, and particularly on the societal conflicts provoked by changes in the electricity billing infrastructure. She has a strong interest in the innovation processes around the devices of measure and billing (from technical design process to professionals, activists and consumers uses) as interfaces between electricity companies and customers. Her research is based on empirical data (more than 135 interviews and observations) and an immersive research of more than four years within EDF Lab. Her publications include: « La « mise en société » du compteur communicant Linky », in *Pratiques sociales et usages de l'énergie* (Lavoisier, 2016).

James Faulconbridge is a Professor of Transnational Management at Lancaster University. He is an economic geographer by training, and is interested in professional work, including the way building design professionals develop the knowledge that informs their design decisions. His recent publications focus on how sustainable building design knowledges get made (*Transactions of the Institute of British Geographers*) and on the globalisation of sustainable building design knowledges (*Area*).

Catherine Grandclément is a Researcher at EDF R&D (Research Group on Energy, Technology and Society). A sociologist who studies the politics of energy demand from below, she investigates sites and objects such as energy efficient homes, smart meters and energy displays and the consumerisation of the kilowatt-hour. Her recent publications include: (Palgrave, in press) 'Transitioning through markets', (with Nadaï, A. et al.,) in *Energy Transitions: a socio-technical inquiry*; and (2015) 'Negotiating comfort in low energy housing: the politics of intermediation', *Energy Policy*, (with Karvonen, A. and Guy, S.).

Conor Harrison is an Assistant Professor in the Department of Geography and the Environment and Sustainability Program at the University of South Carolina. He is an economic geographer with expertise on the geographical political economy of electricity in United States and the Caribbean. His recent publications have examined the intersection of electrification, racism, and profitability in the context of the American South, as well as renewable energy transitions in small island developing states.

Charlotte Johnson is a Research Associate at the UCL Energy Institute. She is an anthropologist specialising in energy infrastructure and urban transitions. Her recent publications include: 'District heating as heterotopia: tracing the social contract through domestic energy infrastructure in Pimlico, London', *Economic Anthropology*; and 'The moral economy of comfortable living: negotiating individualism and collectivism through housing in Belgrade', *Critique of Anthropology*.

Fanny Lopez is an Associate Professor at the National School of Architecture (ENSA) city & territoires at Paris Marne-la-Vallée and a member of the Laboratory infrastructure architecture and territory (LIAT) at ENSA Paris-Malaquais. She is an historian of architecture and urbanism (Ph.D. University of Paris-I Panthéon Sorbonne), with expertise in environmental and energy questions. She recently publised *Le rêve d'une déconnexion, de la maison autonome à la cité auto-énergétique* (La Villette, 2014).

Janine Morley is a Senior Research Associate in the DEMAND Centre at Lancaster University. She is a sociologist who studies the relationships between everyday practices, infrastructures and resource-use, with particular expertise in domestic energy demand and information technologies. Her recent publications include: (2017) 'Technologies within and beyond practices, in Hui, A., Schatzki, T. and Shove, E. (eds.) *The Nexus of Practices: connections, constellations, practitioners*; and (2015) 'Demand in my pocket: mobile devices and the data connectivity marshalled in support of everyday life, (with Lord et al.,). Her Ph.D. thesis is entitled 'Diversity, dynamics and domestic energy demand: a study of variation in cooking, comfort and computing'.

Alain Nadaï is a Research Director at CIRED-CNRS (Paris). An interdisciplinary social-scientist, his focus is on the processes of energy transition, looking at the socio-technical construction of actors, spaces and entities in these processes. His recent publications include: (in press: Palgrave) *Energy Transitions: a socio-technical inquiry*, (eds. with Labussière, O.); 'French policy localism: surfing on "positive energie territories" (Tepos)', *Energy Policy*, (with Labussière, O. et al.), and; (2015) 'Wind power and the emergence of the Beauce landscape (Eure-et-Loir, France)', *Landscape Research*, (with Labussière, O.).

Magali Pierre works at EDF R&D in the social sciences research team GRETS (Groupe de recherche, Energie, Technologie et Société). She is a sociologist with expertise on the emerging market for electric vehicles, the charging infrastructure and the changes in the users' mobility system and in the fleet managers' organisation. Her recent publications include: (2015: KIT Scientific Publishing) 'How professional and private individuals use and charge their EV' (with Fulda, A. S.) in Schäuble J., Jochem, P. and Fichtner, W. (eds.) *Cross-border Mobility for Electric Vehicles,* and; (2011) 'Driving an electric vehicle. A sociological analysis on pioneer users', *Energy Efficiency*, (with Pierre, M., Jemelin, C. and Louvet, N.).

Jenny Rinkinen is Senior Research Associate in the DEMAND Centre at Lancaster University. She is a social scientist with expertise on theories of social practice, everyday life studies and renewable energy technologies. Her recent publications include: (2015) 'Object relations in accounts of everyday life', *Sociology*, and; (2016) 'Stacking wood and staying warm: time, temporality and housework around domestic heating systems', *Journal of Consumer Culture* (with Jalas, M.). Her Ph.D. thesis is entitled 'Demanding energy in everyday life: insights from wood heating into theories of social practice'.

Antti Silvast is a Research Associate at Durham University, working for the National Centre for Energy Systems Integration (CESI) and based in the Department of Anthropology. He is a sociologist with expertise on energy in society, large technological systems, and infrastructures. His recent publications include: (2014) 'Keeping systems at work: electricity infrastructure from control rooms to household practices', *Science & Technology Studies,* (with Virtanen, M.), and (2013) 'Energy in society: energy systems and infrastructures in society', *Science & Technology Studies*, (with Hänninen, H. and Hyysalo, S.).

Mattijs Smits is an Assistant Professor at the Environmental Policy group at Wageningen University and Research (the Netherlands). He is a human geographer interested in social practices, energy transitions, renewable energy policy and politics, development and carbon markets, both in the Global South and in the Global North. He is author of the book *Southeast Asian Energy Transitions: Between Modernity and Sustainability* (Routledge/Ashgate, 2015).

Nicola Spurling is a Lecturer at Lancaster University. Her background is in sociology and anthropology. Her research looks at the processes by which working lives, daily lives and everyday mobility have changed since 1950, and their implications for experiences of time, the products of social practices and energy demand. At present she is focused on the insights that such analyses offer to futures thinking. Recent publications include 'Interventions in practices', in Y. Strengers and C. Maller (eds.) (Routledge, 2015); and *Sustainable Practices: social Theory and Climate Change*, (eds. with Shove, E., Routledge, 2013).

Yolande Strengers is an Associate Professor at the Centre for Urban Research, RMIT University, Melbourne. She is a social scientist with research expertise spanning the disciplines of sociology, human-computer interaction design, and science and technology studies. Yolande has extensive experience researching how smart energy systems, demand management strategies and home automation shape everyday practices in residential settings. Recent publications include *Smart Energy Technologies in Everyday Life* (Palgrave Macmillan, 2013); and (2015) 'Curious energy consumers', *Journal of Consumer Culture*.

Matt Watson is a Senior Lecturer at the University of Sheffield. He is a human geographer with expertise in understanding the systemic relations between everyday practices, technologies, spaces and institutions to advance understandings of social change in relation to sustainability. Empirically, this work has encompassed energy, food, waste and personal mobility. His publications include: *The Dynamics of Social Practice* (with Shove, E. and Pantzar, M., Berg, 2012); and (2012) 'How theories of practice can inform transition to a decarbonised transport system', *Journal of Transport Geography*.

ACKNOWLEDGEMENTS

This work was supported by the Engineering and Physical Sciences Research Council (grant number EP/K011723/1) as part of the RCUK Energy Programme and by EDF as part of the R&D ECLEER Programme.

PART I
Evolving infrastructures

1

INTRODUCTION – INFRASTRUCTURES IN PRACTICE

The evolution of demand in networked societies

Elizabeth Shove, Frank Trentmann and Matt Watson

This book is about the connections between infrastructures and daily life. In modern societies, there are few social practices which do not depend on infrastructures in one way or another. Getting to work, having a daily shower, communicating with friends and family, cooking a meal and much else of what we do depends on power grids, water mains, broadband services and other networked features of the built environment.

On a global scale, these arrangements are responsible for massive and growing levels of energy consumption. According to the US Energy Information Association (2016), by 2040 total world consumption of marketed energy is expected to have increased by 48% from 2012. Worldwide internet use is also escalating: in '2017, there will be more internet traffic than all prior internet years combined' (Hosting Facts, 2016). These figures are indicative of the extensive and profound interdependencies between infrastructures and contemporary ways of life.

The aim of this book is to make these interdependencies visible and to chart their evolution – past, present and future. While few would dispute that infrastructures matter, the precise ways in which they enable, sustain or change what people do has attracted remarkably little thought and analysis. Ironically, the very triumph and ubiquity of infrastructures in modern industrial societies has made it difficult to see how their component parts intersect with the social practices which shape them and on which they depend. Pylons, pipes, wires, electric charging points, gas stations and grids – these can be physically imposing sights, but in the analysis of daily life, they might just as well be invisible.

In Western societies today, consumers routinely take infrastructures for granted despite the fact that without them, vital flows of people, goods and information would come to a standstill. Equally, infrastructure experts rarely trouble themselves to understand the many and varied social practices which create demand for infrastructures in the first place. Instead, providers and policy makers tend to treat the resources and requirements of 'modern life' as some underspecified, generalised need.

The chapters in this collection take issue with this collective amnesia and show that much can be learned by explicitly attending to how infrastructures and practices are woven together. Such analyses are vital to understand how modern societies came to operate the way they do. Such knowledge is not only about the past, however. It is just as critical for anyone who is seriously thinking about what infrastructures might look like in the future and how networked societies might confront coming challenges including climate change.

Conceptualising infrastructures in practice

In detailing the relations between infrastructures and practices, contributors draw on established bodies of work but move beyond them in critical ways. That demand has to be constructed alongside systems of provision and supply, for example, is not a new observation, especially not for those who have studied infrastructures-in-the-making and as sites of innovation, investment and system building. In his classic book, *Networks of Power* (1983), Thomas Hughes noted how important it was to establish the need for electricity alongside the means of producing and distributing it. At the same time, Hughes' analysis remained limited to the first step in a much bigger story of the making of demand. While his account of infrastructures crosses over the threshold of the home and considers the development and diffusion of powered appliances, the actual impact of these devices and of electric lights on daily routines in households and offices remains in the dark. To understand how people consumed energy, and how much energy they consumed, we surely need to know what people did with the resources provided. By bringing analyses of practices into discussions of infrastructures, this book makes a contribution to that larger story.

This emphasis on social practices – which are shared across space and time – sets our approach apart from those who concentrate on 'users'. Within science and technology studies, the 'user' is an important figure (Oudshoorn and Pinch, 2003; Hyysalo, Jensen and Oudshoorn, 2016), featuring as the necessary 'decoder' of artefacts and devices (Akrich, 1992; Silverstone, 1993; Suchman, 2007), and as the potential co-producer or co-designer of things in action. In the context of debates about sustainability, the 'prosumer' – part producer, part consumer – is similarly significant. Acknowledging that consumers have an active and not only passive part to play in the use of technologies is important. However, more is required to show how forms of infrastructural provision co-constitute 'needs' and practices, and to understand how these emerge and circulate (Shove, Pantzar and Watson, 2012). For example, a century and a half ago, taking a bath, let alone a daily shower, did not exist as a recognised practice in industrial societies. Today, the daily, or even twice daily shower is the dominant norm (*Health Science Journal*, 2016). What happened in between these moments is that infrastructures and practices spurred each other on and became entangled in a dynamic that simultaneously constitutes particular ways of life and related patterns of consumption.

Such examples force us to question conventional but all too easy distinctions between supply and demand and between technology and consumption. Rather than treating such categories as fixed or given we take a more fluid approach and define infrastructures as material arrangements that enable and become integral to the enactment of specific practices (Shove, 2017). This status is unavoidably provisional: the range of networks and systems that figure as 'infrastructures' changes as practices evolve. In following these processes and in showing how electric power becomes embedded in daily life, how car parking spaces facilitate driving and how wood stoves or central heating structure the rhythm of the day, contributors highlight forms of interaction and mutual shaping that are largely absent from policy analyses and from popular debates about present and future needs.

In developing these ideas, contributors challenge dominant and deeply held positions in economics and engineering. In economics, demand generally refers to the utility of goods or services for an individual or a company and is expressed in the price a buyer is willing to pay. There are situations in which such a definition makes sense but for an understanding of the demand for energy this line of thinking is rather unsatisfactory. A lot of energy consumption relates to practices that are routine and relatively immune to changes in price, unless these are catastrophic.

In engineering, demand is described and measured in standardised units: in thousand tonnes of oil equivalent (ktoe) or gigawatt and terawatt hours. Whilst national statistics provide useful snapshots of total energy use, they are silent about exactly what people were doing and hence about the different activities that make up aggregate demand. They are consequently unable to reveal the relationship between people, practices and products in the creation of demand across time and space.

Rather than assuming that the demand for the resources and services that infrastructures enable is 'out there', waiting to be met, contributors show that ideals and habits of 'normal' comfort, mobility and communication have changed greatly over time and diverge widely, including among societies enjoying similar levels of wealth and development. To give just a few illustrations, over recent decades, the norm of heating and cooling indoor spaces to around 22°C all year round has become widely established; the technologies and equipment of 'office work' have been transformed, and new mobile technologies are taking hold with varied consequences for what people do, when and where.

There is an established tradition of analysing transitions like these as instances of socio-technical regime change and of explaining how incoming technologies or fuels take the place of previous incumbents (Correlje and Verbong, 2004; Geels, 2005). Rather than characteris-ing 'innovation journeys' of this kind, contributors examine infrastructural changes as part of the shifting nexus of practices, hence their interest in links, tensions and ongoing forms of co-existence.

Investigating infrastructures in practice

The bonds between infrastructures and practices are not 'hard-wired' or fixed. Instead, it is more helpful to picture what Fine and Leopold (1993) call 'systems of provision', including the organisational routes through which goods and services are produced, distributed and delivered. These are not innocent arrangements. Rather, infrastructures are literally shaped by unequal contests over places, resources and rights (Graham and Marvin, 2001; Graham and McFarlane, 2014; Trentmann and Carlsson-Hyslop, 2017). The outcome of these struggles is, in turn, relevant for what services are provided, who has access to them and at what cost. Whilst the interests of city authorities and utilities do not always coincide, both are deeply involved in planning, constructing, reconfiguring and operating urban networks (Coutard and Rutherford, 2010). The chapters in this book take these ideas a step further, showing how the politics of provision connect with parallel developments in changing practices that are, in turn, integral to the co-evolution of demand.

This approach serves to highlight the ongoing transformation and the *variety* of infrastruc-ture–practice relations. In Western societies, the term 'infrastructure' conjures up images of centralised power systems, massive utility companies and huge investment projects, often under-written by the state. And for good reason: these have shaped the physical as well as institutional form of utility provision. However, other configurations have existed and are possible, too. Even in Western Europe, centralised, state-owned public systems represent but one chapter in a longer story which initially began mainly with private monopolies in the nineteenth century and has been moving back towards similarly fragmented, privatised models since the 1970s. Alongside such divisions of labour between state and market and between public utility and for-profit service providers the roles of consumer and provider are constantly on the move, generating tensions at every imaginable interface: between tenants, heat meters and heating providers in Belgrade (Johnson, 2018); between electricity consumers, smart meters, and electricity providers in France (Grandclément et al., 2018; Danieli, 2018); and between office workers, office infrastructures and standards of office design in the United Kingdom (Cass, Faulconbridge and Connaughton, 2018). As we show, even the most durable looking infrastructures require repair and even the most rugged have a restless existence, always depending on the continued enactment of the various practices on which demand for them depends.

Large-scale networked infrastructures do not just exist to cater for the present; they are also designed to meet anticipated future needs. At the time of writing the estimated cost of the controversial Hinkley Point C, the first of a new generation of nuclear power stations to be built in Britain, will be at least £18 billion ($24 billion) – the equivalent of 60% of what the British government spends in a year on transport and more than 50% of its spending on housing and the environment. Such enormous investment assumes that demand for electricity will continue to grow. But what if energy modellers and planners were to anticipate the opposite: a decline in energy intensive habits and practices? If they made different assumptions about need and demand, much of the British government's rationale for Hinkley Point C would disappear. In this as in other cases, infrastructural arrangements are much more than material artefacts, fixed in the here and now. They cast a shadow on the future, laying the foundations for daily practices in years and decades to come.

Questions about the politics, the varieties and the futures of infrastructural provision and practice run through the book as a whole. In addressing them, contributors combine empirical cases and disciplinary approaches situated at the intersection of social and historical studies of consumption and provision, science and technology studies, social theories of practice and schools of political economy and economic geography. Rather than seeking to include examples from all possible 'sectors' or from all parts of the world we have selected studies that illuminate a wide range of configurations and processes through which resources, infrastructures, appliances and practices cohere and change. The variety of historical periods discussed and the juxtaposition of chapters based on archival analysis, interview-based research and participant observation adds to the richness of the work and allows us to showcase the value of different sources and methodological approaches.

The structure of the book

The book is divided into five parts linked by mini-introductions, which guide the reader through the chapters and explain how each contributes to the core themes on which we focus. In Part I, 'Evolving infrastructures', we introduce guiding questions and terms of analysis and provide a critical overview of how infrastructures and practices intersect at different scales (Coutard and Shove, 2018). Subsequent chapters develop this conceptual framework in different ways.

Part II, 'Varieties of infrastructures', gives a sense of the diversity of infrastructure-practice configurations. The first two chapters highlight the practicalities of provision, detailing the development of electric wiring in the USA (Harrison, 2018), and more recently in Thailand

and Laos (Smits, 2018). The next pair consider issues of scale, examining localised and networked 'infrastructures' of wood-based heating (Rinkinen, 2018), and reviewing architectural debates about self-sufficiency in the Western world (Lopez, 2018). In combination these cases and examples provide fresh insight into the intersection of multiple systems and scales of provision, and into the varied routes through which infrastructures are woven into the temporalities of social life as well as the politics of provision.

Part III, 'Standards, planning, adaptation', investigates the key processes through which infrastructural arrangements take the shape they do: exactly how are infrastructures designed and modified, and how are expectations of service and practice folded into systems and technologies of provision? The chapters in this section look at the role of 'standards' in office buildings (Cass, Faulconbridge and Connaughton, 2018), the planning process in new towns (Spurling, 2018), the erratic history of central heating in the UK (Carlsson-Hyslop, 2018), the shifting politics of district heating in Belgrade (Johnson, 2018), and the emergence of the internet (Morley, 2018). Together these chapters show how formal procedures, voluntary standards and emerging conventions define and shape infrastructures, and how these, in turn, are implicated in the normalisation of changing and often escalating expectations of service.

Part IV, 'Drawing boundaries and managing networks', focuses on the roles and responsibilities accorded to the state, planners/designers and the market in making and managing infrastructural relations. In this section, case studies of the electric vehicle market and the 'smart' electric meter (Grandclément et al., 2018; Danieli, 2018) reveal contemporary uncertainty, innovation and change at the point at which consumers and providers meet. Studying these especially sensitive interfaces shows how infrastructures are implicated in the reproduction and reshaping of social categories and divisions, and vice versa.

Part V, 'Steering, managing and disrupting demand', takes a closer look at deliberate efforts to shape and manage infrastructure-practice relations, now and in the future. Chapters in this section examine efforts to balance supply and demand in real time (Silvast, 2018); via prices and tariffs (Strengers, 2018), and in times of nation-wide disruption and crisis (Chappells and Trentmann, 2018). As well as situating infrastructures and their management within and as part of more extensive social and political relations, these chapters highlight the malleability of supply-demand relations, and the flexibility of energy-demanding practices, past, present and future.

And it is to the future that the book's final chapter turns. From what we have learned about the evolution of demand in networked societies, it is clear that although certain infrastructures are massive, expensive and extensive, they are never stable. Instead, they are subject to multiple forms of boundary making, contestation and ongoing negotiation. Given the need to reduce carbon emissions, the question is whether conjunctions of infrastructures and practices might be deliberately steered in a more sustainable direction, and if so, how and how far. That question leads to others about how deeply or irreversibly systems and expectations of universal, 'always on' provision have penetrated the fabric of daily life. Since future infrastructures are being made today, we emphasise the importance of analysing and challenging visions and interpretations of 'normal' practices inscribed in seemingly innocuous models, plans and targets.

References

Akrich, M. (1992) 'The de-scription of technical objects', in Bijker, W. and Law. J. (eds.) *Shaping Technology/Building Society*. Cambridge: MIT Press.

Carlsson-Hyslop, A. (2018) 'The construction of central heating in Britain', in Shove, E. and Trentmann, F. (eds.) *Infrastructures in Practices: the dynamics of demand in networked societies*. London: Routledge.

Cass, N., Faulconbridge, J. and Connaughton, J. (2018) 'The office: how standards define "normal" design practices and work infrastructures', in Shove, E. and Trentmann, F. (eds.) *Infrastructures in Practices: the dynamics of demand in networked societies*. London: Routledge.

Chappells, H. and Trentmann, F. (2018) 'Disruption in and across time', in Shove, E. and Trentmann, F. (eds.) *Infrastructures in Practices: the dynamics of demand in networked societies*. London: Routledge.

Correlje, A. and Verbong, G. (2004) 'The transition from coal to gas: radical change of the Dutch gas system', in Elzen, B., Geels, F. W. and Green, K. (eds.) *System Innovation and the Transition to Sustainability*. Cheltenham: Elgar. pp. 114–136.

Coutard, O. and Rutherford, J. (2010) 'The rise of post-networked cities in Europe? Recombining infrastructural, ecological and urban transformations in low carbon transitions', in Bulkeley, H. et al., (eds.) *Cities and Low Carbon Transitions*. London: Routledge. pp. 107–126.

Coutard, O. and Shove, E. (2018) 'Infrastructures, practices and the dynamics of demand', in Shove, E. and Trentmann, F. (eds.) *Infrastructures in Practices: the dynamics of demand in networked societies*. London: Routledge.

Danieli, A. (2018) 'The French electricity smart meter: reconfiguring consumers and providers', in Shove, E. and Trentmann, F. (eds.) *Infrastructures in Practices: the dynamics of demand in networked societies*. London: Routledge.

Fine, B. and Leopold, E. (1993) *The World of Consumption*. London: Routledge.

Geels, F. W. (2005) *Technological Transitions and System Innovations: a co-evolutionary and socio-technical analysis*. Cheltenham: Elgar. Northampton, MA, Edward Elgar Pub.

Graham, S. and Marvin, S. (2001) *Splintering Urbanism: networked infrastructures, technological mobilities and the urban condition*. London: Routledge.

Graham, S. and McFarlane, C. (2014) 'Introduction', in *Infrastructural Lives: urban infrastructure in context*. London: Routledge. pp. 1–13.

Grandclément, C., Pierre, M., Shove, E. and Nadaï, A. (2018) 'Contentious interfaces: exploring the junction between collective provision and individual consumption', in Shove, E. and Trentmann, F. (eds.) *Infrastructures in Practices: the dynamics of demand in networked societies*. London: Routledge.

Harrison, C. (2018) 'Wires', in Shove, E. and Trentmann, F. (eds.) *Infrastructures in Practices: the dynamics of demand in networked societies*. London: Routledge.

Health Science Journal (2016) 'Shower every day, science says …' Available at: www.thehealthsciencejournal. com/shower-every-day-science-says/ (Accessed 29.08.16.).

Hosting Facts (2016) 'Internet facts and statistics'. Available at: https://hostingfacts.com/internet-facts-stats-2016/ (Accessed 15.08.16).

Hughes, T. P. (1983) *Networks of Power: electrification in Western society, 1880–1930*. Baltimore; London: Johns Hopkins University Press.

Hyysalo, S., Jensen, T. E. and Oudshoorn, N. (2016) *The New Production of Users: changing innovation collectives and involvement strategies*. London: Routledge.

Johnson, C. (2018) 'District heating in Belgrade: the politics of provision', in Shove, E. and Trentmann, F. (eds.) *Infrastructures in Practices: the dynamics of demand in networked societies*. London: Routledge.

Lopez, F. (2018) 'Self-sufficiency in architectural and urban projects: towards small-pipe engineering', in Shove, E. and Trentmann, F. (eds.) *Infrastructures in Practices: the dynamics of demand in networked societies*. London: Routledge.

Morley, J. (2018) 'Unleashing the internet: the normalisation of wireless connectivity', in Shove, E. and Trentmann, F. (eds.) *Infrastructures in Practices: the dynamics of demand in networked societies*. London: Routledge.

Oudshoorn, N. and Pinch, T. J. (2003) *How Users Matter: the co-construction of users and technologies*. Cambridge, MA: MIT Press.

Rinkinen, J. (2018) 'Chopping, stacking and burning wood: rhythms and variations across practice', in Shove, E. and Trentmann, F. (eds.) *Infrastructures in Practices: the dynamics of demand in networked societies*. London: Routledge.

Shove, E. (2017) 'Matters of practice', in Hui, A., Schatzki, T. and Shove, E. (eds.) *The Nexus of Practices: connections, constellations, practitioners*. London: Routledge. pp. 155–168.

Shove, E., Pantzar, M. and Watson, M. (2012) *The Dynamics of Social Practice: everyday life and how it changes*. London: Sage.

Silvast, A. (2018) 'Co-constituting supply and demand: managing electricity in two neighbouring control rooms', in Shove, E. and Trentmann, F. (eds.) *Infrastructures in Practices: the dynamics of demand in networked societies*. London: Routledge.

Silverstone, R. (1993) 'Time, information and communication technologies and the household', *Time and Society*, 2(3): 283–311.

Smits, M. (2018) 'Situating electrification: examples of infrastructure-practice dynamics from Thailand and Laos', in Shove, E. and Trentmann, F. (eds.) *Infrastructures in Practices: the dynamics of demand in networked societies*. London: Routledge.

Spurling, N. (2018) 'Making space for the car at home: planning, priorities and practices', in Shove, E. and Trentmann, F. (eds.) *Infrastructures in Practices: the dynamics of demand in networked societies*. London: Routledge.

Strengers, Y. (2018) 'Prices as instruments of demand management: interpreting the signals', in Shove, E. and Trentmann, F. (eds.) *Infrastructures in Practices: the dynamics of demand in networked societies*. London: Routledge.

Suchman, L. (2007) *Human-machine Reconfigurations: plans and situated actions*. Cambridge: Cambridge University Press.

Trentmann, F. and Carlsson-Hyslop, A. (2017) 'The evolution of energy demand in Britain: politics, daily life, and public housing, 1920s–1970s', *Historical Journal*, 1–33.

US Energy Information Administration (2016) 'International energy outlook'. Available at: www.eia.gov/forecasts/ieo/world.cfm (Accessed 15.06.16).

2

INFRASTRUCTURES, PRACTICES AND THE DYNAMICS OF DEMAND

Olivier Coutard and Elizabeth Shove

Introduction

In this chapter we challenge mainstream policy and engineering approaches which suppose that consumers' needs for resources such as energy, water or data precede the development of infrastructures, and that the task of governments and firms alike is to predict (or uncover) and provide for these needs. Instead, we contend that infrastructures, the social practices they sustain, the devices and appliances involved and the patterns of demand that follow are interlinked and that they mutually influence each other. To give a very simple example, being connected to an electricity grid enables people to engage in a multitude of power-dependent practices and hence supports the reproduction of these practices and the energy they call for, in turn justifying the development, perpetual extension and continuous operation of relevant electricity supply infrastructures. Despite this interweaving, academic and policy discourses routinely split matters of supply and demand apart, treating each as separate sites of enquiry and intervention. Discussions about how to improve efficiency are consequently divorced from an understanding of how practices such as those relating to heating, cleaning, cooking, personal care or communication develop. Similarly, debates regarding the growth of complex networked infrastructures (Hughes, 1983; Mayntz and Hughes, 1988) or of 'post-networked' cities (Bulkeley et al., 2013; Coutard and Rutherford, 2013, 2016) take place aside from parallel theories of consumption and from accounts of how complexes of social practice emerge and disappear (Shove, Pantzar and Watson, 2012). Within science and technology studies, infrastructures remain a core topic of concern, but often with an emphasis on infrastructures in the making or as carriers of social and institutional politics and values (Star, 1999). As a result, there is relatively little analysis, and hence understanding, of exactly how infrastructures, appliances and practices co-evolve.

We argue that such analysis is essential for understanding why demands for energy, water or data have historically tended to increase with the development of large networks and how they might decline in the future. In developing such an approach, we describe three ideal-typical configurations: one associated with ever-expanding infrastructures, growing resource consumption and increasingly demanding practices; the second with modified and sometimes shrinking infrastructures that sustain and stabilise current practices, but that do so more efficiently and with fewer resources than before; and the third implying more or less radical changes in practices that entail or that are associated with more or less radical disconnection from some – typically, electricity – but not all (typically, not the internet) infrastructures viewed as being essential to the reproduction of everyday life in old-industrialised Western societies.

We first outline and elaborate upon the proposition that infrastructures and practices mutually shape each other in contingent and variegated ways. We then examine the three ideal-typical configurations and discuss how infrastructure-practice relations play out in each case. We end by commenting on the scope for engendering arrangements that would be much less carbon-intensive than those with which we are familiar today.

Conceptualising infrastructural configurations

Our approach is informed by a handful of concepts drawn from social theories of practice and from theories of materiality and of networked systems. We build on four related ideas and observations. First, we argue that, rather than simply meeting pre-existing needs, infrastructures shape relations between practices, material artefacts and related concepts of service (e.g., of comfort, convenience) in time and space; reciprocally, established practices shape and sustain specific infrastructural configurations. Second, we emphasise that infrastructures are multi-purpose: they enable many practices at once. Equally, many practices involve the simultaneous or sequential use of several infrastructures: for example, taking a shower typically requires (usually grid-supplied) energy, piped, pressurised water and a connection to a sewer system (or septic tank). Third, this enabling is always mediated by appliances of one kind or another, for example, people do not 'use' electricity in some raw form. Instead, demand happens when electrically powered devices or material arrangements become integral to the conduct of specific practices. Needs and demands for power or for other resources such as water or data are not abstract; they are formulated in relation to social practices enacted at particular places and times (Shove and Walker, 2014). Fourth, as networks become an essential part of cooking, lighting, computing or heating, etc., the need for reliable supply becomes multiply embedded and increasingly important in daily life (Nye, 2010), giving rise to new forms of network dependence. As a consequence of these four features, infrastructures, appliances and practices co-evolve over time.

From this point of view, the extent and timing of *resource consumption* is a consequence of the range of resource-demanding practices: of when, by whom and on what scale they are enacted and the relative efficiency of the devices and appliances involved. As others have observed (including Kline (2000) who studied 'technology and social change in rural America' in the first half of the twentieth century), appliances like freezers, showers and computers have a critical role in mediating between the infrastructures and networked systems of provision that bring power to the socket, water to the tap or data to the port and the ongoing conduct of specific practices.

As Kline (2000) convincingly argues, rural Americans' increased use of electricity was not the result of some spontaneous acknowledgment of the superiority of electricity over other sources of energy. Rather, it was the outcome of an active process of promotion and domestication of electric appliances with many remarkable successes and some spectacular failures in a context in which electricity as a source of energy was, at least initially, highly contested.

The diffusion of network-dependent appliances – that is, appliances using grid electricity, tap water or telephone lines – have helped to foster the emergence, the reproduction and the reinforcement of modern domestic standards of comfort, convenience, cleanliness and communication. To achieve this result, appliances draw power, data and even water and convert them into *services* which become central to the conduct of daily life. This takes different forms. Consider electricity supply. In some cases, the need for grid-supplied power arises from a process of delegation typically from a human (or from human labour) to an appliance. This is, for instance, the case with laundry, many aspects of which are now undertaken by a machine, which, incidentally, also requires pressurised water supply. Many other practices (mowing, drilling, hoovering, trimming one's beard or hair) have come to depend on the use of powered rather than hand-operated devices. Electrification is often, but not always, associated with the provision of additional features – as when telephones become cordless or linked to an answer-phone or when doors are held in place by electronic or electromagnetic locks. In some of these situations, powered variants enable (and reflect) the emergence of new practices. For example, fridges and freezers have had a critical role in transforming systems of food provisioning and feeding/eating practices within and beyond the home (Rees, 2013). In addition, some, but not all of these practices and appliances have no 'unpowered' prehistory. As these various examples suggest, there are significant differences in *how* powered technologies have (re)constituted practices and *when*, in the life of a practice, this (re)shaping occurs.

As processes of co-development or co-evolution of infrastructures and practices take hold, the reliability of supply becomes an important dimension, even a condition, of contemporary *dependence* on networked systems. Indeed, as a system becomes more reliable and taken for granted, additional uses of the system (or the connection of new appliances), often requiring high reliability of supply, are facilitated, hence increasing dependence as people (as practitioners) are bound into certain *infrastructural/technological systems* and into sets of *institutional relations* that surround and constitute the process of 'using' electricity today.

As outlined above, attending to the relation between infrastructures, appliances and practices depends – at a minimum – on paying simultaneous attention to the form of infrastructural provision, the range and design of intermediating appliances, their role in the conduct of different practices and the relation between consumers and relevant institutions and systems of provision. In the rest of the chapter, we use these ideas to structure an account of three infrastructure-practice configurations (summarised in Table 2.1). But before going further, and to avoid misunderstanding, we add a cautionary note: in taking this approach, our aim is to distil and describe features of the relation between infrastructure and practice that appear to be relevant and important for a discussion of the emergence, persistence and possible decline of demand. Although we refer to a handful of empirical cases, these have an illustrative role in what is an essentially conceptual, and at times speculative, exercise.[1]

Extending infrastructures: transforming practices and increasing demand for resources

The historical development of large infrastructure systems in Western societies appears to follow a common pattern of escalating demand, increasing the value of services and/or decreasing unit costs of provision. The details vary, reflecting the specific combination of economies of scale, scope and club inherent to the network technologies deployed, but the

TABLE 2.1 Three ideal-types of infrastructure-practice configuration

Types of configuration	1. Extending infrastructures	2. Adapting or shrinking infrastructures	3. Reconfiguring infrastructures, appliances and practices
Dimensions of configuration	Introducing network-dependent appliances; establishing increasingly resource-demanding practices and supporting the extension of these practices; increasing resource consumption.	Introducing efficient appliances; perpetuating current resource-demanding practices; stabilising or decreasing resource consumption.	Entailing alternative forms of resource supply; sustaining and co-producing different practices in time and space; drastically reducing resource consumption.
Infrastructural provision	Supply/design/investment is predicated on increasing resource demand: predict and provide; which in turn facilitates, even causes, increase in demand.	Does not suppose growth in resource demand: less resource is needed to deliver valued services (because of improved/increased resource efficiency).	Different forms are possible. Examples could include self-supply of energy (and water); often intermittent access to the internet (and the telephone); valued practices entail minimal use of resources.
Focus of utilities/ providers, business model	Selling volumes.	Selling volumes and services, including resource-efficiency services that reduce the demand for volumes; diversification and/or territorial expansion of utility providers.	Potentially irrelevant, there could be diverse forms and institutions of provision.
Network dependent appliances	Proliferation, diversification, becoming embedded in many practices/enabling new practices that generate demand.	Behind the scenes efficiency, unchanging level of service, aim to reproduce current practices, compensation of demand growth in some areas (e.g., computing, communications) by decline in others (e.g., heating).	Devices might include hand-powered appliances; appliances that use very little energy or water or that involve the reuse of resources as part of reproducing 'low carbon' practices.
Relation between social practices and networks	Widespread diffusion of network-dependent practices, generating new meanings, technologies, competencies and daily rhythms.	No change to already power-, pressurised water- or electronic communication-dependent practices.	Different practices in time and space with regard to comfort, convenience, cleanliness, communication/connection (limited lighting and heating; intermittent communication, etc.).
Relation between consumers and the process of provision	Providers require little of consumers: relations are mediated by meters, bills, etc. Production of network-supplied resources is remote.	Providers require little of consumers: relations are mediated by meters, bills, etc. Production of network-supplied resources is remote.	Provision requires time, work, skills and involvement from consumers. Production of some of the necessary resources might be local.
Demand for resources	Ever increasing.	Shrinking – up to a point.	Reducing and remaining at low level.

prevailing idea is that infrastructures develop to meet pre-existing needs. This is at odds with the fact that those involved in making 'big' networks and systems of water, power or communications are also actively involved in building demand on a correspondingly massive scale. As writers like Forty (1986) or Kline (2000) have shown, the need for electricity or other networked technologies does not exist in the abstract, nor is consumption simply determined by availability, accessibility and affordability. Rather, it is an outcome of complex processes of demand-making and reciprocal influence between supply and demand, in which network-connected appliances and devices become available, accessible, affordable, desirable and then embedded in multiple social practices and hence in the conduct of daily life.

Strategies like those of predict and provide – in which planners anticipate future 'need' and build capacity capable of meeting it – have acted as self-fulfilling prophecies: generating the very forms of demand to which investments and infrastructures are allegedly a response. The history of energy supply and of related domestic appliances provides ample evidence of this, as illustrated in the following examples.

Consider, first, the early development of the domestic use of gas in Paris from the late 1880s (see Chatzis and Coutard (2005) for a more detailed account). In less than two decades, the proportion of Parisian dwellings equipped with gas supplies jumped from barely 5% in 1888 to two thirds in 1905 (Berlanstein, 1991: 52). The main driving force behind this massive expansion of gas supply was the competitive threat created by the development of electricity. After the first experiments with electrical street lighting in Paris, the same very rich Parisians and the same trendy department stores that had promoted gas lighting over oil lamps turned to electricity. The Parisian Gas Company (PGC) management was soon convinced that its future rested on the growth of its domestic market. The PGC's first major commercial move occurred in 1887:

> [That year], the company reached out to the sixty-five thousand apartment dwellers, almost all in luxury buildings, whose residences were near a mounted main. Management did so by offering to install at its expense the internal pipes, a kitchen lighting fixture, and a stove. ... By 1905, 137,000 new customers had accepted the offer of free installation of fixtures. ... Hardly any apartment that rented for more than five hundred francs was without gas.
>
> *(Berlanstein, 1991: 55–56)*

But this first offer, because it was limited to a minority of the population, was not in itself enough to turn gas into a mass consumption commodity. This was to be achieved by the second commercial step taken by PGC:

> With the prodding of city hall, the company took the monumental step of democratising gas use in 1894. It created the fee-free program: residents of apartments renting for less than five hundred francs annually would not have to pay for the installation of pipes, the rental of a meter or upkeep of equipment. Eventually, the company even excused them from leaving a deposit. ... Eighty percent of the new customers after 1894 came to the PGC as a result of the policy. Fee-free customers also accounted for 80 percent of the growth in gas consumption after 1895.
>
> *(Berlanstein, 1991: 56)*

Another example of how demand is actively produced is provided by studies of rural electrification in the United States in the inter-war period when networked electricity supply was being developed. In the United States (as in other Western societies), home economists, also known as home electrification specialists, were hired by utility companies and public electrification bodies. These agents were charged with the mission of 'pushing electricity' (Kline, 2000: 178). The progressive engineer Morris Cooke, the architect of the US Rural Electrification Agency (REA), remarked in 1935, as quoted by Kline, that

> our big job is to build up the psychology of the generous use of electricity – a few lights in a home is not rural electrification. … Really to electrify rural America we must adopt every possible means for building up its use.
>
> *(Kline, 2000: 178)*

In order to promote the use of electricity in activities on the farm, the US Rural Electrification Agency organised a 'Farm Equipment Tour' from 1938 to 1941. The 'REA Circus', as it was informally called, is described by Kline (2000: 181) as the REA's Utilisation Division 'major promotional effort'. In the Tour,

> male agricultural engineers demonstrated water pumps, milking machines, milk coolers, feed grinders, ensilage cutters, corn shellers, chicken brooders, soil-heating cables, safe wiring, household plumbing, and such novel devices as a rotating drum with rubber 'fingers' that plucked chicken – a popular attraction. Female home economists demonstrated household lighting, 'efficient' kitchen arrangements, and electric refrigerators, hot plates, rosters, ranges, coffeemakers, washing machines, irons, vacuum cleaners, and radios. They also supervised the lucrative all-electric lunch tent.
>
> *(Kline, 2000: 181)*

A third example is provided by Ruth Cowan's (1983) seminal study of household technology. Cowan demonstrates that home electrification had transformative effects – not just by making washing and cleaning 'easier', but by changing the very nature of domestic practices and the conventions and expectations associated with them. In the cases she describes, 'labour saving' technologies co-developed with new, more exacting standards, meaning that although energy demand and the use of electrically powered household equipment increased significantly, the time American women spent on domestic chores did not reduce. In effect, the development of new infrastructures and the diffusion of new appliances helped establish new interpretations of 'normal' comfort and cleanliness. Studies of practices such as Cowan's demonstrate that material elements and technologies are in part constitutive of the practices they enable.

Our last example concerns a later phase in the history of electricity supply. From the 1970s, Électricité de France (EDF), the French national utility, actively promoted electric heating. This campaign was quite directly related to a problem of overcapacity that resulted from major investment in nuclear power generation combined with an unanticipated decrease in the rate of growth in national electricity demand following the 1973 oil and economic crisis. Faced with this situation, EDF needed to develop new uses for the electricity it produced, hence the decision to focus on domestic heating. This strategy proved extremely effective at the time: from the late 1970s into the 1990s, more than 40% and up to 70% (72% in 1988) of new built dwellings were equipped with electric heating in France (Bouvier, 2012: 38). Yet it was to be strongly criticised soon afterwards for its low efficiency and its high cost especially for households. As this case shows, dominant technologies are not inherently superior to other available, but more seldom adopted, alternatives.[2]

On the whole, at least in old-industrialised countries, coexisting processes of active mediation (between infrastructures and appliances and between appliances and practices) have sustained the advent of conventions, practices and expected standards of comfort, convenience, cleanliness and connectivity that are distinctly resource-intensive[3] to maintain. In what has become a repeating pattern, related systems of provision are reproduced at different scales: in networks of power, water and data; in building design (plumbed in, connected, wired) and in the details of kitchen and bathroom planning, for example. Such arrangements are also advocated and promoted by the media (in the name of progress and modernity), by the utility industry (in the name of their business interests) and by governments and public bodies (in the name of economic, social and spatial development). Connected and powered devices and appliances have consequently become firmly integrated into the fabric of daily life: being essential to what are seen to be 'basic needs', as well as to societal rhythms and expectations, especially in terms of reliability, with substantial implications for the functioning of the networks on which the fulfilment of these needs depends.

In short, the ubiquitous development of networked infrastructure systems has been as a rule (even in more recent instances such as the internet), a self-reinforcing process acting on the multiple dimensions (material, symbolic, cognitive) of multiple practices. And in one way or another, it has brought these practices into line with the interests (and ambitions) of network service providers – that is, in generating ever-growing demand for access to networked infrastructures, and for the services they make possible. Although the dominant narrative of the last century or so has been one of escalating demand rooted in infrastructural systems requiring the emergence of ever more energy intensive practices, other narratives and trajectories can be imagined, and there are already increasingly significant counter tendencies.

Adapting or shrinking infrastructures: stabilising practices

In general terms, demand for networked services and resources is still rising, but in certain places and sectors, other trends and dynamics are taking hold. For example, electricity consumption has stagnated and even slightly decreased in Europe since 2007.[4] Some factors accounting for this unprecedented situation reflect competition from other energy suppliers or from self-provision. However, some point to decreasing demand, including the consequences of the 2008 economic crisis (poorer households and, especially, less prosperous businesses use less energy) and the effect of public policies aimed at curtailing energy demand and promoting efficiency in order to reduce CO_2 emissions.

In France, for example, total electricity consumption has remained stable at just under 480 TWh per year since 2010, having previously increased steadily until 2007. Whatever the reason, any stabilising or decline in demand challenges the suppliers' traditional business model, which depends on selling ever larger quantities of resources. As a consequence – and sometimes also as one of the causes – of such decline, strategies have been developed based on the provision of 'energy services', including 'energy efficiency solutions' which promise to generate and perhaps increase supplier revenue despite selling less volume.[5]

The ability to profit from selling energy services depends on the potential for increasing the efficiency with which such services are delivered. Exploiting such opportunities, in turn, depends on reaching beyond generation and distribution, getting involved in selecting and operating 'appliances' and sometimes reconfiguring buildings and the contexts in which they are used. An energy services company will, for example, design a tailor-made 'solution' for typically large-scale energy consumers, such as a more energy-efficient heating or cooling system, or industrial process, that will result in the supplier selling less energy to its client. This involves some reshuffling of utilities' roles and responsibilities, but it seems that within this immensely complex sector, there is considerable scope for 'non-traditional' business models and for new and existing organisations to carve out niches for themselves and to remain profitable in the context of stable or reduced resource consumption.

Taking a broader view, there is nothing new about the idea of capitalising on demand reduction. Policies and markets for 'energy efficiency' have been actively developed and implemented from the 1970s oil crisis onwards. Then, as now, there was, and there still is, money and political gain to be made from investing in products which use less energy than those they replace.[6] Lower energy appliances have entered the market, governments have developed and promoted energy labelling schemes and standards, and the fluctuating economics of 'payback periods' have justified the adoption and installation of devices which reduce consumption. Whilst many of these measures have been adopted in a wider context of *growing* demand, there is no denying their impact. For example, swapping 45 million incandescent bulbs for lower energy compact fluorescent alternatives reduced Mexico's energy demand by over 3,000 GWh a year (SENER, 2015). In addition, and in contrast to previous scenarios in which gas or electric heating was simply added to existing buildings, regulations and design strategies have been adjusted to conserve fuel and power. The emergence of the Passive House 'concept' and related low energy standards exemplify this trend (Passive House Institute, 2015).

In combination, the widespread introduction of more efficient appliances and systems has the potential to diminish consumption in ways that matter for the operation and (re)design of power or water supplies. Conventional infrastructures of provision might shrink or be rearranged as the profitability of suppliers becomes less and less dependent on the quantity of gas, water or electricity that is sold. And, as observed above, the pursuit of efficiency is compatible with an income growth strategy. Even so, it is important to notice that efficiency policies, efficient products and energy service providers exist in a space that is defined and limited by the shared ambition of *reproducing current standards and practices*, although with a lesser use of resources.

The adoption of lower energy technologies almost always involves some minor modification in practice. For example, people adjust to fluorescent or LED lighting and they get used to washing machines that take longer to run than their predecessors. Similarly, interpretations of 'normal' service are always in flux. In particular, in areas of daily life where practices are more obviously on the move or where there is as yet no shared understanding of 'need' – as has been the case with IT or digital connectivity over the last decade or so[7] – the concept of efficiency is more contested. But when efficiency measures relate to established practices, they are generally introduced and positioned with reference to a shared understanding of proper provision. Because of this, discourses of efficiency go hand in hand with a persistent commitment to the project of maintaining current ways of life and associated interpretations of progress and growth. These commitments reproduce socially and culturally embedded understandings of 'networked normality' – including expectations that power is always 'on', that there is permanently reliable communication and that the rhythms and interdependencies of 'modern' living are here to stay.

This is not a passive stance. In so far as the efficiency agenda is designed to meet present needs with fewer resources, it has far-reaching and powerful consequences: helping to pre-serve and reproduce what are treated as taken-for-granted, non-negotiable standards. On the one hand, this means there is no deliberate programme of actively extending energy demand by 'powering' new or existing practices, as was the case before. Equally, there is no intention of undermining existing regimes of institutional relations, networked systems, consumer-provider roles or related complexes of social practice.

In short, there is evidently some flexibility in how infrastructures are configured and in how the material elements of practices are defined and delivered. As a result, it is sometimes possible to increase appliance efficiency behind the scenes and without substantially affecting the ongoing conduct of related practices. How much scope there is for *decoupling* resource consumption from service provision, and where this potential lies, varies from one practice to another. At the same time, that scope is limited by the shared ambition of reducing resource demand *without* compromising service delivery associated with 'normal' practices. The irony is that far from being natural or inevitable, contemporary interpretations of need and (standard) service are themselves outcomes of previous infrastructural configurations.

This is not the only possible strategy. In so far as 'needs' are made and not simply there, and to the extent that infrastructures and appliances help constitute practices (which then depend on them), analyses of configurations which enable and generate *different* complexes of social practice promises to provide new insights into the malleability of the practice-infrastructure nexus.

Reconfiguring infrastructures, appliances and practices

We began by noticing that the supply-driven imperative for ever-increasing resource demand can falter. Recent trends suggest that future infrastructure-practice configurations need not rest on an economic model of ever-increasing resource consumption, nor do they need to perpetuate current interpretations of 'normal' practice. There is, for example, growing recog-nition among climate change experts and policy-makers that improvements in energy effi-ciency will be *insufficient* to meet carbon emissions targets and that more radical changes may be required. In this context, it makes sense to wonder whether infrastructures, appliances and practices might be reconfigured in ways that call for very much less consumption.

Looking back, the proliferation of individual household appliances (toasters, freezers, wash-ing machines, air conditioning, etc.) is in keeping with an assumption of increasing energy (and water) consumption. Looking ahead, it is possible to envisage systems and technologies that enable more collective forms of provisioning (for example, shared laundries, district heat-ing systems), increasingly IT-based, partly 'dematerialised' services or less energy-intensive systems (unfrozen food chains) or novel forms or standards of provision (wearing insulation, reducing the volume of heated or cooled space).

Greater geographical proximity between energy supply and demand might, in addition to improved supply efficiency, favour correspondingly localised variations in practice – as distinct from expectations of homogenous 'standards' and conventions. These might better reflect spe-cific conditions, such as the local climate, along with local resources, constraints and opportuni-ties more generally. For example, in hot countries we might imagine the return of the siesta, the habit of closing the shutters during the daytime, new conventions of clothing or a re-greening of urban environments. More generally, the multiplication of diverse local configurations might facilitate social innovation and the emergence of novel infrastructure-practice arrangements that prove better adapted to the prevailing conditions.

Since everyday practices interact in time, in space and through diverse social and material systems, significant and widespread reductions in demand for (increasingly networked) resources imply correspondingly systemic innovation and change. In thinking about the types of transformation involved, it is important to recognise that there are already extensive variations in how seemingly shared practices are enacted and that these variations are, to an extent, reflected in the amount of resources that different social groups consume. People living 'off grid' (which in general means off energy grids) are at one end of this spectrum. These currently 'extreme' cases are often and perhaps necessarily small scale and they are, to an extent, precisely characterised by being set apart from and defined in contrast to the 'mainstream'. We do not consider 'off-gridders' as models to follow, in a normative way. Rather we use them for analytical purposes. From this point of view, the experiences of voluntary 'off-gridders' provide insights into the types of reconfiguration at stake. In particular, they highlight issues of time and labour, space, institutional involvement and change in the organisation of everyday life. Furthermore, by emphasising notions of autonomy – metabolic and political – off-gridders tend to question contemporary (Western) standards of material consumption and waste that support and are supported by prevailing infrastructural arrangements.

Off-grid experiences suggest that being deprived of networked supplies increases the time, effort, attention and often money spent in providing one's own water and energy, and in communicating with others or disposing of one's waste. For example, the overall time and work involved in domestic chores is greater when using hand- rather than grid-powered appliances. This has further implications for the rhythm of daily life. Amongst other things, it means that less is done in any one day, fewer tasks are accomplished and each calls for greater dedication and effort. One relevant insight is that there are different ways of evaluating the costs and also the benefits of seemingly slower ways of life and of more direct interaction with seasonal variations of heat and light (Vannini and Taggart, 2013b). A second is that whether seen as a step 'back', a drop in standards or an advance, lower-power living entails a range of quite significant changes in the temporal ordering and organisation of what people do.

The use and experience of space is also key. Full central heating has reinforced a notion of space- rather than person-heating and has enabled the spread of people and of energy-demanding practices around the home. Those who live off-grid tend to use space in different ways, often concentrating activities around more localised sources of heat and light. Such arrangements are associated with specific interpretations of what it means to be comfortable and of how this might be achieved. Vannini and Taggart reach the following conclusion, based on a study of 159 off-gridders:

> as the experiences of off-grid homes show, in no way is domestic visual comfort achievable only by flicking on an electric lightbulb powered by distant sociotechnical assemblages. Comfort is, in fact, not a uniform experience and off-gridders' practices show vividly what it means to achieve it differently, in variable intensities and through alternative entanglements of nature and culture.
>
> *(Vannini and Taggart, 2013a: 1076)*

These experiences underline the negotiability of thermal and visual comfort: as new interpretations take hold, these become the benchmarks against which other arrangements are judged.

Third, Vannini and Taggart's analysis of off-gridders' experiences highlights patterns of organisational and material (in)dependence. The social and institutional arrangements associated with networked infrastructures are significantly rearranged by off-gridders, especially those who simultaneously occupy the roles of producer, distributor and consumer. These strategies are sometimes, but not always, an expression of political commitment involving a rejection of the state, a reluctance to interact with global corporations and some resistance to mainstream ways of life (van Vliet, Chappells and Shove, 2005). Whatever the reasoning and approach, those who produce the electricity they consume are differently positioned from those who are enmeshed within and hence dependent on the reliable functioning of much more remote systems and institutions of provision.

Many future patterns are possible, but in combination, these observations suggest that significantly lower energy configurations of infrastructures and practices are likely to involve new temporal rhythms, the emergence of new concepts and understandings of space and service (and related ecologies of materials and 'appliances' broadly defined) and different forms of social and organisational interdependence. Off-grid experiences also highlight important differences *between* practices and their relation to variously networked forms of power. As already mentioned, there are many ways of heating, lighting, cooking or communicating and an array of potentially relevant appliances and fuels. Different practices are marked by different histories and forms of power dependence. In some cases, there is ample scope for material substitution, for compromising or reinterpreting standards of performance and service or for falling back on old methods – for example, washing by hand or using a hand-powered drill (De Decker, n.d.). More generally, practices and related appliances are increasingly linked in various ways. These forms of interdependence are normally invisible. But as extended power cuts reveal, water supplies routinely depend on an electrical supply, as do gas heating systems, automatic garage doors or mobile phone masts.

Practice-specific and practice-connective features are both important in thinking about where and how more extensive resource demand reduction might begin and about the possibilities for establishing alternative configurations. In this context, existing methods of 'service provision' illustrate the scope for enabling certain practices in different ways necessitating less energy and resources – for example, via forms of efficiency.

Whilst these methods are typically designed to mimic standards which are, in effect, born of an age of energy and resource plenty, the examples of off-grid reconfiguration discussed above indicate that other formulations are possible. For example, the increasing digitalisation of relations between infrastructures and their use(r)s may facilitate a transition from one-size-fits-all infrastructural environments to a much greater variety of tailor-made arrangements, thus opening new 'spaces' in which a corresponding variety of infrastructure-practice configurations might evolve. These new spaces may be unattractive or remain dormant when energy prices are low, but prove to be extremely valuable under conditions of more or less sudden and large rises in energy prices or increasing constraints on energy use.

Configuring the future?

In this chapter we have presented three 'ideal typical' configurations of infrastructures and practices and we have done so as if these forms were of equal status and as if they could be detached from specific situations and historical contexts. We have used this scheme to argue that networked infrastructures do not necessarily constitute 'technologies of growth' (type 1) and in particular that they do not necessarily call for and support ever more service- or resource-intensive practices. Under specific conditions, 'shrinking' infrastructures (type 2) may prove profitable for utility companies, users and the environment (in terms of resource use) alike. Both these configurations (type 1 and type 2) help reproduce specific concepts of 'normal' practice, laying down multiple, sometimes reinforcing, tracks of 'path dependence'; representing 'sunk costs' in terms of hardware and – perhaps more powerfully – anchoring normative visions of everyday life. By contrast, the third formulation 'reconfiguring infrastructures' (type 3) entails and depends on establishing practices that are positioned in opposition or at least as an alternative to those associated with mainstream infrastructural provision.

Looking across all three forms, the question is whether it is possible to imagine and realise future scenarios in which infrastructural developments go hand in hand with significant transitions in practice resulting in a systemic decline in demand for energy or other resources.

In this chapter we have argued that any move in this direction depends on a better understanding of how scenarios of growth, persistence, decline or disconnection are formed through the interaction of variously obdurate (or variously dynamic) business models, systems of provision, material arrangements and complexes of social practices. We conclude that whatever arrangements take hold in the years ahead, one thing is sure: they will be informed by past and present concepts of progress, by institutions and systems of provision and by a material legacy of buildings, generators, pipes and wires. In making some trajectories more likely or seemingly more viable than others, this accumulation of infrastructure-practice configurations throws shadows deep into the future. At the same time, the fact that infrastructures enable and co-constitute diverse social practices and that they do so through multiple forms of active mediation ensures a measure of restless, ongoing and potentially steerable change.

Notes

1   Throughout the chapter, the discussion is based on the supply and use of infrastructure services in the domestic sphere. We do not discuss in any depth the (potential) dynamics of practices in the manufacturing or service sectors, even though they represent a significant share of total resource use.
2   This scheme was subsequently criticised given the cost and financial burden of using all electric heating and the problems this presented especially for rural households, which had few other options and which generally lived in larger and more poorly insulated dwellings than their urban counterparts.
3   Compared with those they replaced.
4   For the statistical information in this and the following paragraphs, see RTE (2015).
5   Other strategies include expanding the supplier's service area and/or diversification into other sectors (utility or otherwise). See, for example, Florentin (2015).
6   See, for example, the work of the International Energy Agency (2015) which treats 'efficiency' as a fuel or the ambitions of the European Council for an Energy Efficient Economy (n.d.), which claims on its website's homepage that 'since the 1970s, energy efficiency has contributed more to our economic prosperity than any other single source of energy supply'.
7   These examples currently have more in common with 'type 1' configurations of expanding infrastructures and growth.

References

Berlanstein, L. (1991) *Big Business and Industrial Conflict in Nineteenth Century France: a social history of the Parisian Gas Company*. Berkeley: University of California Press.
Bouvier, Y. (2012) «Les ambiguïtés de la communication d'EDF au temps des économies d'énergie», *Annales historiques de l'électricité*, 1(10): 31–42.

Bulkeley, H., Castán Broto, V., Hodson, M. and Marvin, S. (eds.) (2013) *Cities and Low Carbon Transitions*. London: Routledge.

Chatzis, K. and Coutard, O. (2005) 'Water and Gas: early developments in the utility networks of Paris', *Journal of Urban Technology*, 12(3): 1–17.

Coutard, O. and Rutherford, J. (2013) 'The rise of post-networked cities in Europe? Recombining infrastructural, ecological and urban transformations in low-carbon transitions', in Bulkeley, H., Castán Broto, V., Hodson, M. and Marvin, S. (eds.) (2013) *Cities and Low Carbon Transitions*. London: Routledge. pp. 107–125.

Coutard, O. and Rutherford, J. (eds.) (2016) *Beyond the Networked City: infrastructure reconfigurations and urban change in the North and South*. London: Routledge.

Cowan, R. S. (1983) *More Work for Mother: the ironies of household technology from the open hearth to the microwave*. New York: Basic Books.

De Decker, K. (n.d.) 'Hand powered drilling tools and machines'. *Low-Tech Magazine*. Available at: www.lowtechmagazine.com/2010/12/hand-powered-drilling-tools-and-machines.html (Accessed 21.12.15).

European Council for an Energy Efficient Economy (n.d.). Available at: www.eceee.org (Accessed 28.12.17).

Florentin, D. (2015) '"Shrinking networks?" Les nouveaux modèles économiques et territoriaux des firmes d'infrastructure face à la diminution de la consommation'. Unpublished Ph.D. dissertation. Paris: LATTS.

Forty, A. (1986) *Objects of Desire: design and society, 1750–1980*. London: Thames and Hudson.

Hughes, T. (1983) *Networks of Power. Electrification in Western society 1880-1930*. Baltimore, MD: Johns Hopkins University Press.

International Energy Agency (2015) 'Energy efficiency market report'. Available at: www.iea.org/publications/freepublications/publication/energy-efficiency-market-report-2015-.html (Accessed 28.12.17).

Kline, R. (2000) *Consumers in the Country: technology and social change in rural America*, Baltimore, MD: Johns Hopkins University Press.

Mayntz, R. and Hughes T. (1988) *The Development of Large Technological Systems*. Frankfurt am Main: Campus.

Nye, D. (2010) *When the Lights Went Out: a history of blackouts in America*. Cambridge, MA: MIT Press.

Passive House Institute (2015) 'Home page'. Available at: http://passiv.de/en/ (Accessed: 24.06.16).

Rees, J. (2013) *Refrigeration Nation. A history of ice, appliances, and enterprise in America*. Baltimore, MD: Johns Hopkins University Press.

RTE (2015) *Bilan prévisionnel de l'équilibre offre-demande en France, édition 2015*. La Défense: Réseau de Transport d'Electricité (RTE). Available at: www.rte-france.com/sites/default/files/bp2015.pdf (Accessed 19.12.15).

SENER (2015) 'Piloting energy efficiency and behaviour policies in México'. Available at: www.iea.org/media/workshops/2015/eeuevents/behave1103/S1SantiagoCreuherasMexico.pdf (Accessed 24.06.16).

Shove, E., Pantzar, M. and Watson, M. (2012) *The Dynamics of Social Practice: everyday life and how it changes*. London: Sage.

Shove, E. and Walker, G. (2014) 'What is energy for? Social practice and energy demand' *Theory, Culture and Society*, 31(5): 41–58.

Star, S. (1999) 'The ethnography of infrastructure', *American Behavioral Scientist*, 43(3): 377–391.

van Vliet, B., Chappells, H. and Shove, E. (2005) *Infrastructures of Consumption: environmental innovation in the utility industries*. London: Earthscan.

Vannini, P. and Taggart, J. (2013a) 'Domestic lighting and the off-grid quest for visual comfort', *Environment and Planning D: Society and Space*, 31(6): 1076–1090.

Vannini, P. and Taggart, J. (2013b) 'Off-grid living: voluntary simplicity or involuntary complexity?' *Huffington Post*. Available at: www.huffingtonpost.ca/phillip-vannini-and-jonathan-taggart/offgrid-living-voluntary-_b_3497138.html Posted 25 June 2013. (Accessed 28.12.17).

PART II

Varieties of infrastructures

There are many ways in which infrastructures and practices constitute each other. Rather than characterising infrastructures by what they provide, for example, mobility, waste management, water, communications etc. the following chapters introduce readers to methods of identifying and analysing different *forms* of infrastructural configuration.

In conventional terms, infrastructures appear as substantial, relatively durable entities in their own right. This tends to underestimate the many provisional and dynamic connections between people, organisations, material arrangements, appliances and practices involved. Star and Ruheleder (1996) contend that infrastructures have certain defining characteristics: they are embedded in other social arrangements and structures (and have emerged from them); they have a background or invisible supporting role in relation to other materials/appliances; they have distinctive features of reach or scope, and they are entwined with social conventions of practice. In their words, 'the configuration of these dimensions forms "an infrastructure" which is without absolute boundary on a priori definition' (Star and Ruhleder, 1996: 113). The chapters in this section develop a similarly *relational* approach.

Scale is an important feature of all such relations. While it is now common to recognise that systems of provision and consumption shape each other, few have considered the ways in which this works out at different *scales*. In writing about the cables of which electricity grids are made, Harrison takes up this challenge, showing how high and low voltage parts of the USA electricity network connect, how producers and consumers are 'wired' together and how this changes over time. Rather than there being 'one' system, variants and combinations arise and disappear *within* 'the' grid, and within the fabric of the home. Smits explores similar issues in relation to the more recent arrival of electrical power in villages in Laos and Thailand. Read alongside each other, these two chapters show that what is ostensibly 'the same' – namely electricity provision to households – is woven into distinctive moments and historical configurations of domestic, political and commercial practice. 'Normal' provision is a constantly moving target, shifting as networks are modified and extended, and as notions of need evolve.

How the roles of 'consumer' and 'provider' are defined and the points at which they intersect are part of this dynamic (see also the section on boundaries). Differing relations between consumers and providers are explored by Rinkinen, who writes about methods of heating with wood, and Lopez who traces ideas about autonomy, self-sufficiency and collective provision. Scale is again critical. Large and extensive networks, like district heating with wood pellets, or centralised grids, link many consumers with distant providers. By contrast, the work of provisioning is more visible where households are more directly involved. There are ongoing debates about the social and political costs and benefits of 'small' versus 'large' networks and as Lopez describes, arguments about the merits of self-sufficiency vs centralised supply swing back and forth.

Combinations of infrastructural relations – some 'large' and some 'small' – are generally discussed in relation to issues of political economy, ideology and state versus corporate power. New questions come into view when broadening the perspective to include infrastructures-in-use. For example, as Rinkinen and Smits demonstrate, more and less centralised forms of provision have a bearing on the temporal order and rhythm of daily life. This works in different ways. People who heat their homes with wood are often locked into seasonal cycles of chopping and storing fuel. Other temporal relations and rearrangements follow from the provision of reliable mains power but again this is not a simple or one-dimensional process. The socio-temporal transformations associated with electric lighting are, for instance, quite unlike those related to the 'arrival' of a television (Smits). More broadly, the significance of having automatic central heating or access to a TV is tied up with symbolic meanings and interpretations of convenience and modernity, and with precisely when, where and in what context infrastructures are introduced and changed.

Multiple methods are required to catch sight of the kaleidoscopic rearranging of infrastructural relations and to characterise the diverse forms and conjunctions that arise as a result. Of the four chapters included in this section two take an historical approach, with Harrison offering a history of technology, and Lopez a history of ideas. Rinkinen and Smits work with case studies and interviews, using these to compare processes of village electrification on the one hand, and the relation between self- and central provisioning on the other. In combination these chapters introduce new ways of thinking about how dominant and marginal systems and scales of provision intersect. They examine infrastructures as living systems that are entwined with the temporal order of society and with the dynamics and politics of provision and practice.

Reference

Star, S. L. and Ruhleder, K. (1996) 'Steps toward an ecology of infrastructure: design and access for large information spaces', *Information Systems Research*, 7(1): 111–134.

3

WIRES

Conor Harrison

Introduction

Imagine walking through the front door of a newly built suburban home in the United States today. You are often met with a chandelier hanging from a vaulted ceiling. The lights of the chandelier are controlled by a bay of switches directly adjacent to the front door. One switch may control the chandelier lighting, the other a light outside the front door, while another light illuminates the front hallway. Walking down the hallway one looks down to the right and sees a small table on which smart phones and other electronic devices are connected to a mess of black wires for their daily refill. The black wires lead down to two electrical sockets just above the baseboard; both are occupied. As you enter the kitchen, you are again met by several light switches. These operate different sets of overhead lights, one over the sink, and another over the granite topped kitchen island. Against the back splash are several more sets of sockets. These accommodate an array of appliances as they are called upon: the toaster, the blender, the can opener or hand mixer. A glance at the microwave reveals a blinking 12:00; the clock was never reset after the power flickered during one of the frequent summer thunderstorms that affect the area.

Now imagine the brief panic that storm caused at the local power company's control centre. High winds caused a tree limb to fall on the power lines of the local distribution system, knocking it out of commission. Grid operators leapt into action, power was re-routed, the limb was removed, the line repaired, and all has been functioning normally since. Normal operation is a 1,000 MW coal plant located 150 miles from the home that is now humming along seamlessly. Other scattered natural gas plants break up the peak load, turning on and off as needed on a daily basis. Various reservoirs and diesel generators have additional spare generation capacity if needed. But the big power plant is the coal fired one, producing electricity that leaves on high voltage transmission wires at 240,000 volts. As these wires approach the city, the electron flow is stepped down and subdivided at substations and transformers, and then spread out along the local distribution system at 120 volts. Electricity enters homes, is divided onto various circuits, and circulates via a web of hidden wires. It is available at socket outlets but only really appears as light, as the spinning blades of a blender, as a recharged smart phone, or as the endlessly blinking 12:00 on the microwave.

Electricity networks make western high energy lifestyles possible (Nye, 1998; Huber, 2013). However, the contribution of electricity generation to climate change has revealed this infrastructure to be rather problematic. Each blink of the 12:00 on the microwave requires a tiny pulse of electrons, charging phones require a small stream and the constantly cold refrigerator a small river. In aggregate these demands, when combined with the multitude of other electricity using practices, constitute a veritable ocean of electricity consumption (and thus, a regime of fossil fuel based electricity generation and emissions of CO_2), ebbing and flowing as people wake up, go to work, cook dinner and go to sleep (Walker, 2014).

During the twentieth century electricity consumption in the United States increased dramatically (Nye, 1998). Attempts to chart this process have involved calculating additions to generation capacity or estimating the number of electric appliances on sale at stores but so far, little has been written about the infrastructure of wires itself. In this chapter, I trace the history of both high voltage electricity transmission wires and systems of home wiring to show how wiring evolved alongside and also anticipated future electrical practices. High voltage transmission wires work at a regional scale, bringing together often distant sites of electricity production and consumption. By contrast, systems of residential wiring function at the scale of the home, where concerns over fire safety intersect with those of standardisation, flexibility and convenience. Though organised around quite different considerations, both systems have been designed to facilitate and encourage increasing residential electricity demand.

In developing an account of wiring infrastructures, I draw on archival material from General Electric (GE), a leader in the development of high voltage transmission and interior wiring. In particular, I make use of materials and oral histories collected by John Winthrop Hammond, the GE publicist and author of the internal GE history *Men and Volts* (1941). In the section on high voltage transmission I describe how transmission problems were conceived and addressed by GE engineers, focusing on problems of early electrification but also plans for future electricity consumption. Then, switching scale to the home, I focus on changes to the National Electrical Code during the first half of the twentieth century, highlighting the need for wires capable of safely meeting the growing demands customers and electrical equipment manufacturers were placing upon them. I conclude by commenting on a contemporary iteration of wiring technology, the so-called 'smart grid', and point to the continued importance of wires in the co-evolution of electricity consuming practices and technologies of transmission.

High voltage transmission

At the fourteenth meeting of the Association of Edison Illuminating Companies in 1898, W. S. Barstow of Brooklyn Edison presented a paper entitled 'The development of a transmission system'. In his paper, Barstow remarked that the Edison low voltage three wire system was useful 'as long as cities were closely built up and of limited area, or as long as the supply company confined itself to the "cream" of the district' (Barstow, 1898: 1). However, Barstow noted, the profile of loads in Brooklyn was changing. System planning had been haphazard. When one plant's generation capacity was maxed out, another plant was built. Each newly constructed plant had its own distribution grid. In Barstow's opinion, this method of system expansion had to be abandoned. In its place he proposed a system with multiple generating stations serving a single grid.

While this sounded ideal, the problem, Barstow admitted, was the kilowatt. In his estimation:

> A kilowatt is a peculiar creature. It is somewhat human in its character, in that it likes to go where it is not wanted, and prefers to return home by the shortest cut possible rather than travelling great distances.
>
> *(Barstow, 1898: 3)*

What's more, under high voltage, the kilowatt becomes particularly unruly: 'at 6,000 volts it requires a very respectable place' (Barstow, 1898: 3) in order to stay where the engineers wanted it to be. The respectable place that Barstow was describing was a wire, most often copper, as well as the various switches, fuses and insulators that are needed to keep the kilowatt on the path most system engineers' desire.

Billions of kilowatts found a respectable place to travel in the years after Barstow's address. However, as Hughes (1983) points out, high voltage transmission wires often functioned as a reverse salient, holding back advancement of the overall electricity system. The frequent spatial mismatch between sites of electricity production and consumption compounded Barstow's dilemma. Cities and factories using the most electricity were often not located near prime falling water or coal mining sites. The mobility of coal meant that coal powered electricity was the norm in many eastern US cities. Yet a considerable amount of the cost of coal to the end user came from its transport (Jones, 2014). Hydropower, by far the cheapest source of electricity, was often hundreds of miles away from electric loads. For example, newly developing cities in the western US such as Los Angeles and San Francisco had little nearby coal but were potentially powered by 'white coal' (Hughes, 1983), electricity generated from falling water high in the distant mountains.

For electricity system planners the first 30 years of the twentieth century was largely a period of working out ways to move cheap power over long distances. What became evident in early experimental work was that the solution depended on high voltage transmission. Voltage can be thought of as a measure of electrical pressure that can produce a force. To understand the importance of voltage to electricity transmission, a common analogy is to think of a hose of a certain width. Assuming that width is fixed, at any given time, under a certain pressure, some amount of water can pass through the hose to the opening at the end. However, if the water pressure is increased, a larger amount of water can flow through the hose faster, meaning it comes out of the end with greater force. In electricity transmission the same is true. Voltage is the measure of how much electrical 'pressure' can be passed through a wire to its end point. Higher voltages (greater pressure) mean that more electricity gets to the end point through the same width wire. But, just as a hose may start to disintegrate if the pressure is too great, high voltages produce a number of different stresses on electrical wires and can cause damage to them and to their surroundings.

Others have written about the movement of energy. For example, Hughes (1983) describes the emergence of regional electricity systems, Jones (2014) has examined the movement of coal, petroleum and electricity and its significance for mid-Atlantic regional economic development, and Needham (2014) has argued that high voltage transmission lines were central to the uneven development of the American Southwest. I share the views of those who conceptualise transmission wires as vectors of convergence, bringing together distant sites and scales of electricity production and consumption. However, my focus is not on the overall electricity system or regional development but on the incremental design changes of high voltage wires, and the co-evolution of wires and electricity consumption more generally. In addition, transmitting electricity at high voltages has always required thinking about insulation, and particularly the interactions of insulation with electric currents.

Since the first experiments with electric lighting, wire insulation has been a critical issue. Recalling an early installation of arc lights in Cincinnati, Professor Elihu Thomson (whose Thomson-Houston company would merge with Edison Electric to form General Electric) described a line transmitting 'some 14,000 or 15,000 volts, and no special precaution had been taken to insulate for this relatively high pressure'. Not surprisingly, on starting up the motor producing the electric current immediately burnt out (Thomson, 1908: 2). Other electricity pioneers also underestimated the need for insulation. At a party hosted at the New York home of William K. Vanderbilt, an early user of electricity supplied by Thomas Edison, nearly 20 fires started because of faulty uninsulated wiring (Hammond, n.d. a).

Despite early challenges with wiring insulation, Edison caught on before long. In 1886, Edison Electric's manufacturing of wires and cables was moved to Schenectady, New York, and soon insulation made from combinations of lead, jute, various waxes and oils, and vulcanised rubber was being employed to coat wires (Hammond, 1925). Later, various impregnated papers were used as insulation because of their flexibility. Edison's workshop developed a lapping machine for the purpose of wrapping wires with the new paper insulators (Black, 1983). By the mid-1900s, insulating materials changed once again. Wiring manufacturers used asphaltum varnish and pasted mica, applying them to wires via a slow baking process. Manufacturers were able to increase the baking temperatures, a shift that helped to eliminate the varnish solvents that degraded the insulation (Lee, n.d.). GE and other wiring manufacturers continued making incremental improvements in insulating materials and manufacturing processes. Rectangular wire began to be used, which allowed for more copper to be placed in the same space within the electrical apparatus (Hammond, 1925). All of these changes improved the consistency and reliability of the insulators, thus eliminating many mechanical failures in electricity transmission.

A second major challenge engineers faced was the fluctuating demand for electricity. Social practices that consume electricity have a particular temporality leading to peaks and troughs in consumption. Copper and aluminum, like other compounds, tend to expand when they are heated and contract when they cool. Varying flows of electric current through wires produce the same heating and cooling effect. As a result, in a typical three core cable (in which three wires are wrapped around each other), under low electron flows the wires are cool, tightly wound, and completely protected by the insulating compound. However, when the cable is under heavy load, the strands heat and tend to expand. When electric loads drop, the wires cool and contract. The constant expansion and contraction can degrade the insulating compound and create space between the wires. This space then allows for electric discharges between the wires, stressing the insulating compounds, and charring the insulating paper. The result is either high electricity losses or line failure (Black, 1983).

Engineers addressed this problem through design changes that wrapped the cables with a linen or cloth tape that had a bare copper wire woven into the fabric. This kept the expansion and contraction of the line to a minimum and greatly decreased line failure (Black, 1983). As this example shows, the temporal organisation of electrically demanding social practices shaped the design of the electricity infrastructure, and the construction of the wires involved.

Better wiring insulation enabled increased transmission voltages and distances in the years around 1900, leading to changes in the economic geography of electricity system planning

(Hughes, 1983). For example, California's Bay Area could now harness hydropower from the Sierra Nevada Mountains. In 1894, convict labour from Folsom, California helped to connect Sacramento with a power source 23 miles away at 10,000 volts. By July 1900 Oakland and San Jose, CA were connected by a 150 mile transmission system at 60,000 volts. Slightly more than a year later Oakland was connected 142 miles to the town of Colgate on the North Yuka River by a 40,000 volt line. The growing Southern California cities of Pasadena and Los Angeles also looked to hydropower, and in 1897 were connected 81 miles to a hydro plant in the Santa Ana Canyon by a 33,000 volt transmission line (Hughes, 1983). Increasing transmission voltages increased the resource peripheries of cities across the United States. Yet with growing urban electricity consumption cities were demanding access to still more power, and thus to wires capable of transmitting it.

In the years leading up to 1907, high voltage transmission wires tended to experience extremely high line losses above 60,000 volts. Electrical engineers identified the problem as corona loss. As GE Engineer F. W. Peek describes in *Dielectric Phenomena in High Voltage Engineering*, if voltage along a line is gradually increased, 'a voltage is finally reached at which a hissing noise is heard and, if it is dark, a pale violet light can be seen to surround the conductors' (1915: 48). Once the voltage becomes sufficiently high, if several transmission wires are hung close a spark can move from one wire to the next. Initially spark-over occurs at points along the wire that have dirt or irregularities, but when the voltage is high enough it occurs all along the line. Spark-overs can eventually damage transmission lines, but for most utilities the primary problem with so-called corona loss is that usable electricity dissipates as heat, light and sound (Peek, 1915).

Peek's (1915) extensive testing on corona loss revealed several factors that influenced the rate electricity was lost along transmission wires. Some, including altitude, humidity and temperature, were outside the control of electrical engineers. Others were not. After years of testing, Peek and others found that the spacing and physical arrangement of wires proved critical. If wires were arranged symmetrically along a plane losses started at lower voltages than if they were arranged in an equilateral triangle. The diameter of the wire was also important. Wires with greater diameter were able to sustain greater voltages without significant corona loss. Wire manufacturers began developing thicker wires, and eventually moved to hollow core stranded wires.

But as large diameter wires came into greater use, another problem emerged. Larger diameter wires were heavier meaning that the size and number of support insulators used in hanging them had also grown. Early versions, known as pin type insulators, were most often a single, large, cone-like porcelain insulator holding lines on top of cross arms. In order to provide insulation from ever higher voltages, these had to be increased in size: some were as large as two feet in diameter and three feet in height. In combination with more robust wires, the weight of the electricity transmission apparatus became too heavy for wooden towers.

In response, most power companies turned to steel towers, which were stronger but also more expensive to build. The strength of steel meant that the spans between towers could be greater so fewer towers could support the same amount of wire. This decreased the number of support insulators needed, but the cost, size and fragility of large pin type insulators remained a problem. A 1906 paper presented at the American Institute of Electrical Engineers convention by GE Engineer E. M. Hewlett proposed an alternative system that used steel towers with long spans of wires supported by 'suspension type' insulators. In the suspension type system, rather than a single large insulator on top of the cross arm, the wire was hung from a number of smaller (initially only ten inches in diameter), lighter, and simpler insulators descending from the cross arms. This design allowed the electrical stress to be distributed among the insulators (Hewlett, 1906). As was the practice at GE, after obtaining patents, a commercial version was developed – the Hewlett insulator – and voltages quickly increased above 100,000 volts (Hammond, n.d. b; n.d. c; n.d. d).

Again better insulation enabled higher voltages, and higher voltages meant more power could be moved. The impact was again most visible in the western United States. In 1913, using suspension insulators, the Southern Sierras Power Company (which would be absorbed by Southern California Edison) built a line from Bishop Creek, California to San Bernardino (229 miles) that would later be extended to Yuma, Arizona, a total distance of 539 miles. The same year Southern California Edison put into operation a 241 mile long line with voltages of 140,000. Ten years later, voltages on these lines were increased to 220,000 volts, and a continuous transmission connection of 2,300 miles was created between Vancouver, Canada, Billings, Montana and Yuma, Arizona.

General Electric estimated that, 'by 1935 all of the water powers that are within economic reach of the bay region will have been developed and put to use'. The aforementioned interconnections 'of all great powers and markets generally through the Far West' (Press Release, n.d.) was essential to enable continued growth to meet existing 'needs' and to accommodate utilities and electrical equipment manufacturers' visions of future demand. By the early 1920s, plans emerged on the East Coast for electricity-led economic development based on long distance high voltage transmission. Two such competing plans, Giant Power and Super Power, called for regional electrification via giant power plants located in Pennsylvania's coal producing regions (thus eliminating the costly transportation of coal) that would transmit electricity to manufacturing and population centers on the eastern seaboard (Hughes, 1983; Murray, 1921).

During the 1920s, electricity consumption was increasing year on year, and largely continued to do so over the next 50 years. The ability to use long distance transmission to tap into prime sources of electric power – whether from falling water high in mountains or from seams of coal far underground – was central to this mission. The 'grow and build' strategy (Hirsh, 1989), wherein power companies 'grew' electricity demand and met it by building ever larger plants, was in turn predicated on the ability to transmit power efficiently across space. Early twentieth century advances in high voltage transmission meant that the unruly kilowatt was increasingly tamed, although as Bennett (2005) and Nye (2010) make clear the kilowatt has never been entirely domesticated. The shape that high voltage transmission wires ultimately took was a reflection of both the timing and scale of electricity consumption – as represented by the demand curve – and a vision of an increasingly electrified future.

While the focus to this point has been on moving electricity across long distances at high voltage, electricity cannot be used in this form. Instead, it has to be stepped down via transformers to voltages suitable for local distribution networks, and ultimately fed into the wiring system of the home. Interior wiring – which is just as vital for the development of electrical power – had a trajectory of its own.

Interior wiring

The combination of multiple generators, high voltage transmission, substations, transformers and low voltage distribution solved many problems for utilities. Thanks to a network of high voltage wires, the challenge of generating enough electricity to meet peak demands could be spread across a variety of suppliers. In addition, multiple distribution systems could be combined efficiently through power sharing agreements that enabled utilities to buy and sell power to one another as guided by each utility's time of peak demand. However, all these developments depended on building and establishing the demand for electricity and the means to use it.

In the early twentieth century most people continued to use candles or gas lights for indoor lighting, meaning that management of natural light was crucial. Aspiring early twentieth century homemakers wrote to publications such as *House Beautiful*, an interior decorating magazine first published in 1896 and still published today, asking for advice. A typical letter is below:

Please give me a full scheme in how to decorate the living-room in the following cottage:

> The living-room faces south by a little east, has three good windows with small diamond-cut glass in the top sash (Queen Anne), besides the light in the door and the side-lights in the same. It will have plenty of light, but no direct light, being covered with porches.
>
> *(House Beautiful, 1905: 33)*

In this letter, and in many others to *House Beautiful*, considerable attention is paid to *natural* light – the location and size of the windows, the orientation of the home – but not to *artificial* light that is today used to illuminate houses night and day. By one estimate, in 1915 only 8% of residences in the United States were wired for electricity (Croft, 1915).

The electrification of homes was not a uniform or seamless process: materials and methods were rarely homogeneous, wiring systems were often incomplete, and typically comprised a mélange of solutions layered over one another. In this section, I describe how the United States' National Electrical Code attempted to standardise home wiring for safety and to accommodate and anticipate the growth of residential electricity demand starting in the early twentieth century. Alongside discussion of the changes in code I review efforts to boost the use of electricity in homes by improving residential wiring infrastructure. Home wiring systems, I show, have been central in shifting consumer attention away from electricity itself and towards the 'benefits' electricity is meant to provide.

There is more than one way to wire a house, and many of them are not safe. Improperly insulated wires can lead to fires. Overloaded circuits can cause outages and damage appliances. Realising that faulty wiring posed a hazard to users and thus to the nascent industry, in the early 1890s the primary American electrical manufacturers trade group, the National Electric Light Association, developed a set of rules to guide wiring installations. Almost simultaneously, the National Board of Fire Underwriters and the Underwriters National Electrical Association produced their own set of rules. In 1896, a group was formed to produce a single 'National Code' on electrical installations, which was published in 1897. This code was adopted by the National Board of Fire Underwriters, which was later absorbed into the National Fire Protection Association (NFPA) (Grant, 1996). Still under the guidance of the NFPA, the National Electrical Code continues to be periodically updated.

In the early twentieth century the committee updating the Code was comprised of representatives from the electricity, fire protection and insurance industries. Though this membership was intended to ensure that the outcome would balance diverse concerns, this was not always achieved. Writing about the electrical code in 1912, engineer and author Thomas McLoughlin laments that while 'the Code addresses itself first, last and all the time to fire risks' it 'is not officially concerned at all with economy, convenience, correct illumination or the ordinary every-day reliability of the work'. Further, '[w]iring may be far too small for bright light, and yet fully meet Code requirements' (1912: 1).

In subsequent years the Code's authors became more involved in enabling electricity consumption, going so far as to mandate a minimum number of electrical outlets per room. The National Electrical Code, and related specifications of safe wiring practice, can thus be viewed as the outcome of a contested process in which the interests of expanding demand are confronted with those of minimising risk.

The first electrified homes were most often wired on a single circuit, meaning that all lighting and whatever appliances were being used were connected to the same loop of wire. One of the first methods of home wiring described in the Code was called 'knob and tube wiring'. The 'tube' was an insulating tube made of porcelain and designed to protect the wires as they ran through a home's wooden support frame. The 'knobs' were a series of cleats to which wires were anchored as they ran along walls. Although prevalent during the first three decades of the twentieth century, knob and tube methods were phased out in new construction during the 1930s and replaced by non-metallic (commonly called NM) and armoured cable systems. NM cable systems consisted of individual wires wrapped in a cotton braid that was impregnated with varnish or tar. By the 1950s, the cotton braid was replaced by synthetic fabrics, and in the 1960s by thermoplastics. However, many homes retained knob and tube systems through to the 1970s.

The shift away from knob and tube was about safety and the efficiency with which NM cable systems could be installed, but it also reflected increasing demands placed on home wiring. Evidence of this can be seen in the work of American engineer Terrell Croft, author of a 1915 handbook on wiring old houses. Croft's work addressed both technical and commercial issues, coaching utilities and contractors on the proper techniques of selecting and running wires, and explaining how to drum up wiring business. He advised power companies to offer special deals on home wiring, claiming that money lost on wiring would be made up in added revenues. He encouraged the use of salesmen with minimal training in the technicalities of electricity; too much specialist knowledge confused potential customers, he argued. Croft (1915) goes to great lengths to explain that even previously wired houses could and should be rewired in order to keep up with new demands and the changing ways electricity was being consumed.

By the 1920s, new appliances and applications for electricity were constantly being introduced. In the 1928 'Report of the Electrical Committee of the National Electrical Code', Chairman A. R. Small noted the difficulty of keeping up with changing practices, stating that the code document is 'as alive as is the use and application of electricity in buildings, a report even three months old cannot be considered in a frozen state' (Small, 1928: 141). Overloaded circuits, appliances operating at different frequencies and currents, and intermittent electricity supplies created stress on existing wiring. A problem with a single appliance could cause an outage for an entire residence, and new appliances were emerging that had different electrical requirements. The solution in most cases was to install multiple circuits. In the 1930s Westinghouse introduced the circuit breakers most homes use today, although they did not come into widespread use until the 1960s. Separate circuits enabled appliances with a heavy demand for electricity – ovens, heaters and dishwashers – to be more easily incorporated alongside lighting (Dini, 2006).

The National Electrical Code reflected the increasing number of electrical appliances that required more power sockets in homes. Reference to the number of power sockets (receptacle outlets) recommended in family dwellings first appeared in the 1933 Code. Householders were advised to fit outlets in every room in the house so that no point on the wall, as measured horizontally, would be more than 15 feet from an outlet. Two years later, this recommendation was made mandatory for newly constructed homes. In 1937, just four years after it was first introduced, the 15 foot recommendation was changed to a mandatory ten feet. In 1940 this distance was again altered, with the Code now requiring that one outlet should be provided every 20 linear feet along the wall. In 1956, the distance was decreased to 12 feet. Finally, in 1959, the Code deemed that no point measured horizontally along the floor should be more than six feet from a power socket. This requirement remains in place today (Dini, 2006).

While new houses incorporated the latest innovations, wiring in older homes represented a layering of previous practices and materials. For example, Croft (1915) describes retrofitted homes that had exposed wires connecting new outlets and fixtures. In the 1928 update to the National Electric Code, DeWitt Rapalje of the Railroad Insurance Association of New York argued that the focus should be code enforcement, particularly of 'the bootleg electrical industry' (Small, 1928: 147). In his view, uninspected jobs performed by 'unauthorized persons' had the potential to cause a black eye for the electrical industry as a whole.

This theme is echoed in GE's 1922 publication *Home of a Hundred Comforts*, with the importance of electric wiring was described in detail. Properly wiring a home prepared the homeowner for the electric present – 'No matter where you are, you need electrical service in some form' (General Electric, 1922: 6). Wiring also prepared a home for an infinitely more electrified future. In GE's terms, 'Complete wiring is nothing more than making provision in your house for all the electric lights and appliances that you … may some day want to use' (General Electric, 1922: 2).

This depended on a wiring aesthetic designed to enhance rather than diminish the home's beauty. For GE, hiding the wires behind walls helped focus on the appearance of the appliances in use: 'The cords are almost entirely hidden and do not mar the fine effect of the appliances that are being used' (General Electric, 1922: 9). While much time and effort was spent convincing housewives of the importance of the vacuum cleaner, ensuring the availability of power sockets and sufficient wiring to handle the load was just as important.

To GE, complete wiring was essential for a comfortable and modern life. To further this goal, GE, in conjunction with a number of other electrical equipment manufacturers, joined forces to create an advocacy group called the Society of Electrical Development. Throughout the 1920s the Society produced a number of training and advertising campaigns designed to build electricity use in homes. One such campaign focused on increasing the number of 'adequately wired houses'. 'For years', the Society explained:

> there has been a persistent demand for a satisfactory method of educating the public to a proper understanding of the necessity for installing adequate wiring to provide for convenient electrical service. A standard of safety has been established by the National Electrical Code but no authoritative standard for convenient service has heretofore been offered as a guide to the public.
>
> *(The Society for Electrical Development, 1924a: unpaginated pamphlet)*

Insufficient wiring, the Society argued, had been an obstacle to sales of lighting, fixtures and appliances. This meant that sales of electricity were not what they could be. The Red Seal plan, as it was called, was a programme designed to celebrate houses that had been 'adequately wired', as certified by the local electrical league. The idea was that homes that were Red Seal certified could be advertised by real estate agents and building contractors as having met rigorous criteria, and would be more attractive to home buyers. This matched the Society's overall plan to increase and improve existing wiring. In 1924, the Society estimated that 7.5 million American homes had wires, but 'that every wired house is a potential prospect for more wiring' (The Society for Electrical Development, 1924b: 3).

Over time, wiring was concealed, more outlets were mandated in every room, multiple circuits were introduced to accommodate different types of energy demand, and an over-all concept of an 'adequately wired' house was introduced. Electrical manufacturers sought to promote the 'electrical modernisation' of the home and introduced a range of devices designed with consumer convenience in mind. This is most evident in the design of the ubiquitous light switch present in nearly every American home today. The 'Tumbler Switch', as GE termed it, took convenience and ease of use to a new level. Rather than fumbling with a dial or even pushing a button, the tumbler switch provides light in an instant and without thought – 'Here your hand rests on this group of switches the moment you have crossed the threshold. See! You illuminate the hall brilliantly' (General Electric, 1922: 5). In the *Home of a Hundred Comforts*, its ease of use is further described:

> Notice how easily this GE Tumbler Switch operates. You can't miss that one little pro-jection, and it moves – literally – at the touch of a finger ... It is the most convenient type of switch ever designed. If your hands are already occupied, you can tip it just as easily with your elbow.
>
> *(General Electric, 1922: 14)*

In the United States, electrical modernisation of the home was advanced by the creation of the Federal Housing Administration (FHA) in 1934. With the American economy flounder-ing in the early 1930s, the FHA sought to resuscitate the housing market by insuring mort-gages offered by local commercial banks. In order for a mortgage to be insured, the FHA set a number of requirements including the provision of electrical service in line with the National Electrical Code (Tobey, 1996). In other words, without modern electrical service – circuits for light and power as well as numerous outlets in each room – a home could not be easily bought or sold.

Electrifying homes called for new forms of expertise, standardisation, and collaboration among utilities, equipment manufacturers, homebuilders, electricians and the wires them-selves. What was the desired outcome? Again, the *Home of a Hundred Comforts* makes this clear: 'Electrical service, completely installed, is as elastic as your own movements' (General Electric, 1922: 19). Whether cleaning, cooking or entertaining, the home had become a site for electrified social practices.

Wiring the future

The high voltage transmission and household wiring systems described in the previous sec-tions were organised around a straightforward set of requirements. The infrastructures of transmission and household wiring were designed to ensure electricity would be reliable, affordable and capable of being provided at scale. The wires in these systems facilitated and anticipated the movement of electricity from a small number of producers to relatively distant consumers.

Recent years have seen a new set of demands placed on electrical wiring by both consumers and producers, resulting in the so-called 'smart grid'. Smart grids are typically defined as communications-enhanced electricity networks that can seamlessly integrate, modulate and adapt to the behaviours of producers and consumers. Advocates position them as a technological solution to a diverse set of challenges including climate change, power company profitability and cybersecurity (Clastres, 2011). In contrast to the one way systems of wiring described above, 'smarter' systems are better able to handle distributed forms of generation, identify the exact location of outages or line damage, and provide instant feedback on power consumption for customers and utilities alike. While typically considered a network of wires with communications capabilities, smart grids depend on interaction with meters, monitors and storage solutions, and hence with the movement of electricity at both high and low voltages (see chapters by Danieli and Grandclement et. al. in this volume).

For many utilities, smart grids are a potential solution to the problems of profitability and of delivering reliable electricity supply in the face of more distributed sources of generation (Warrick, 2015). In the realm of high voltage transmission, the drive to incorporate renewable energy is forcing grid operators to accommodate smaller and intermittent power supplies. Smart technologies are being designed to better modulate transmission frequencies and cool highly burdened transmission lines. These and other solutions seek to optimise efficiency and limit transmission losses by diagnosing system breakdowns and predicting future demands (WIRES, 2011; United States Department of Energy, 2014).

In low voltage household wiring systems, smart grids are viewed by utilities as electricity demand optimisers, shifting (but not eliminating) loads to times of cheaper electricity production. For consumers, optimisation may mean decreasing electricity consumption altogether (Davito, Tai and Uhlaner, 2010; Wang and Wang, 2013). Either way, the concept of the smart grid gives wires a new role in managing and orchestrating the supply and demand of electricity.

Does this entail 're-wiring' the relationship between electricity producers or consumers? Or are smart grids simply the latest iteration of electricity infrastructure designed to facilitate ever-increasing electricity consumption? The outcome is unclear, and will likely remain so for some time. What is clear is that the social practices that make up electricity consumption are thoroughly interwoven with the wires that facilitate the movement of power.

References

Barstow, W. S. (1898) 'The development of a transmission system', *Minutes of the 14th Annual Meeting of the Association of Edison Illuminating Companies*. Presented at the Annual Meeting of Edison Illuminating Companies.

Bennett, J. (2005) 'The agency of assemblages and the North American Blackout', *Public Culture*, 17: 445–465.

Black, R. M. (1983) *The History of Electric Wires and Cables*. London: Peter Peregrinus.

Clastres, C. (2011) 'Smart grids: another step towards competition, energy security and climate change objectives', *Energy Policy*, 39(9): 5399–5408.

Croft, T. (1915) *Wiring of Finished Buildings*. New York: McGraw-Hill.

Davito, B., Tai, H. and Uhlaner, R. (2010) 'The smart grid and the promise of demand-side management', in *McKinsey on Smart Grid: Can the Smart Grid Live up to Its Expectations*. New York, NY: McKinsey & Company.

Dini, D. (2006) *Some History of Residential Wiring Practices in the U.S.* Northbrook, IL: Underwriters Laboratories Inc.

General Electric (1922) *Home of a Hundred Comforts*. Bridgeport, CT: General Electric.

Grant, C. (1996) The Birth of NFPA. Available at: www.nfpa.org/about-nfpa/nfpa-overview/history-of-nfpa (Accessed 14.12.15).

Hammond, J. W. (1941) *Men and Volts: the story of General Electric*. Philadelphia: JB Lippincott Company.

Hammond, J. W. (1925) Development of insulated wire and cable, Information from W. S. Clark. MiSci Collection, Hammond Papers, L1865.

Hammond, J. W. (n.d. a). Edison Electric Light Company, Information from J. E. Bartlett of Patent Department. MiSci Collection, Hammond Papers, C224.

Hammond, J. W. (n.d. b) Transmission line development – derived from testimony of Prof. Charles F. Scott in 1917 suit against Ohio Brass Co. over patent. MiSci Collection, Hammond Papers, L2125.

Hammond, J. W. (n.d. c) Transmission – Hewlett suspension insulator. Extracts from testimony and briefs in patent suit of Hewlett vs. Louis Steinberger. MiSci Collection, Hammond Papers, L2177.

Hammond, J. W. (n.d. d) Transmission line practice – development. MiSci Collection, Hammond Papers, L2108.

Hewlett, E. M. (1906) 'A new type of insulator for high-tension transmission lines'. Presented at the American Institute of Electric Engineers, Niagara Falls, New York.

Hirsh, R. (1989) *Technology and Transformation in the American Electric Utility Industry*. New York: Cambridge University Press.

Huber, M. (2013). *Lifeblood: oil, freedom, and the forces of capital*. Minneapolis: University of Minnesota Press.

Hughes, T. (1983) *Networks of Power: electrification in Western society, 1880-1930*. Baltimore: Johns Hopkins University Press.

Jones, C. (2014) *Routes of Power*. Cambridge, MA: Harvard University Press.

Lee, E. S. (n.d.) Letter from Harry Winthrop Turner to Mr. E. S. Lee of GE. MiSci Collection, Hammond Papers, L5262.

House Beautiful (1905) Letter to Editor. Vol. 33, July 1905.

McLoughlin, T. S. (1912) *Questions and Answers on the National Electrical Code: a key and index to the official code*. New York: McGraw-Hill.

Murray, W. S. (1921) *Superpower System for the Region Between Boston and Washington, by W.S. Murray and Others*. Washington, DC: U.S. Geological Survey Professional Paper 123.

Needham, A. (2014) *Power Lines: Phoenix and the making of the modern Southwest*. Princeton, NJ: Princeton University Press.

Nye, D. (1998) *Consuming Power : a social history of American energies*. Cambridge, MA: MIT Press.

Nye, D. (2010) *When the Lights Went Out: a history of blackouts in America*. Cambridge, MA: MIT Press.

Peek, F. W. (1915) *Dielectric Phenomena in High Voltage Engineering*. New York: McGraw-Hill.

Press Release. (n.d.) MiSci Collection, Hammond Papers, L2182.

Small, A. R. (1928) Report of the Electrical Committee of the National Electrical Code. Boston: National Fire Protection Association.

The Society for Electrical Development. (1924a) *A National Residence Market Survey: Wired Homes in the United States (Customers vs. Population)*. New York: The Society for Electrical Development.

The Society for Electrical Development. (1924b) *The Red Seal Plan: a program to promote adequate wiring for convenient electric service in the home*. New York: The Society for Electrical Development.

Thomson, E. (1908) Extracts from 'A Retrospect'. *General Electric Interview*. MiSci Collection, Hammond Papers, L1602.

Tobey, R. (1996) *Technology As Freedom : the new deal and the electrical modernization of the American home*. Berkeley: University of California Press.

United States Department of Energy. (2014) 'Smart grid investments improve grid reliability, resilience, and storm responses'. Washington, DC: United States Department of Energy.

Walker, G. (2014) 'The dynamics of energy demand: change, rhythm and synchronicity', *Energy Research & Social Science*, 1: 49–55.

Wang, Z. and Wang, S. (2013) 'Grid power peak shaving and valley filling using vehicle-to-grid systems'. *IEEE Transactions on Power Delivery*, 28: 1822–1829.

Warrick, J. (2015) Utilities wage campaign against rooftop solar. *Washington Post*. Available at: http://wapo.st/1DX2eRt?tid=ss_mail&utm_term=.c0cd931cc7ae (Accessed 28.11.17).

WIRES. (2011) 'Smart transmission: modernizing the nation's high voltage transmission system. Working group for investment in reliable and economic electric systems'. Available at: www.smartgrid.gov/files/Smart_Transmission_Modernizing_Nation_High_Voltage_Electri_201107.pdf (Accessed 14.12.15).

4

SITUATING ELECTRIFICATION

Examples of infrastructure-practice dynamics from Thailand and Laos

Mattijs Smits

Introduction

This book makes the point that infrastructures are more flexible than commonly assumed. This is especially so in the Global South, where infrastructures are often highly dynamic and visible due to rapid economic and population growth (McFarlane, 2010). Images of newly built metropoles in China immediately come to mind, but one could also think of the spectacular increase in the rate of household electrification in Laos from 15% in 1995 to 79% in 2011 (EdL, 2012). The fast pace of new development or upgraded infrastructures, such as electricity networks, sewage systems or roads has repercussions for the ways people live their daily lives. These rapidly changing situations allow us to catch sight of how infrastructures trigger the emergence, disappearance and transformation of specific practices, and of how these developments are, in turn, important for infrastructural configurations.

The chapter explores features of this infrastructure–practice dynamic through two village-level case studies of rural electrification in Thailand and Laos. In both cases, different 'layers' of electricity infrastructure entered the villages in time frames of a few decades. Sometimes new infrastructural arrangements replaced existing ones, for example, after breakdown; at other times, new layers were constructed alongside what was already there. In-depth fieldwork, involving interviews, homestays, and (participant) observations, provided revealing insight into how infrastructures, practices and demand co-evolved in these two cases.

In detail, the chapter examines the emergence and development of new and 'electrified' practices, such as watching television and lighting, considering these with reference to rapidly changing infrastructure in the two cases. The arrival of new arrangements often heralds the disappearance of others. I therefore consider parallel instances in which infrastructure was abandoned, phased out or taken away, as a result of changing practices. In moving between these themes, and in considering systems and politics of provision alongside shifting relations between variously electrified practices, the chapter bridges between concepts associated with sociotechnical innovation, with political ecology, and with accounts of emerging complexes of social practice.

At the most basic level, we can identify three different kinds of rapid infrastructural change: (1) the development of new transmission lines, sewage systems and roads where there was nothing before; (2) the upgrading of infrastructure, referring to situations in which infrastructures are replaced by newer, bigger or otherwise improved systems; (3) the breakdown of infrastructure, either temporary or permanent, in which the system is suddenly or gradually no longer available. This chapter deals mainly with the first and the third kind. However, rather than focusing only on matters of supply and infrastructural investment, and rather than concentrating exclusively on the social, political and environmental relations (Robbins, 2012) which influence the types of infrastructure provided, the aim is to detail the dynamic interaction between supply and demand. This requires paying attention to the subtleties of the social and environmental costs and benefits of specific infrastructural projects; and of how material innovations work out in practice – which areas of daily life are affected, which are not, and how do changes in what people do figure in the future constitution of demand? In working within and between these lines of enquiry the chapter connects the analysis of everyday practices with issues generally considered to be in the realm of (political) economy.

Observations from the case study sites provide fresh insight into 'electrification' as a varied and situated process, the characteristics of which depend on how existing practices and conventions are modified, on a range of appliance-practice relations, and on institutional arrangements through which electricity is provided and through which it has effect in daily life. Amongst other things, the chapter shows that practices do not change automatically at the point of electrification. Instead, pathways of electrification are mediated through different practice-dynamics which involve more than just 'material' changes. As the two cases show, the meaning of electrification is also bound up with the practicalities of specific infrastructural configurations, including state control and related systems and economics of provision. Both cases demonstrate that demand is not autonomous, or somehow isolated from the means of provision, instead infrastructural development itself can prompt further energy demand, as existing practices are 'electrified' and as new ones develop. In some situations, it is the emergence of newly electrified practices that leads to the 'need' for new infrastructure.

Introducing case studies of infrastructure-practice dynamics in Thailand and Laos

What happens to social practices when electricity arrives? To explore these questions I focus on two case studies from Thailand and Laos, both involving rapidly changing electricity infrastructures and also rapidly changing practices.[1]

Both countries have seen significant infrastructural development over the last few decades, including rural electrification. Rural electrification was (virtually) completed in Thailand towards the end of the twentieth century (Shrestha et. al., 2004), whereas in Laos this process is still underway (Bambawale, D'Agostino and Sovacool, 2010). An estimated 79% of all households and 69% of all villages were electrified in Laos in 2011 (EdL, 2012). The two cases described below allow me to explore the dynamics of infrastructures and practices, and identify some of the theoretical challenges involved in conceptualising these interdependent processes.

The first case is a village in Northern Thailand which is called Mae Kampong. The village is only an hour and a half drive from Chiang Mai, in Northern Thailand. Before 1982 there was almost no access to electricity in the village. People used kerosene and gas lamps for light in the evening. Only a few people had diesel generators or car batteries for lighting or to watch TV, and these were used for no more than a few hours a day. In 1982, a 20 kW micro-hydropower generator was constructed, funded by USAID. Simultaneously, a cooperative was set up to carry out maintenance, collect money and manage the revenue from the hydropower system. With this system installed, the sparse and patchy household electricity infrastructure was replaced by a village mini-grid, serving about 150 households. Following an increase in demand and to enable the electrification of a nearby village, a second 20 kW micro-hydro turbine was added to the existing powerhouse in 1988. In 1998, a third generator (40 kW) was installed further downstream, again increasing the capacity of the local energy system.

While talks about connection to the main electricity network started in the 1990s, it was not until 2002 that Mae Kampong was connected to the network of the Provincial Electricity Authority (PEA), the utility that serves all areas outside of the Bangkok metropolitan area. Part of the delay was caused by resistance from people in the village who wanted to keep their own electricity infrastructure. Faced with these objections, the PEA decided to construct a new grid in parallel to the existing infrastructure. For most people, this parallel grid extended into their houses, meaning that they would have separate wiring to connect appliances to either one or the other supply; for example, the electricity from micro-hydro might be used for powering some lights and one or two sockets, while the television and fridge would be on PEA electricity. Others opted to have a control switch in their house, to enable them to switch their domestic supply from one source to the other. In both situations, people would pay separate bills to PEA and to the village cooperative managing the micro-hydropower system. While the consumption of electricity from the micro-hydropower generators had decreased by 2011, people had not stopped using it.

Before saying more about how these systems played out in practice, I describe the key features of supply in my second case.

This second case is Nam Ka village, in Xieng Khouang province in northern Laos. Like many villages in northern Laos, most of the population are from an ethnic minority (in this case Hmong). As with Mae Kampong, the village is located close to the provincial capital. Until 1995, only a few people had access to a private electricity supply, based on either pico-hydropower turbines and/or the odd diesel generator. In 1995, the Chinese Xinhua News Agency Development Corporation funded a micro-hydropower plant near the village and built a village mini-grid, much as in Mae Kampong. All households were connected for free, but a small monthly fee was collected for maintenance. However, the micro-hydropower generator broke down in 2003, forcing some people to go back to using their own diesel generators and pico-hydropower for electricity. Unable to afford these options, the majority reverted to using pinewood torches and small diesel lights.

In 2006, the system was selected for renovation by a public-private coalition of a Lao-German company, an NGO and an international engineering company. Making use of some of the existing micro-hydropower infrastructure – the small concrete dam, the forebay (water tank) and the penstock (intake pipe) – they installed a new micro-hydropower system and a new village mini-grid. They also introduced electricity meters, a relatively high connection fee and fixed tariffs per kWh used. Unlike Mae Kampong, the poles and wires of the existing system were not kept. When the new mini-grid started working in 2007, only 59 house-holds out of 101 wanted – or could afford – to pay the connection fee required. However, 31 households managed to acquire 'illegal' access to electricity through one of their neighbours or family members via a shared connection (RISE, 2008).

While connection to the main grid was not envisioned for many years, dissatisfaction with the connection fee and high tariffs, and the resulting low revenues for the company led to discussions with the national utility Electricité du Lao (EdL) about a national grid connection. Finally, a deal was made for the NGO and the company to share in the costs of a national grid connection and the village was connected to mains electricity in 2010. The existing mini-grid infrastructure was then taken over by EdL. Following this development, almost all households were connected by 2011, perhaps because of the lower cost of connection and tariffs, and perhaps because of interest-free loans from the NGO.

Infrastructures, appliances and practices

These narratives of supply and provision give a sense of the rate at which electricity infrastructures can change. In the case of Mae Kampong, the village went from only a few personal electricity generators in 1982 to grid connection 20 years later. In Nam Ka, this process went even faster, from almost no electricity infrastructure in 1995 to almost complete electrification in 2010. These developments went hand-in-hand with rapidly changing practices. For example, the existence of an electricity infrastructure simultaneously transformed existing practices, like lighting, and enabled 'new' ones, such as watching television.

The following discussion concentrates on the introduction and practice of watching television. It does so in that televisions are often the first large appliances to be acquired when electricity becomes available, and because televisions also figure as pervasive and powerful symbols of modernity.

At this point it is useful to distinguish between infrastructure and appliance. While they both play a role as material elements of practices (Shove, Pantzar and Watson, 2012) and are part of socio-technical networks, it makes sense to separate them for analytical purposes. Infrastructures, such as electricity networks, have been called 'first order' socio-technical systems (de Wit et. al., 2002). Electric appliances often need such first-order systems to function. In other words, when analysing something like the diffusion of televisions, and the practices associated with them, commentators often take first-order systems for granted, and simply focus on the appliances. However, both play a crucial role in the evolution of practices, as this chapter – and indeed, the book – shows.

Watching television

Figure 4.1 shows the penetration rate of televisions in the two villages. The diffusion of televisions is quite closely matched to the provision of electricity, outlined above. However, the graph shows that some people used diesel generators to power their television, and thus acquired one before the micro-hydropower generators were installed. In other words, there is no direct relation between the uptake of these appliances and the development of a collective electricity infrastructure. Second, not all households wanted or were able to afford a television at precisely the moment when electricity became available, explaining the increases in the years after installing the systems. In Nam Ka, a television was often the only electrical appliance people had in their homes, in addition to a couple of light bulbs. The longer history of access to electricity in Mae Kampong partly explains why there are more electrical appliances and a greater variety of them as well.

What is it that people are doing when watching television? In the case study villages in rural Thailand and Laos, people are rarely alone in the living room (the key space in which the television is located), a feature which makes watching television part of a broader set of social

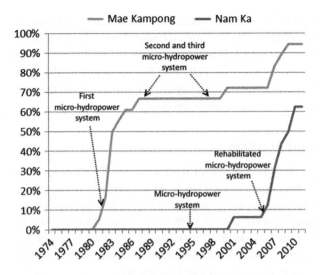

FIGURE 4.1 First year of television ownership of 16 (Nam Ka) and 18 (Mae Kampong) respondents.

relations. In both villages, before the electricity infrastructure came in, the few houses that had a television set (connected to a diesel generator), would be popular sites of social gathering. To pay for the diesel, the owners of the televisions would sometimes ask for a small fee from those who joined them. Given the costs involved of buying a television set, the generator and the fuel, the owners of such systems would most likely enjoy a good position in the social hierarchy of the village. Indeed, it would often be the head of the village, or people of the local elite (e.g., members of the village committee) who would be the first to get a television. In both villages, even after many homes acquired their own reliable source of electricity, people would still frequently gather to chat and watch soap operas or comedy shows together.

However, actively watching is not the only mode of 'viewing'. In some of the households that were observed, the television was often on in the background, just to break the silence or because it was considered 'normal'. People occasionally paid attention to what was happening on the screen, but ignored it completely at other times. This form of watching happened in the two villages, especially when the electricity tariffs became less significant, either because they reduced, or because they became a smaller part of a household's disposable income.

There are other ways in which televisions figure in the conduct of daily life. Devices like televisions also provide access to certain cultural images. For example, television gives people in rural Thailand ideas about what 'normal' life is like in urban Bangkok. This is a significant development in that until recently few would have the means or opportunity to visit the capital. Since Thai television channels – especially soap operas – are also very popular in Laos, such images are not limited to people in Mae Kampong. While it is impossible to trace the impact of these diffuse influences on village life in any detail, many interviewees were of the view that electrification had far reaching consequences. For example, people in Nam Ka explained that partly as a result of television (and of electrification) it was no longer common to wear traditional (ethnic Hmong) clothing. Others talked about the influences – some positive, some negative – of television on children and their education.

As these instances suggest, the novelty of watching television and the forms it takes evolve over time; in effect, it shifts from being the centre of attention to something that is on in the background. At the same time, the appliance is not inert: it provides access to an extensive repertoire of ideas and cultural images. By implication, these shifts follow the normalisation of electric power. From this point of view, television watching is interesting in that there are no pre-electric versions, and no forms of the practice that do not depend on the existence and availability of this key device, and of the means to power it.

Electric and other forms of lighting

The infrastructure-practice dynamic is different for lighting (compared to television) which has many pre-electric forms. In this case, 'second order' devices (light bulbs) are combined with 'first order' infrastructures in ways that reconfigure existing practices. These combinations result in what we might call altered or electrified arrangements. Before the availability of an electric infrastructure, people in Nam Ka and Mae Kampong would live, work and read by daylight, or by the light of open fires or candles. Relying on non-electric light sources calls for a range of related skills including those involved in maintaining and trimming candles, or in keeping a fire alight, both of which generally give a lower quantity and quality of light than that provided by an electric bulb. One of the clear benefits of having access to electricity, and one often mentioned in interviews in Mae Kampong, was the option to continue working at night, and especially to continue work on preparing *miang* tea, which is traditionally one of the main economic activities in the village. The villagers would pick the tea leaves during the day, steam them in the late afternoon for several hours and then sort and package them during the evening.

In detail, the meaning of 'good' or sufficient light was not an abstract concept: rather it was related to the types of light-demanding activities involved. For example, interviewees' indicated that the meaning of 'necessary' light, meaning the minimum amount required to read or work during the night, is flexible and changed over time. In the two case study villages, people would often start with one or two light bulbs, typically one in the kitchen and one in the bedroom. As they got more used to electric lighting, they would – if their budget and the systems allowed for it – expand the number and types of lights, for example, having a light outside, installing CFL lights, and so on. In this way, the availability of an electric infrastructure apparently led to a 'ratcheting' of demand, as new ideas about the 'normal' amount of light took hold (Shove, 2003).

Changes in lighting arrangements are not necessarily gradual. Indeed, rapidly developing infrastructure can swiftly transform the ways in which people use light and how lighting in turn transforms the rhythm of the day. In Nam Ka, people mentioned leaving their lights on day and night when their micro-hydropower generator was renovated and more capacity became available. However, when the first bills arrived, which were very high, they used their lights (and television) much more sparingly. When the price of power dropped again as a result of getting access to mains electricity a few years later, some loosened this strict control. As this example shows, the dynamics of practices involving electric appliances (lamps, TVs) are intertwined with the broader system of provision.

The dynamics of supply and demand

One of the ways in which changing practices affect systems of provision is by fostering or perhaps requiring the abandonment of previously vital infrastructures. The case studies of Nam Ka and Mae Kampong show that certain electricity infrastructures were set aside because they were no longer embedded in the conduct of daily life. For example, the arrival of the micro-hydropower system in Nam Ka meant that the pico-hydropower turbines and power lines became redundant. They were taken down and sold soon after the new infrastructure arrived, only to be bought again and put back in place when the micro-hydropower systems failed, as happened some years later. And when the micro-hydropower system was renovated, the old power lines were replaced with new ones in anticipation of growing demand for electricity. More broadly, the role of diesel generators shifted from being the only, localised form of power supply to more of a back-up system or supplement to 'mains' power.

At the same time, as more practices came to rely on electricity, the demand for a stable and reliable infrastructure increased. In the case of Mae Kampong, the installation of the first micro-hydropower generator not only provided electricity to fulfil demand associated with existing (and altered) practices, but also triggered new demand and thereby the 'need' to construct a new turbine. This, in turn, generated further demand, which soon required a second turbine, which led to even more demand and the need for even more electricity generation. In other words, the ratcheting of demand was translated into expanded capacity for supply. While there were initial rules from the village cooperative about the number of lights and other appliances that a household could run, these were abandoned along the way, as they proved difficult to uphold.

In both villages, micro-hydropower turbines were sometimes unreliable in that their operation depended on variable natural conditions. The local operators, with help from other people, would often have to clear branches, leaves and other debris from the water inlet. Over time, and as people became more used to a stable electricity supply, they became more sensitive to the frequency of blackouts and brownouts associated with running a micro-hydropower system.

Again, the significance (or not) of such power shortages depends on the types of practices enacted and the extent to which they depend on constant electrical power. For example, Mae Kampong developed a successful eco-tourism formula based on 'homestays'. The village cooperative developed some guidelines regarding the comfort of tourists, including promising hot showers and a toaster, both of which require a good electricity supply. Many people in Mae Kampong have therefore switched to the more expensive, but also more reliable PEA (mains) electricity. For similar reasons, people in Nam Ka were keen to connect to mains (EdL) electricity as soon as it became available. As the previous discussion of changing expectations of lighting illustrates, these experiences point to a change in the meaning of what a 'normal' supply of electricity is or should be like.

To summarise, infrastructures enable new and different forms of everyday practice including television viewing, and lighting, along with related activities like socialising, working and reading, or hosting tourists. Equally, certain practices depend on the co-existence of different types of infrastructure. To give another example, the rapid increase in the number of mobile phones – which shows some similarities to television (Figure 4.1), but within an even smaller time frame – leads to increased demand not only for sources of power (to charge batteries) but also for radio towers to enable them to function. In some villages in Laos, people have mobile phones, but can only use them in certain spots or even in the next village or town. In other places, such as Nam Ka and Mae Kampong, younger people complained that the area is served by only one or two networks. More ordinarily, road systems have an important infrastructural role in enabling providers to deliver electrical appliances. Systems of finance are also vital in enabling people to purchase new equipment. Within the home things like televisions or refrigerators 'need' space, and may also call for or engender new social relations, new socio-temporal rhythms and new or reconfigured institutions and infrastructures.

The politics of provision

The previous sections have considered some of the dynamic relations between infrastructures and practices, but have not mentioned the politics and practicalities of providing electrical power. Taking a step back, it is possible to see the dynamics of infrastructural provision as the result of a highly political process, with both direct and indirect effects on the configuration of practices.

Critical analyses of the politics and economics of rural electrification in Thailand point to the fact that rapid rural electrification based on centralised electricity production is strongly related to the politics of the Cold War. Greacen (2004) shows that the decision to support centralised over decentralised electricity production was motivated to a large extent by aid money from the United States (US) from the 1960s. During this time, the US supported Thailand in its efforts to resists communist insurgents, both from neighbouring Indochina (Laos, Vietnam and Cambodia), but also from domestic groups (Baker and Phongpaichit, 2014). Electrification of rural villages like Mae Kampong in the 1970s and 1980s can be understood in this way: this village was classified a 'pink area', meaning that the central government was observing it closely for possible 'communist' activities. Extension of infrastructures – such as electricity and road networks – was seen as a way to access and control areas in the north and northeast of Thailand.

In Laos, political-economic accounts also emphasise the role of rural electrification as means of extending state control over remote hinterlands (Evans, 2012), and as a process of territorialisation (Vandergeest and Peluso, 1995). For example, Baird and Shoemaker (2007) argue that such infrastructural developments are an expression of the Lao government's ambition to gain more control over the many ethnic groups in upland and highland areas (Smits and Bush, 2010). Since the end of the Second Indochina War (better known as the Vietnam War) the government has resettled a large number of villages and tried to connect them with roads, electricity, schools and hospitals. While this is done under the banner of development, and often generously supported by donors, there are clear political motives and outcomes.

Political economic analyses generally stop at this point. However, the ambitions of state-led territorialisation only have effect if they are manifested and reproduced in practice. This works in different ways. To illustrate, the state's interests in promoting regimes of administrative ordering (Scott, 1998) are in a sense enacted through the installation of electricity meters. The two cases show that meters are much more than simple devices that count the number of kilowatts used: they also introduce ideas about paying bills, which in turn rely on a (more or less) regular income and the ability to read. As such, electricity meters can be seen as mediating devices between the state or companies and a wide range of every-day practices.

The political nature of electricity metering was foregrounded in Nam Ka when people started tampering with the meters. They did so in order to avoid high electricity bills after their micro-hydropower system was renovated. They were not initially aware of the high costs associated with the 'new' arrangement which in effect privatised what was previously a communal energy system. Suddenly, they had to pay high energy bills and they had to do so on a regular basis, a contrast to the previous arrangement in which costs were allocated and organised much more informally. As a result, the village was divided in two groups, those with and those without effective access to electricity. In this way, the rapid change in electricity infrastructure (and associated institutions of pricing and provision) had a profound influence on the unequal social distribution of electrified practices.

The politics of electricity provision never go away, but as the two cases indicate, they tend to fade into the background, along with the normalisation of 'mains' supply, and with the related 'normalisation' of the relationships involved (e.g., between consumer and provider, between state and utility etc.).

Discussion and conclusion

This chapter focuses on how electrification plays out in contexts of rapid infrastructural change and related infrastructure-practice dynamics, illustrated by examples from two villages, one in Thailand, one in Laos. It shows that electrification does not suddenly happen and change everything. Rather, an electricity system – or several, as in the two cases discussed in this chapter – arrives at a certain moment and starts interacting with existing traditions and lives of diverse and related practices. As such, the consequences of electrification cannot be taken for granted. In practice, the process changes what people do along with their expectations of what is normal.

As these cases illustrate, the consequences of electrification are sometimes mediated by pre-existing material arrangements (as in the case of lighting) or by their absence (as for television). Again, the 'arrival' of electricity means that these material arrangements change, often leading to the requirement for more materials (e.g., more light bulbs, bigger televisions), which in turn triggers the need for more or bigger systems of provision. In most cases the interplay between supply and demand remains largely unnoticed, but as this chapter shows, changes in how electricity is used are of direct consequence for the various decentralised electricity supply systems in Mae Kampong and Nam Ka.

There are other related and also ongoing transformations. As we have seen, the consequences of electrification spill over into various aspects of life. For example, lighting enables people to work later, and can have further consequences for what people do, and for when and where different practices take place. Analysing interactions like these calls for methods of describing and conceptualising the co-evolution of the dynamics of supply and demand, and for identifying the different kinds of interaction at stake. As is often the case, interfaces between infrastructures and practices are politically charged, illustrated here by the multiple functions of electricity metering and of related infrastructures and technologies that are integral to forms of business practice and state control. Comprehending these relations depends on seeing them not as 'fixed' arrangements but as configurations that are constantly on the move, and that bridge between seemingly 'small' and 'large' scales of social and political organisation. A conventional political account of provision would, for instance, notice the effect of the Cold War on the provision of electricity infrastructure in Thailand. However, it is important to realise that systems and technologies of supply are not simply outcomes or expressions of 'large' political-economic forces. Rather, they are constituted and reproduced through the practices of different stakeholders, acting in relation to each other and their environment (Peck, 2004). In highlighting these and other points of connection, this chapter shows how issues traditionally considered to be in the realm of political economy (such as infrastructure) can also be conceptualised in terms of practice theory and related concepts of materiality, consumption and provision.

Note

1   These two cases, and others, are discussed in more detail in Smits (2015).

References

Baird, I. G. and Shoemaker, B. (2007) 'Unsettling experiences: internal resettlement and international aid agencies in Laos', *Development and Change*, 38(5): 865–888.

Baker, C. and Phongpaichit, P. (2014) *A History of Thailand*. 3rd Edition. Port Melbourne: Cambridge University Press.

Bambawale, M., D'Agostino, A. and Sovacool, B. (2010) 'Realizing rural electrification in Southeast Asia: Lessons from Laos', *Energy for Sustainable Development*, 15(1): 41–48.

de Wit, O., Cornelis, J., van den Ende, M., Schot, J. and van Oost, E. (2002) 'Innovation junctions: office technologies in the Netherlands, 1880-1980', *Technology and Culture*, 43(1): 50–72.

EdL (2012) *Electricity Statistics 2011*. Vientiane: Statistic-Planning Office, Business-Finance Department, Electricité du Laos.

Evans, G. (2012) *A Short History of Laos: the land in between*. Revised edition. Chiang Mai: Silkworm Books.

Greacen, C. (2004) *The Marginalization of 'Small is Beautiful': micro-hydroelectricity, common property and the politics of rural electricity provision in Thailand* (Ph.D. Thesis). Berkeley: Energy and Resources Group, University of California.

McFarlane, C. (2010) 'Infrastructure, interruption, and inequality: urban life in the global South', in Graham, S. (ed.) *Disrupted Cities: when infrastructure fails*. New York: Routledge.

Peck, J. (2004) 'Geography and public policy: constructions of neoliberalism', *Progress in Human Geography*, 28(3): 392–405.

RISE (2008) *Report of Observation the Village Grid in Ban Nam Kha*. Phonesavan: Rural Income through Sustainable Energy (RISE) Project.

Robbins, P. (2012). *Political Ecology: a critical introduction*. 2nd edition. Malden, MA: Blackwell.

Scott, J. (1998) *Seeing Like a State: how certain schemes to improve the human condition have failed*. New Haven: Yale University Press.

Shove, E. (2003) 'Converging conventions of comfort, cleanliness and convenience', *Journal of Consumer Policy*, 26(4): 395–418.

Shove, E., Pantzar, M. and Watson, M. (2012) *The Dynamics of Social Practice: everyday life and how it changes*. London: Sage.

Shrestha, R., Kumar, S., Sharma, S. and Todoc, M. (2004) 'Institutional reforms and electricity access: lessons from Bangladesh and Thailand', *Energy for Sustainable Development*, 8(4): 41–53.

Smits, M. (2015) *Southeast Asian Energy Transitions: between modernity and sustainability*. Abingdon: Routledge.

Smits, M. and Bush, S. (2010) 'A light left in the dark: the practice and politics of pico-hydropower in the Lao PDR', *Energy Policy*, 38(1): 116–127.

Vandergeest, P. and Peluso, N. (1995) 'Territorialization and state power in Thailand', *Theory and Society*, 24(3): 385–426.

5

CHOPPING, STACKING AND BURNING WOOD

Rhythms and variations in provision[1]

Jenny Rinkinen

Introduction

While advocates of renewable energy are struggling to persuade people to install solar panels, heat pumps and other novel and smart energy solutions, a long-lived form of heating is enjoying something of a renaissance. Heating with wood is often considered a laborious and archaic form of heating, yet many find aspects of it fascinating. One indication of this is the popularity of Lars Mytting's book *Norwegian Wood: Chopping, Stacking and Drying Wood the Scandinavian Way* (2015), a surprise bestseller of the mid-2010s including in countries outside Scandinavia. The sheer success of Mytting's book tells us something about the allure of heating with wood, whether it is based on the aesthetics of a log fire, the activities associated with logs, such as chopping, stacking and burning wood – or something else. This allure and efforts to understand it are often marginalised in more mainstream, more technologically centred discussions of energy use.

If we are to take the project of understanding wood heating seriously, it is revealing to compare it with other forms of heat provision. For this task, the concept of a 'system of provision' is especially useful in that it highlights the interaction between production and consumption, and reminds us that relations between resources, providers, intermediate technologies and consumers' roles vary greatly depending on how provision is organised. Even when infrastructures consist of relatively stable and spatially extensive material arrangements, they differ in terms of the division of labour between people and material objects, the circulation of resources, and the forms of service involved. For example, with some forms of wood heating, consumers play a much more active role than they do when provision is more centralised (Southerton, Chappells and van Vliet, 2004).

In recent writing, ideas about systems of provision have been used to address questions about the design and delivery of *services* – rather than focusing only on the world of goods and the handling of commodities (Shove, 2003). For example, studies of changing electricity networks have advanced thinking about how demand evolves and escalates through and as a part of changing forms of provision (van Vliet, Chappells and Shove, 2005). Whilst such analyses have helped reveal the interlinking of production and consumption, the temporal implications of such systems are rarely discussed. For example, how do different forms of provision relate to temporal patterns of consumption and how is the work of heating synchronised and sequenced with other activities? These are important questions in that rhythms of consumption and provision are crucial for analysing and distinguishing between infrastructural arrangements and for conceptualising the development of demand associated with them. Better understanding of these interlocking temporalities is consequently vital for understanding how infrastructural arrangements are entwined with patterns of demand. Equally important, such an approach treats the provision of infrastructural arrangements as a dynamic achievement, and not only an outcome of past forms of investment and organisation.

This chapter explores these themes by delving into the world of heating with wood. Though not often considered in discussions of infrastructures, this example is used to show how different scales and forms of provision relate to scales and forms of consumption, and how infrastructural arrangements configure the timing and distribution of the work involved. Both aspects are relevant for conceptualising diverse and changing scales of provision: from continent-wide networks to smaller scale forms of embedded production (van Vliet, Chappells and Shove, 2005). In addition, and as explained below, this strategy depends on conceptualising infrastructures not as static features but as dynamic arrangements that reflect the temporal ordering of practices (Shove, Watson and Spurling, 2015).

In what follows, the term 'infrastructure' is not used in the traditional sense of referring to obdurate, collective and typically hidden technological systems. Instead, I use it to describe material arrangements that underlie and in part constitute distinct patterns of consumption and work. The distinction between material arrangements that are more 'infrastructural' than others reflects the extent and manner in which they are rooted in the natural and built environment.

In developing this approach, I work with the inter-related concepts of *scales* and *rhythms of provision*. 'Scale' is a matter of lesser and greater spatial-temporal spread (Schatzki, 2014: 17). Size and scale are achieved only via connections that work through many sites (Latour, 2005); a phenomenon that is larger in scale therefore embraces a network of relations among practices and material arrangements that is more spread out than is the case for one of a smaller scale (Schatzki, 2011: 8). The notion of scale is useful for distinguishing between alternative material arrangements. For example, with energy provision, scale has implications for the reliability of supply and for the escalation of demand, both of which are important in thinking about what infrastructures are for and what they enable.

'Rhythms of provision' is used to describe the rate at which activities or sequences reoccur and the temporal rhythms according to which systems of provision are maintained and replenished. Whereas *scales of provision* refers to the diversity of interconnected systems, and the spatial and temporal reach of infrastructures, *rhythms of provision* are outcomes of the flows of labour, services and resources that infrastructures support and depend on. As such, they entail temporal patterns of provision, consumption and associated forms of work.

The rest of this chapter uses these concepts to structure a discussion of specific material-practice relations involved in heating with wood in Finnish private houses. Drawing on the author's studies of small-scale wood heating in Finland (Jalas and Rinkinen, 2016; Rinkinen, 2013, 2015), this chapter contributes to an understanding of infrastructures in practice that foregrounds the connectedness of demand with patterns of consumption on the one hand and systems of provision on the other.

The studies involved an analysis of small-scale wood heating, as well as the role of wood heating during infrastructural disruptions. They draw on a pre-existing archive of diary accounts written by Finns on selected days in 1999 and 2009 that were collected by the Finnish Literature Society. The call for diary entries invited contributors to describe 'the ordinary day of the Finn'. Although there were no special instructions to write about heating, the diaries contain numerous detailed descriptions of logs, stoves and methods of keeping warm. This qualitative material provides a subtle account of the everyday as experienced and reported by 'ordinary' people, such as workers, farmers and elderly people (Rinkinen, Jalas and Shove, 2015). Though not written with this question in mind, the diaries consequently offer revealing insights into the ways in which infrastructures and systems of wood-provisioning interact with the practicalities of home heating.

The chapter starts by introducing two scales and forms of wood-based heating provision – small-scale wood burning and large centralised systems – and examines these with respect to the temporalities of provision and demand. Insights from these examples are then used to produce a more refined account of relations between practices and materials especially as these relate to themes of flexibility and convenience. The concluding discussion develops a more sophisticated understanding of the varieties of infrastructural arrangements and their implications for the co-evolution of demand.

Small-scale heating – it warms you twice

In cold countries such as Finland, it is common to use solid wood for space heating in detached houses. Even though the housing stock in Finland is relatively new, wood-based heating forms the backbone of a system within which other technologies are integrated. Finland even witnessed a 20% increase in the use of small-scale heating with wood in private houses between 1994 and 2008 (Torvelainen, 2009). In 2014, wood was the second most common energy source for heating residential buildings, accounting for 15% of total use of energy, and wood fuels were the largest source of energy overall, representing 25% of total national energy consumption (Statistics Finland, 2014a, 2014b). Small-scale wood heating is also common in other Nordic countries such as Sweden (Swedish Energy Agency, 2015), and though still marginal in the UK, it is becoming more widespread there (MacLeay, Harris and Annut, 2014). Despite wood burning being a very traditional way of keeping warm, new methods and technologies for heating with wood are constantly being developed.

Historically, the most basic method of using wood for heating is to burn logs on an open fire, in a wood stove, or in a dedicated fireplace. These techniques involve 'infrastructures' at the smallest scale: wood is burnt in a separate fireplace/stove in each room that is heated, and the fire is only lit when there is a need for heat. However, even in these situations, the simple act of putting another log on the fire represents the end-point of a more elaborate sequence. From this point of view, practices of wood heating encompass skills, meanings and materials related to the acquisition and management of wood fuel, including logging, storing, fire lighting and the use and regulation of stoves, fireplaces and boilers to manage indoor temperatures. Wood burning in this extended interpretation is an historically, culturally and socially complex practice – something that is coordinated with many other aspects of life and that many people have grown up with.

In cases of small-scale wood burning, the actual work or labour involved in making heat does not happen elsewhere, or in some distant, centralised factory: rather, it is typically carried out by the end-user in, or close to the specific locales that need to be warmed. The work involved in managing this kind of heating has a number of distinctive temporal features (Jalas and Rinkinen, 2016). When organised on a small scale, wood heating requires planning and physical effort, and what can be called a 'harvest-when-available and store-until-required' mentality. For instance in Finland, people who heat with wood often source logs from their own forest, or buy them from a provider who supplies them dried or wet, chopped or solid, piled or loose. Chopped logs can take two winters to 'season', and during this time they need to be stored somewhere and under conditions that enable them to dry out. The temporal cycles of wood-related work can be illustrated with extracts from the diary data in which two men vividly describe the labour of heating:

> At 10:20 I straighten myself up and light up the central boiler, fuelled 2/3 with wood and 1/3 with lump peat. The lump peat is damp after a rainy summer, even too damp and icy. Probably half of the heat energy goes to drying! The wood that was chopped in May is almost dry. The firewood is sourced from our own forest 24 kilometres away or from closer, clearing the logging areas in others' forests. Sourcing firewood is mainly a healthy functional exercise. An elderly man like myself has to be careful not to hurt himself. Logging requires skills and strength, and one needs to stay calm.
>
> *(SKS diary 1999/42469, man, retired)*

> After four o'clock I toughen my mind. The frost has hit minus fourteen degrees Celsius, but one has to drag oneself to the wood pile. My back does not like this and my fingers get cold, but the remaining firewood is of such size that it needs to be chopped. I manage to make half a wheelbarrow of chopped wood and get an idea to heat the sauna.
>
> *(SKS diary 1999/41200, man, employed)*

These extracts illustrate how the temporality of the work involved in heating is strongly linked to the characteristics of wood as a fuel. This takes various forms. For example, burning wood calls for regular attention when the fire is lit. By comparison, the tasks involved in preparing the fuel (logging, storing logs) are spread over the year, but with the heating season in mind. These aspects are linked to the ability to store heat and the supply of wood, which dictate the intervals of related activities.

More immediately, wood heating has an impact on the temporal and spatial ordering of social life within the home. Using a fire to keep warm is a matter of management, adjustment and moderation. Patterns of (wood) consumption vary and indoor temperatures fluctuate depending on these rhythms of 'control' (Royston, 2014; Wallenborn and Wilhite, 2014), as illustrated by the following diary entry:

> I escape to the basement to light the boiler... I have to add wood every hour so the fire wouldn't go out. Regardless, during hard frost this flimsy house cools down by morning. This winter's lowest temperature in the living room after a night has been 14 Celsius degrees. Once the fire is lit I get back upstairs.
>
> *(SKS diary, 1999/38740, woman, on sick leave)*

The rhythms of wood heating are to an extent linked to the rhythms of nature. The next two quotations show how the work of heating is aligned with the weather:

It snowed lightly in the morning. The frost turned close to zero and it was easier to chop the logs. Three ovens eat a lot of wood when it is cold. The water of the well froze over on the surface. It was easy to break, easier than fixing the frozen water pipe. Wood heating, well water, and outdoor toilet are not popular nowadays but I like it here. From the upstairs window I can see the valley, bluish in the afternoon light. Stunning view, quietness, and a peaceful rhythm of life. There is physical work and mental work – a balance.

(SKS diary, 1999/12078, woman, unemployed)

The weather forecast shows minus 20 degrees and snow for tomorrow in Eastern Finland. I must light up the baking oven in the morning, it balances the heat when it is windy and snowy. At the same time I can bake bread and buns and cook food in the oven.

(SKS diary, 1999/199953, woman, retired)

In sum, small-scale wood heating consists of a bundle of distinctive, temporally orchestrated practices through which the materiality of wood and stoves, and the surrounding rhythmic events and practices coordinate the daily life of those who heat with wood. From the above quotations it is also obvious that the mentalities of the rhythms – such as the balance of physical work and the joy of synchronising – matter a lot to some of those who heat with wood. Discovering these rhythms depends on learning about a range of everyday practices including how logs are chopped, dried, split, stored and finally burnt in fireplaces of different scales and types. These activities and rhythms are quite unlike those associated with more centralised forms of energy and infrastructural provision, including systems which also involve the use of wood, for example, as a fuel for district heating.

Scaling up – less work for the householder

Whilst the use of wood in small-scale domestic heating has increased overall, its role as the main or supplementary form of heating has changed. Methods of using wood for heat have developed in ways that relate to, and that resemble material arrangements that would be conventionally described as 'infrastructural' (being large scale, networked and involving extended systems of provision). These new wood-based heating technologies mimic methods of provisioning, control and temporal organisation previously associated with other fuels.

While solid firewood (logs) remains the main form used in open fireplaces, tiled stoves, cast iron stoves and baking ovens, it is now possible to burn wood in other ways. Central wood-fired boilers are commonly used to heat individual homes or even small communities. As well as using wood pellets or chips as fuel, these systems make the burning process more efficient, and link to technologies that spread heat more evenly across the room. Such innovations have relocated the 'work' of heating with wood and have done so across various spatial scales.

Within the home, boilers have shifted the function of generating heat away from the living room to a backstage area: that is, to where the boiler is situated. Boilers can be at quite some distance from the living area of the house. Centralised arrangements also relocate the source of the timber, where it is stored and how it is treated. Central boilers typically use wood in the form of processed chips or pellets usually ordered from a commercial provider. While central boilers have reduced the number of fires that need to be managed, the spatial separation of the dedicated boiler room from the places that are to be heated has created new problems of monitoring and control.

Central boiler systems represent one option. However, wood is also used as a fuel in biomass plants within even larger scale networks. Bio power plants that are used to generate electricity and/or as part of district heating schemes are multi-fuel factories, powered by clean wood along with surplus from forestry like stumps and limbs. Compared to small scale heating with wood, district, central and direct electric heating are forms of provision in which the consumer has a more passive role. In centralised or large scale systems, relations between practices like those of harvesting, storing, fuelling and controlling heat from wood are less obvious, less familiar to the end-consumer, and more difficult to grasp: their temporal rhythms are also of an entirely different order.

In addition, from the householders' point of view, large-scale infrastructures offer a form of heating that is 'flat': the service is constant and always on. When such systems fail, their underlying temporalities come to the fore. However, when they function normally, they are invisible, falling into the background having become embedded in daily life (Mau, cited in Graham, 2010: 7).

On all these counts, the spatial and temporal qualities of large-scale provision differ greatly from those associated with small-scale wood heating. As explained above, those who harvest, store and burn wood locally are tied into a series of seasonal, weekly and also daily rhythms. By contrast, those who buy heat or power 'ready-made', and who are connected to a centralised system of provision do not need to make time for the work of heating. Instead, relevant rhythms are entirely those of consumption: of when to put the heating on, or off, and how the thermostat or controls are set. As described above, centralised, large-scale provision contributes to an industrial temporality in which production and consumption are worlds apart.

Rhythms of provision and material-practice relations

What can we learn from these spatially and temporally distinctive ways of organising heat? And what insights do these cases provide for an understanding of how demand evolves within systems of provision organised around different infrastructural arrangements? In addressing these questions I begin by reflecting on the status of objects and infrastructures before commenting on concepts of convenience, and the types of flexibility associated with different forms of provision.

At first sight, the practice of burning logs has little or nothing to do with the concept of infrastructure. Small-scale heating with wood is a mode of provision in which certain forms of work and service provision are closely intertwined. Those who burn wood on this scale are involved in a constant balancing act between supply and demand: managing logs and keeping a fire going requires active work, the details of which determine when, where and how much warmth is delivered. This is quite unlike the separation of consumption and production that characterises systems of provision organised around large-scale infrastructures of generation, distribution and supply.

Second, whereas traditional notions of infrastructure emphasise material arrangements that are relatively invisible and that enable a 'comfortable' setting in which diverse practices are enacted, small-scale wood heating depends on a dynamic bundle of inter-related activities, each involving distinctive material, spatial and temporal arrangements. Rather than a condition that enables or that is a material element of other practices, heating with wood involves a sequence of bodily interventions: it is a practice, or better, a set of practices in its own right.

Despite these points of contrast, there are areas of overlap and similarity. Highlighting these helps detail the relations between material arrangements, 'infrastructures' and practices.

In small scale and in centralised systems of heat provision, wood enters the 'infrastructure' (broadly defined) and comes out as heat. However, the relation between devices in the background ('infrastructure' as it is usually understood), and those that are in the foreground and interacted with directly (e.g., appliances, stoves etc.) is clearly not the same. For example, small-scale heating is a combination of foregrounded devices such as stoves and fireplaces, and background arrangements such as the fabric of the house itself, along with backup provision in the form of an electricity network. In this context, the fuel – solid firewood – has a distinct and tangible presence. In more centralised forms of provision, appliances, fuels and related material arrangements all remain in the background.

As the scale of provision increases, the definition of appliance and infrastructure becomes more complicated. For example, does a central boiler count as part of the background infrastructure or as an appliance that users engage with directly? This question forces us to think about what it is that flows when resources or services move through systems of provision: at what scale, in which form and by the aid of what kind of work do trees turn into logs or pellets and then to heat?

The discussion above shows that these flows respond to spatial and rhythmic patterns of provision and consumption. Conventional infrastructural arrangements like wood-fired central or district heating systems may be more static and more invisible than things in use (like a wood-store or an open fire) but they too affect the movement, positioning and timing of labour, resources and services. When provision is centralised households interact with items at the 'end' of the line, such as switches, air conditioners and radiators, these being what Shove and Chappells refer to as the 'sensitive fingertips' of extensive infrastructural systems (Shove and Chappells, 2001). Where provision is localised, the relation between these devices, their control, and the resources they consume is much more immediate.

These arrangements and differences prompt further reflection on recent methods of conceptualising infrastructure. There has been a tendency to think of infrastructures as enabling systems – platforms that support a huge variety of potential services and activities, and that are not tied to any particular rhythm or pattern of activity. Whilst individual practices have a temporal rhythm (cooking, lighting), modern infrastructures are designed to be (largely) a-temporal, to function equally all year round, and throughout the day. Ideal infrastructures consequently flatten natural and other rhythms and situate the provision of heat, power or water within a technically mediated sphere (Jalas, Rinkinen and Silvast, 2016).

These aspects of separation do not mean that supply and demand, or supply and the resources on which it depends are really fractured. Instead, it means that the temporal, technological and institutional configurations we observe are structured in ways that divide responsibilities, obligations and labour along certain lines. For example, the recurring maintenance and operation of large technical systems reflects natural annual and daily cycles as well as socially negotiated expectations of comfort. Meanwhile, in offering 'flat' and uniform provision, large technical systems order and enable distinctive patterns of everyday life. Whatever form they take the key point is that all such systems involve a complex interplay between and with the practices involved in providing and 'consuming' heat.

To summarise, different modes of heating with wood demonstrate the variety of infrastructural arrangements through which heating services are provided, and reveal a range of more centralised and more localised solutions. In thinking about how these arrangements are structured, the question of scale is key. As wood is burnt at different scales, there are related differences in terms of the division of labour, material arrangements, resources and service flows, and in how methods of heating with wood overlap, merge and suffuse with other material arrangements.

Associated rhythms of provision and consumption have further implications for a discussion of materiality, infrastructure and the temporal ordering of social practices. As we have seen, forms of heating differ significantly in how, when and where labour is divided and distributed along more and less extended supply chains. The experiences of those who burn wood on a small scale suggest that although the heating process may be sequential (the fire has to be lit, kept going etc.) the work of provisioning also has a temporal order of its own. Moving between the different scales of wood-based heating (localised, centralised) it is obvious that the work entailed is differently distributed in time and space, and between humans and machines.

Because logs need to be cut, chopped, dried and relocated, wood heating resembles what Vannini and Taggart (2016) describe as onerous consumption. Sure enough, those who burn wood on a small scale report on home-based patterns of life that are to an extent organised around the tasks involved in using solid wood as a source of heat (see Jalas and Rinkinen, 2016). Once established, these configurations of attention, time and labour 'make sense' and 'hang together'. But as the experiences of new homeowners who are unfamiliar with wood burning demonstrate, adapting to the demands of a fire or a stove, and to localised systems of provision depends on also adapting their everyday routines (Rinkinen and Jalas, 2016).

As concepts of comfort and expectations of time use change, so the perceived advantages of different heating systems wax and wane. For example, forms of district and central heating have enabled people to disconnect from the effort of keeping their home comfortable, and given them the flexibility to engage in diverse patterns of work and leisure. Such arrangements appear to fit well with the temporal organisation of urban ways of life, so much so that other more demanding systems of provision would be quite disruptive. In this context, the growing use of small-scale wood heating seems to indicate a somewhat puzzling trend away from convenience and towards 'onerous' consumption. These experiences counter the idea that there is widespread societal interest in increasing convenience, and suggest that 'demanding' practices such as domestic wood heating can be valued for the satisfaction they afford. For some people an onerous form of heating is a source of tension and trouble, but not for all. It seems that the apparent inconvenience of living with the temporal demands of wood heating can be defined in other ways, especially if this method of warming the home is culturally accepted and if it is taken to be normal.

Shifts and differences in how wood heating is interpreted do not happen in isolation. If more decentralised systems become normal, other arrangements, including methods of building design and regulation evolve in support. From this point of view, changes in provision and in the 'infrastructure' of daily life are enmeshed in shifting social and cultural conventions and in related divisions and allocations of time and labour. As outlined here, recognising the interdependence of temporal rhythms, and the flexibility and patterning both of heating and daily life helps make sense of the persistence and positive appeal of what look like inconvenient, laborious and physically demanding practices. In brief, wood-based heating creates rhythms in everyday life that can be a source of pleasure, even for people living within an increasingly flexible and interconnected global society.

Staying warm represents a very concrete accomplishment and as we have seen, some associate the experience (and the work involved) with feelings of efficacy and satisfaction. Such accomplishments and experiences are not measured in terms of effectiveness or economical value: rather they are part of the aesthetics and meaningfulness of everyday life. What others might count as inconvenience is tolerated (or rather not defined as such) if its role in the temporal order of the day or the year is accepted and taken as 'normal'. All these facets together explain why convenience (as in time saving) is not an always over-riding goal.

Methods of heating are also important in defining meanings of comfort and the rise of wood heating suggests that some people are accepting significantly variable indoor temperatures. Over the past century there has been a shift from local, on-site heating to large-scale heat provision (e.g., from gas or electricity) and to technologies, building designs and regulations organised around the goal of delivering even temperatures throughout the day. One consequence is that standardised interpretations of comfort are increasingly inscribed in the infrastructures of home heating. As others have argued, more exacting understandings of comfort have been taking hold, and have done so in ways that reflect and influence the design and organisation of centralised systems (Shove, Walker and Brown, 2014). As a result, it has become normal to expect the stable provision of constant heat, and it has become normal to be situated as a passive consumer at the end of long, complicated and (from the consumer's view) inflexible chains of provision. Small scale heating with wood counters these trends.

These observations present something of a dilemma for those seeking to promote the use of renewable fuels, including wood. On the one hand, centralised systems have the potential to make sustainable energy transitions easier, for instance, by switching fuels behind the scenes. On the other hand, changes of this nature maintain regimes in which consumers are separated from the work involved in keeping warm, and in which the relation between supply and demand remains distant and highly mediated.

The wider message from this investigation of heating with wood is that distributed renewable energy technologies might be taken up even if they entail new or different temporal rhythms. This is because 'convenience' is a relative concept, not an absolute goal, and because not all future infrastructures need to be invisible, 'easy to use' or dependent on the distancing and outsourcing of time and labour. This conclusion extends the scope of what could and should be included in the valuing of a range of infrastructural systems, and highlights the significance of viewing them not in isolation from but in the context of other aspects of daily life.

Note

1   This chapter develops some of the ideas presented in my Ph.D. thesis, entitled *Demanding Energy in Everyday Life: insights from wood heating into theories of social practice* (Rinkinen, 2015).

References

Graham, S. (ed.) (2010) *Disrupted Cities: when infrastructure fails*. London: Routledge.

Jalas, M. and Rinkinen, J. (2016) 'Stacking wood and staying warm: time, temporality and housework around domestic heating systems', *Journal of Consumer Culture*, 16(1): 43–60.

Jalas, M., Rinkinen, J. and Silvast, A. (2016) 'The rhythms of infrastructure', *Anthropology Today*, 32(4): 17–20.

Latour, B. (2005) *Reassembling the Social. An Introduction to Actor-Network Theory.* Oxford: Oxford University Press.

MacLeay, I., Harris, K. and Annut, A. (2014) *Digest of United Kingdom Energy Statistics 2014.* A National Statistics publication. London: TSO. Available at: www.gov.uk/government/uploads/system/uploads/attachment_data/file/338750/DUKES_2014_printed.pdf (Accessed 28.12.17).

Mytting, L. (2015) *Norwegian Wood: Chopping, Stacking, and Drying Wood the Scandinavian Way.* London: Maclehose Press.

Rinkinen, J. (2013) 'Electricity blackouts and hybrid systems of provision: users and the "reflective practice"', *Energy, Sustainability and Society*, 3(1): 1–10.

Rinkinen, J. (2015) *Demanding Energy in Everyday Life: insights from wood heating into theories of social practice.* Ph.D. dissertation. Aalto University School of Business. Helsinki: Aalto Print.

Rinkinen, J. and Jalas, M. (2016) 'Moving home: houses, new occupants and the formation of heating practices', *Building Research and Information*, 45(3): 293–302.

Rinkinen, J., Jalas, M. and Shove, E. (2015) 'Object relations in accounts of everyday life', *Sociology*, 49(5): 870–885.

Royston, S. (2014) 'Dragon-breath and snow-melt: know-how, experience and heat flows in the home', *Energy Research and Social Science*, 2: 148–158.

Schatzki, T. (2011). 'Where the action is (on large social phenomena such as sociotechnical regimes)'. Working Paper 1: Sustainable Practices Research Group. Available at: www.sprg.ac.uk/uploads/schatzki-wp1.pdf (Accessed 28.12.17).

Schatzki, T. (2014) 'Practices, governance and sustainability', in Strengers, Y. and Maller, C. (eds.) *Social Practices, Intervention and Sustainability: beyond behaviour change.* London: Routledge.

Shove, E. and Chappells, H. (2001) 'Ordinary consumption and extraordinary relationships: utilities and their users', in Gronow, J. and Warde, A. (eds.) *Ordinary Consumption.* London: Routledge.

Shove, E. (2003) *Comfort, Cleanliness and Convenience: the social organization of normality.* Oxford: Berg.

Shove, E., Walker, G., and Brown, S. (2014) 'Material culture, room temperature and the social organisation of thermal energy', *Journal of Material Culture*, 19(2): 113–124.

Shove, E., Watson, M. and Spurling, N. (2015) 'Conceptualizing connections: energy demand, infrastructures and social practices', *European Journal of Social Theory*, 18(3): 247–287.

Southerton, D., Chappells, H. and van Vliet, B. (eds.) (2004) *Sustainable Consumption: the implications of changing infrastructures of provision.* Cheltenham: Edward Elgar.

Statistics Finland (2014a) *Energy Consumption in Households* [e-publication]. Helsinki: Statistics Finland. Available at: www.stat.fi/til/asen/2014/asen_2014_2015-11-20_tie_001_en.html (Accessed 28.12.17).

Statistics Finland (2014b) *Energy Supply and Consumption* [e-publication]. Helsinki: Statistics Finland. Available at: www.stat.fi/til/ehk/2014/ehk_2014_2015-12-14_kuv_001_en.html (Accessed 08.04.16).

Swedish Energy Agency (2015) *Energy in Sweden* [e-publication]. Stockholm: Swedish Energy Agency. Available at: https://energimyndigheten.a-w2m.se/Home.mvc?ResourceId=5545 (Accessed 29.12.17).

Torvelainen, J. (2009) Pientalojen polttopuun käyttö 2007/2008. (The use of solid wood in detached houses, in Finnish). Metsätilastotiedote 26/2009. Helsinki: Metla.

Vannini, P. and Taggart, J. (2016) 'Onerous consumption: the alternative hedonism of off-grid domestic water use' *Journal of Consumer Culture*, 16(1): 80–100.

van Vliet, B., Chappells, H. and Shove, E. (2005) *Infrastructures of Consumption. Environmental Innovation in the Utility Industries.* London: Earthscan.

Wallenborn, G. and Wilhite, H. (2014) 'Rethinking embodied knowledge and household consumption', *Energy Research and Social Science*, 1: 56–64.

6

SELF-SUFFICIENCY IN ARCHITECTURAL AND URBAN PROJECTS

Toward small-pipe engineering?

Fanny Lopez

Since the end of the 1990s, new variants of infrastructure have emerged in Europe. These 'small-pipe' engineering systems can be disconnected from traditional networks: in this they defy the dominant paradigm of centralised energy distribution and consumption that has been in place for over 100 years. Infrastructures of this type are micro, alternative, self-sufficient and disconnected (Lopez, 2009, 2010, 2014), off-grid or post-grid (Coutard, 2010; Coutard and Rutherford, 2015). Small technical systems are defined in relation to an industrial model of large-scale distribution and to networks that exist at the scale of entire cities and territories and that characterise the provision of services such as water, sanitation and power (Joerges, 1988; Gras, 1993). While large systems have undeniably improved the comfort and sanitary conditions of urban populations (Tarr and Dupuy, 1988), they have also marginalised pre-existing and competing decentralised models.

It is in this context that I want to reflect on the call for autonomy or self-sufficiency. In practice, there are no fixed or given spatial boundaries to autonomy: it can be a goal adopted in relation to a single house, a whole building, a district, a city or an entire region. Discourses around energy self-sufficiency are consequently defined by economic and political considerations as well as technical and symbolic concerns.

This concept of energy autonomy has inspired architectural and urban projects for over a century. Beyond the realm of counter-cultural experimentation, conceptual antecedents can be found as far back as the late nineteenth century. Indeed, as soon as large-scale distribution and connection networks were imposed, dreams of energy autonomy and debates about disconnection appeared (Lopez, 2014). Whether by challenging forms of design and patterns of use, or by reinventing service systems at different scales, self-sufficiency projects question the (re)invention of local infrastructures.

This chapter describes the history of these ideas and gives a sense of their development since the end of the 1960s. It asks: What kinds of lifestyles and daily practices emerge in visions of self-sufficient houses and in plans for systemic disconnection from traditional networks? What lessons can be learned from these small-pipe engineering experiments?

Autonomous or self-sufficient

The word 'autonomy' was initially applied to political relations and was used to describe the deliberate self-government of states and certain communities. In these terms, 'local energy autonomy' refers to the capacity of a local group of actors (like a cooperative or a municipality) to define an energy project including energy production and supply conditions.

The notion of energy autonomy can take one of two forms. The first is secessionist autonomy: this refers to the goal of radical independence and is related to communities of isolationists (certain communities of the 1970s, gated communities, etc.). It is the result of a deliberate policy enacted by a group of individuals within a closed economy. Secessionist autonomy can be likened to autarchy. The second form, which we will call cooperative or generative autonomy, emphasises the potential for pooling and for local connection and collaboration as part of a shared political project on the part of those involved in 'connectable places'. By contrast, the term self-sufficiency refers to a balance between production and consumption.

During the 1970s, many different terms were used to describe projects, buildings or communities that sought disconnection from the network, including: 'autonomous', 'self-sufficient', 'off the grid', 'autarkic', etc. These descriptive terms were often used indiscriminately to describe the same broad dream of disconnection, typically at the scale of the house or small community. In many of these visions, the house represents a symbolic space, the screen on which one can project one's capacity to live in a sustainable manner. For over a century, a number of architectural and urban projects proposed a form of autonomy that was both desired and planned. In such visions, being disconnected was not the same as being beyond the reach of a network – as might be the case with geographically isolated houses which are simply deprived of connections to utility networks.

The visions of the 1970s echo previous discourses and ambitions. For example, in 1912, Thomas Edison presented the concept of a 'Self-Sufficient Electric Country House', an idea that figured in what was at the time an ongoing debate about how electrification might work (e.g., AC versus DC current), and at what scale (New York Times, 1912; Hughes, 1983). Some years later, Richard Buckminster Fuller imagined the disappearance of infrastructural networks in his famous 'Dymaxion House' and other 'Autonomous Living Packages'. During a presentation of the Dymaxion House in New York in 1929, Fuller detailed the energy system. The house was reportedly provided with two septic tanks and a fuel tank. The water was filtered, sterilised and recycled; waste was hermetically packed, stored then sent to the chemical industries, and the toilet functioned without water: 'You press a button, and the air goes out. You press another button, and the air goes in' (cited in Krausse and Lichtenstein, 1999: 94).

The technical descriptions of the systems that Fuller introduced are incomplete. Apart from the structural and functional aspects, major uncertainties remained as to the energy supply: Fuller lacked clarity. The house was described as 'practically independent' or 'semi-autonomous', but Fuller's presentations were studded with phrases like: 'it should be possible', 'we imagined' and the narrative was often told in the future tense. This caution is not surprising: at the time it was not really possible to produce the elements required for a totally autonomous housing unit on an industrial scale. Fuller asserted that self-sufficiency was possible and within reach, but a large part of his work remained theoretical, conceptual and prototypical. The Dymaxion House nonetheless represents the first model of a self-sufficient house in the twentieth century. Although the idea of a house that could generate the energy required by its inhabitants has figured as a technological dream for most of the last century, practical research and experiments in self-sufficiency attracted increasing interest between 1970 and 1980.

American counter-culture visions of autonomy in the 1970s

Aided by technological progress and the critical social-cultural context of the late 1960s, the movement for energy autonomy gained momentum on an international scale after the 1973 oil crisis. A reduction in the consumption of water, energy, materials and food appeared to be an essential response in the face of the predicted exhaustion of non-renewable resources and of climate change caused by energy-consuming and polluting activities. The Club of Rome's publication alerted the public to the fact that resources were finite and that their use left environmental footprints behind. The report questioned the postwar model of growth and affluence in which urban services symbolized a modern technological society and enabled the global spread of Western lifestyles and patterns of consumption.

During the late 1960s and early 1970s, the model of 'modern' technological growth was repeatedly attacked by counter-cultural movements which experimented with alternative ways of living, building, consuming and producing. These movements envisioned 'energy without its technicians and operators', reinforcing also popular slogans like 'architecture without architects' and 'Do it Yourself'. The American counter-culture moved the inhabitant–constructor–producer to the centre of the domestic project (Maniaque, 2011). Many publications and magazines took their inspiration from images of a return to organic domesticity but although various counter-cultural figures argued for independence from traditional utilities very few achieved this between 1965 and 1970.

Symbolically, initiatives and prototypes developed during this period distanced themselves from both the aesthetics and the energy models of Modernism and instead advocated low-tech futurism (Lopez, 2014). For example, the 'Drop City' community, in southern Colorado, was one of the first to experiment, in 1965, with the self-building of zomes, domes and autonomous energy systems, in collaboration with Steve Baer, an expert in thermal physics and the founder of the Zomeworks Corporation. Also from the United States, Michael Reynolds extended self-building, highlighting its vernacular roots and developing a radical discourse on the political challenges of autonomy. After graduating with a degree in architecture from the University of Cincinnati in 1969, he proposed the 'Earthship' concept in 1970 (Reynolds, 1990) and created the Earthship Biotecture Foundation. Reynolds believed that the conventional home had become the victim of an addiction to modern power networks. Once a synonym of social progress and better hygiene, the urban network now appeared as a contagious infrastructure infecting the territory it covered, causing environmental, architectural and urban decline (Figure 6.1).

No matter how Manichaean these statements may appear, Reynolds' ambition of organising the fundamentals of housing around a subsistence economy turned him into a visionary leader of self-sufficiency. His practice was based on the direct use of natural resources supported by a critique of the network and related forms of energy consumption inherited from the nineteenth century.

As the shift toward self-construction indicates, citizens were invited to play their part in a new, more autonomous and private model of housing: one that relied on mutual assistance, free association, decentralisation and self-management. Reynolds and his followers were skeptical about modern construction and modern energy systems in general. They believed that autonomy had to be holistic and extensive, encompassing the economy, politics, society and nature as well as energy. Beyond the house itself, the imperative of self-construction extended to services including, heating systems (thermal solar panels), water tanks and wind energy.

FIGURE 6.1 Michael Reynolds, « Connexion et pollution », 1990.

In order to make a clean break with modern networks, the inhabitants of autonomous homes were expected to be totally (or almost entirely) devoted to the construction, repair, modification and maintenance of makeshift systems.

To sum up, American counter-culture protagonists, active between 1965 and 1970 wanted to limit their social and technical worlds to that which was within their immediate reach. These ambitions were criticised by the mainstream architectural profession as well as by others: it seemed to be a denial of technological progress and of modern expertise and know-how. For the most part, the projects of this period envisaged autonomy on the family scale or that of the small community. There was no dominant typology, but the archetype of the shelter or cabin was common. Often made of recycled materials, these were small domestic modules, rarely with more than one floor.

In some cases, the goal of autonomy and reliance on alternative technologies was at the cost of what counted as 'Western' standards of comfort and was therefore hard to popularise. The technical performance of projects built in the early 1970s in the United States, like Steve Baer's house or Reynolds' Earthship were discussed in several reports. These iconic cases have sometimes been accused of technological denial and architectural impoverishment. For example, Reyner Banham compared counter-cultural technological systems, such as Steve Baer's house, to inefficient spaceships (Banham, 1969: 288). The primitive 'post-carbon hut' advocated by members of the counter-culture was criticised for abandoning modern technology and for imagining an environment far from the city. For Banham, the low energy performance of this type of cabin construction and the daily efforts involved in closing, opening or repairing shutters and solar panels figure as constraints on domestic life.

Even so, the first oil crisis ensured that energy autonomy became a widespread theme in architectural and urban discourse. A new line of publicly funded research emerged, focusing on improving living standards and the production of models and solutions such as the 'Autonomous Housing Project' which sought to attract manufacturers and developers from across the building sector. Launched in 1971 by Alexander Pike, this project undoubtedly helped popularise energy autonomy: it remains a major reference point for those interested in the relationship between the infrastructure and housing.

Making autonomy 'normal': Autonomous Housing Program, Cambridge UK, 1971–1979

Darling, tonight the Kilocalorie was superb,

- It is because of our high density energy battery
- To cook with a digester is really simple
- Now, run the water for your bath, I'll go connect the wind turbine to the compression heat pump.
- Darling, can you also put the goat outside before closing the solar insulation blinds?

This could be the script for the first advertising material for the autonomous house, a research project at Cambridge led by Alexander Pike with the support of the Science Research Council. A revolutionary housing unit.

(Games, 1975: 6)

This fictitious dialogue is how the progressive British magazine *The New Statesman* presented Alexander Pike's vision of autonomous housing (Figure 6.2).

Unlike the cases discussed above, this project was supported by the Science Research Council (SRC) and the Department for the Environment (DoE) and was based at the

FIGURE 6.2 Alexander Pike, Autonomous House Model, 1973.

University of Cambridge in England. For the SRC and the DoE, the study of autonomous housing was part of an international assessment of alternative energy in the 1970s.

The proposed scheme was innovative enough to seduce these funding institutions even though it was seen as being 'too institutional for the counterculture and too utopian for the institute' (Lopez, 2010: 225). Looking back, Pike's now forgotten project proved to be a precursor of contemporary research on self-sufficient buildings (Lopez, 2011).

Before the first environmental crisis and the boom in alternative energy, the Autonomous Housing Project (AHP) was renowned for the expertise and influence of those involved, and for the quantity of documented, technical analysis produced. The AHP adventure started in 1971. Pike's objectives were clear from the outset: to establish a theoretical and critical base that would support the development of autonomous energy services; to develop the necessary tools in order to construct and test a prototype of the Autonomous House; and, finally, to promote its commercial development. Pike was a visionary pioneer, outlining an architectural and town planning programme for the twenty-first century. He followed the technical experiments emerging from the American counter-culture, but without subscribing to them. Pike was also aware of the autonomous ideals enshrined in Steve Baer's house (1965), and developed by the New Alchemy Institute (1965) and the Farallones Institute (1972). In most cases, Pike regretted that technical problems tended to be resolved at the expense of domestic comfort. Pike insisted that a 'typical house could function without connection to any centralised services'. His argument, however, was not a return to a simple or archaic life. 'We defend a very sophisticated "self-sufficiency". We must use all our technical understanding in order to build efficiency in the use of materials and alternative energies' (Pike and Frazer, 1972: 8).

It was this dual challenge – total autonomy and high performance – that the team confronted and that informed their approach to constructing a prototypical home in 1977. The prototype had a floor space of 70 m^2 divided over two stories, with an interior garden of 35 m^2. The structure was built of wood and steel (Figure 6.3).

A wind turbine, satisfying electrical needs, was mounted on a tower located at the centre of the construction, which contained most of the mechanical equipment and utilities. In addition passive solar and geothermal installations provided for space and water heating. Water was purified and stored in tanks, and grey water was treated by reverse osmosis before being evaporated. A Clivus System digester produced methane from organic waste. An article in the American magazine *Popular Science*, in August 1973, marked the beginning of national and international interest in the project.

> You have taken a shower, finished dinner, you are comfortably sprawled in the living room watching the television and that does not cost you a penny! Even more important, you have consumed no non-renewable resources of the planet in order to heat your water, to cook or to light the house. Your house is completely self-sufficient in energy and offers you great comfort. This is Alexander Pike's vision at Cambridge University.
>
> *(Scott, 1973: 4)*

Notwithstanding such media attention, in 1978, the SRC decided not to renew funding for the project: the awarding committee estimated that the achievements had been insufficient. In spite of the proliferation of research on the subject, the reviewers concluded that it was impossible to build a completely self-sufficient house with the technical means available. Pike died suddenly in 1979 and the Autonomous Housing Project died with him. However, it gave

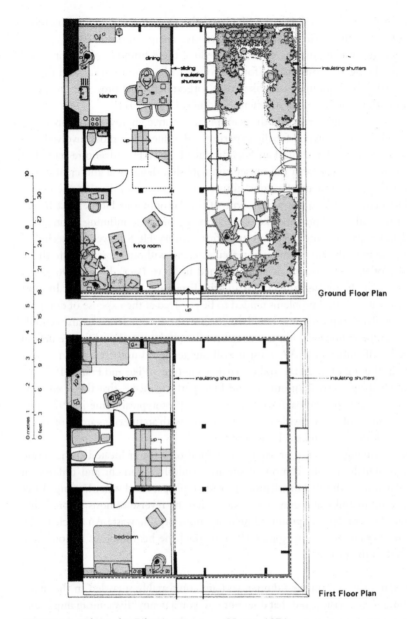

FIGURE 6.3 Alexander Pike, Autonomous House, 1974.

rise to an enduring interest in autonomous homes. From 1973 onwards, architects, engineers and town planners vigorously debated the possibilities of energy self-sufficiency. *Architectural Design* published two issues on 'Autonomous Houses', one in November 1974 and the other in January 1976.

At the end of the 1970s, the idea of energy autonomy for an entire city or the countryside had yet to really take hold. Instead, studies of alternative energy systems tended to focus on specific technologies. The concept of an autonomous house was associated with the idea of a small technical system completely independent of any more extensive network, and with no possibility of being integrated into systems of a larger scale.

Autonomous architecture within urban networks

In the above examples, autonomous architecture was defined and developed in opposition to infrastructural networks. In the mid-1970s, autonomous buildings attracted growing interest from organisations considering networks and distribution systems at different scales. These ranged from universities and public institutions to commercial companies. Whilst the self-builders had generally focused on individual dwellings or communal housing, new experiments in autonomy extended from the family unit to entire cities.

Also working at the start of the 1970s, the French architect and academic Georges Alexandroff, was especially influential in widening debate about appropriate scales of self-sufficiency. Like others of his time, he drew on the work of previous pioneers, including Frank Lloyd Wright, whose ideas about community and self-sufficiency, local resources, natural thermal systems, small-scale dams, etc. were embodied in various projects including his self-sufficient Taliesin and unbuilt schemes for 'Broadacre' city. These schemes, all of which embodied a distinctly American vision of utopia, had very little appeal in Europe's denser urban context, but they did inform concepts of sufficiency across different scales. For example, Alexandroff defended solar power as the main source of energy for those seeking self-sufficiency in dense urban areas as well as in the countryside. For Alexandroff, the building stock was not an inert mass that had to be 'equipped', but a living object that evolved. Looking beyond architectural aesthetics, Alexandroff proposed a new urban order characterised by forms of 'pooling' and energy density. Alexandroff argued that self-sufficiency had to 'work' on the adaptability of its systems and that the scope for moving in this direction depended on the type of urban fabric and the buildings in question. The degree of self-sufficiency sought had to be systematically assessed and energy-related solutions had to be developed at scale, and between buildings (Figure 6.4).

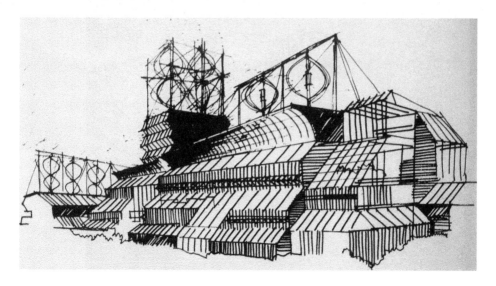

FIGURE 6.4   Georges Alexandroff, Self-sufficient city, 1976.

He covered entire surfaces with solar collectors, wind turbines, Stirling engines or cylindrical-parabolic collectors. Their multiplication and structural dimension took into account the desire for energy performance and for technical innovation: each building would produce the energy needed for itself or its neighbours. Alexandroff displayed a taste for regional development in these plans, with the creation of large-scale energy sources, the wind turbine-reflecting pool, the wind turbine-water tower, fields of reflective collectors or the amphitheatre solar conch, all figuring as visible landmarks in an ecosystem of provision (Figures 6.5 and 6.6).

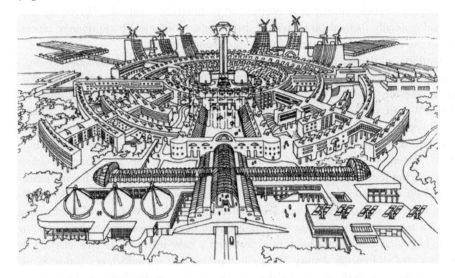

FIGURE 6.5 Georges Alexandroff, Self-sufficient city, 1980.

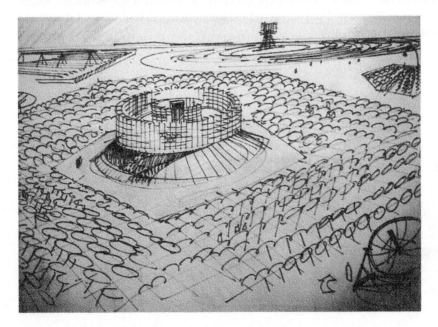

FIGURE 6.6 Georges Alexandroff, Energy Monument, 1976.

Such combined structures reshaped the landscape and traditional infrastructures disappeared. In their place, Alexandroff imagined new networks powered by alternative energy sources including solar and wind. For Alexandroff, energy had to move to the centre of the architectural imagination, after which applied research could be used to demonstrate the technical performance of those systems. Meanwhile, lifestyles and patterns of energy demand were simply not discussed.

It was not always clear how self-sufficiency would work out in practice. In addition, autonomy was not synonymous with ecological benefit, or reduction in the use of resources. As is now obvious, there have been different, not always consistent ambitions. For example, the Dymaxion House was a Fordist design that included technologically futuristic alternatives to traditional networks. For counter-cultural architects, self-sufficiency appealed as a form of self-building in unspoiled lands. It was a way to get closer to natural resources and reduce overall consumption. For Alexandroff, it was about rethinking the nature of the city and urban networks. For the majority of these architects and writers, autonomy was important as a critique of Western energy systems. But for all their visionary elements, these ideas produced no overarching manifesto of the ideal city.

By the end of the 1970s, ideas about energy-related autonomy were small scale, utopian, pluralistic and internally divided. Much thought was given to how to overcome the technical challenges of new energy systems, but much less to the questions of how to switch to a larger scale or of the implications of autonomy for the daily life of an entire community. The critique of large modern systems involved a rejection of top-down control and planning, and a reaction against centralistic policies and large-scale projects. Micro-scales became an essential aspect, also being associated with ideals of participation and 'democracy'. In combination, these movements for autonomy reinforced the idea that the everyday and the domestic was an appropriate scale for architecture.

Forms of social and technical autonomy – contested discourses 1970–1980

As outlined above, 1970s designs for autonomous homes were diverse. Ideology, technical ambition, cost and governance were all matters of disagreement. Even though many writers shared a critique of energy monopolies, embraced alternative energies, and hoped to develop an everyday economy based on biological cycles, market gardening and short distribution networks, they did not agree on the types of political change or on the forms of daily life and 'needs' around which autonomy might become a reality. Whereas the self-builder's movement aimed to promote economic freedom for citizens via the reconstitution of an autonomous and private sphere of action based on mutual assistance, free association, decentralisation and self-management, others distrusted such ideals. Pike, for example, considered autonomy to be an essentially technical challenge. He trusted in industry and mass production: only this would enable him to manufacture his highly sophisticated housing model cheaply and only this would enable him to develop and exploit avant-garde technologies.

For some counter-cultural activists, an autonomous energy economy was a political project designed to generate counter-power, but for Pike, as for Fuller, it was an essentially technological ambition.

Many agreed that total autonomy was difficult to achieve but on a small scale, counter-cultural builder-activists succeeded in demystifying the technical challenges involved by building homes with their own hands. These low-tech experiments may have been wanting in terms of building performance, but they were very accessible in terms of cost and know-how. The development of autonomous buildings therefore involved a curious paradox. On the one hand, there were buildings and communities which were inspired by a social utopian vision but which did not perform well in technical terms. On the other, there were high tech prototypes that were never built due to technical constraints and financial costs.

In 1973, an autonomous home was expensive. For the UK architect Ian Hogan, who specialised in alternative energy, total autonomy at the scale of an individual building was prohibitively costly in mid-1970s.

> If you spend about one thousand pounds in alternative technologies, any house would become 60% self-sufficient. By spending more, let's say three thousand pounds, by adding a heat pump and a windmill for instance, one would achieve 80% self-sufficiency. The last 20% are the most costly and most difficult.
>
> *(Harper and Boyle, 1976: 158)*

While some aspects were plausible, complete autonomy was a triple dead end: to guarantee total independence while maintaining high living standards was financially ruinous, to lower the costs while maintaining the goal of independence resulted in a significant decrease in performance, and, finally, reducing costs while maintaining high performance resulted in only partial autonomy. At the time, these three constraints confounded the pursuit of full autonomy.

Estimates of the relative economic cost of energy-related self-sufficiency differed depending on the state of the network. For example, it might be cheaper to build an autonomous house in an off-grid area than to extend the power network to reach it. But with the expansion of nuclear power and electrification across Europe and the United States, the equations changed again. UK architect Peter Harper advocated a standard kit for an autonomous house, along with house clusters that would enable cheaper forms of collective or semi-collective installations and systems. However, architects like Harper or Hogan were cautious about the prospects of autonomy at an urban scale.

Other debates turned on the social and political merits of different scales of provision: ranging from housing collectives to municipalities. For example, some advocates of self-sufficiency were wedded to ideas of democracy and participation, and to specific concepts of community. Others were not. Pike and Alexandroff distanced themselves from questions of political governance and their approach to urban politics remained highly ambiguous. They believed that some central power should bring about energy self-sufficiency, encourage experimentation, coordinate measures, ensure the management of urban services and lead inhabitants toward a new, energy-conscious domesticity. They called on municipalities to provide special financing for high priority zones and pilot projects and given the technological complexity of their autonomous housing schemes it is perhaps not surprising that construction could not be delegated to the inhabitants. However autonomous homes were to be governed and paid for, they were symbolically positioned as a distinctive type – clearly set apart from dominant forms of urban dwellings.

Meanwhile, in popular representations, self-sufficiency was often characterised, and caricatured, as a little house overloaded with useless and uncontrollable technological devices. The cover of the January 1976 issue of *Architectural Design* took this line (Figure 6.7).

FIGURE 6.7 Monica Pidgeon (dir) « Autonomous houses », *Architectural Design*, January 1976.

Behind the gate, we can see one of Pike's autonomous houses, as well as another building. Cows, a kitchen garden and a biogas digester complete this domestic scene and in the background we glimpse the dark and threatening silhouette of an industrial city. Framed like this the autonomous community promised to protect and guarantee individual interests. The entrance gate with the warning 'Autonomous property, keep out' recalls the enclosed space of gated communities, some of which seceded from the municipality to provide their inhabitants with better services: ecology and autarky often feature as the core principles on which such communities are founded. These and similar stereotypes of self-sufficiency were widely reproduced. For example, the British sitcom, *The Good Life*, which ran from 1975 to 1978 on BBC one, featured a stylish London suburb, in which the Good family decided to transform their home and their suburban way of life in order to live in autarky. Selling fruits and vegetables from the garden, breeding goats and installing windmills were ridiculed as fantastic adventures revealing the impossibility of self-sufficient living amid twentieth-century social and economic structures.

In architecture as in the popular media, the autonomous house retained a deeply ambivalent status. Sometimes celebrated for creating an authentic community without hierarchy the autonomous house was also derided for being anti-social, closing itself off from the city and the world. Given these socially negative associations, autonomy amounted to a form of architectural abdication in which the small individual house was set against the city, and in which off-grid solutions were pitched against large-scale infrastructures of collective supply.

The result is a curiously limited representation of autonomy in which the complexities involved are either overlooked or forgotten. It is also an image implicitly founded on conflict: the individual against the collective, or a community against a region, a country, even the rest of the world. By association, the socio-political model is that of the reduced world of the monastery, the space colony or the gated community. To put it more strongly, concepts of autonomy and autarky are often related to the strategic vocabulary of war. When framed like this, the principal opponent seems to be that of centralised public service, and of collective provision.

Many researchers have examined the social and symbolic significance of the network (electricity, water, communication), often underlining the ambition of cohesion that it expressed. As described, municipal actors were involved in building extensive systems based on the precepts of solidarity, universal access and equality. Gabriel Dupuy defined these networks as the 'technical equipment of urban solidarity' (Dupuy, 1984). Stephen Graham and Simon Marvin also shared this definition in their book *Splintering Urbanism* published in 2001. The network operators guaranteed the supply of a huge amount of energy to be shared by the city's inhabitants; subscribing to the network offered immediacy and stability and entailed participation in a normative and regulatory relationship. From this point of view, the emancipatory potential of autarky and autonomy, whether on the individual scale or that of a small community, seems to be no more than an ideological illusion promoted by those who are committed to an alternative but equally 'social' vision of collective networked provision and solidarity. By contrast, advocates of the 'autonomous house' mobilised images of peace, shared abundance and fertile nature, but in a typically reclusive context. Situated between these opposing visions, the concept of *energy-autonomy* had a more subtle role. On the one hand it complicated the ideal of a narcissistic and individualistic culture, and on the other it also hinted at alternatives to the dominant model of centralised service provision. Seen in these terms, the project of energy self-sufficiency was informed by, but also served to counter the traditional pairing of opposites: connection-sharing versus disconnection-isolation, house–city, etc.

Beyond autonomy: linking small and large-scale provision

At the beginning of the 1980s, protagonists of energy autonomy stressed that technological systems that relied on renewable energy could not be adopted on a large scale. They argued that new economic and social models were required, along with a new politics of provision:

> The problem is not so much the fact that the means of production belong to a power but rather that these means of production and these infrastructures incorporate the entire program and the entire history of capitalism since the 19th century.

The question is therefore not simply one of the necessity of a new energy choice (fossil energies, renewable energies, hybrid systems) but how the technological then the economic and political whole of society is viewed.

(Castoriadis and Cohn-Bendit, 1981: 12)

In other words, the problem was not energy in itself as much as the physical, technical and organisational structures of production and consumption: in short the network and its infra-structures. From this perspective, renewable energies could become the vehicle for another kind of social and political organisation, combining actions and reflections that anticipated new modes of societal organisation. If taken to heart, the strategy of starting from the goal of energy autonomy would greatly expand the scope of the 'environmental question', for example, including the need to redefine lifestyles and traditional modes of consumption and governance. In developing these ideas, Castoriadis and Cohn-Bendit warned that renewable energy technologies were not inherently incapable of being incorporated into large technical systems, or into centralised systems of provision.

The decade between1980–1990 marked the advent of these and other discussions about the scope for integration, and the dilution of certain principles previously associated with energy autonomy. Nevertheless in the early 1990s, the implementation of 'Agenda 21', then the launch of the European Conferences on Sustainable Cities and Towns (with the Aalborg Charter, drawn up in 1994) stimulated interest at every institutional level, also prompting more concrete forms of urban environmental action. This impetus led to the creation of eco-districts, initially in northern European cities.

Today, there is a consensus in favour of hybrid systems of extensive networks and more localised forms of micro-grids. Rather than advocating the autonomy of units or groups of buildings, most European public-private partnerships focus on the sustainability of buildings that are connected to the electricity network and that balance energy demand in real time. The smart grid appears to promise new ways of optimising this relationship and with these possibilities in place questions about the future of energy seem to revolve around intercon-nection: how do you hook small installations up to the network? How can renewable energies become included in large technical systems? One of the questions this raises – most obviously for electricity – is that of network scale. On what scale should autonomy (and therefore the network) be considered: on the scale of a building, a block, a region? And how far should interconnectivity go?

Paradoxically, the survival of the big electrical networks increasingly depends on new forms of interconnection. The majority of public–private European partnerships are, for example, keen to emphasise the resilience of interconnected buildings that are linked to the centralised electricity network. For EDF (the public French energy supplier), being discon-nected is equivalent to being invisible to the network during peak hours: this is a problem since the smart grid is designed to optimise and balance the various interconnections in line with the fluctuating relationship between demand and supply. Accordingly, micro-grids are invited, and sometimes obliged, to be connected to the super-grid. In Bretagne, Kergrid Building (Smart Award 2013), for example, is 'devoted to its network' (Lopez 2015, personal communication, 19 January). At the same time in France, the Pas de Calais-Picardie region hired the American futurologist Jeremy Rifkin to develop a master plan that put regional autonomy at its centre. How can these competing visions coexist? Which systems of service management will emerge?

If self-sufficiency is still justified in environments devoid of any infrastructures, it is much harder to make the case for disconnection in areas already supplied by the network. In a French town outside Nantes, the power struggle by the Abalone group for a complete disconnection of its building from the EDF network shows how difficult it is for total autonomy to be imagined or realised. In this case, the demand for autonomy was seen by EDF as an act of defiance toward existing public services. But again, scale is critical. Micro-grids are proven to be technically viable for a building, a neighborhood, a city, even a region or an island. Celebrated examples now include King's Cross or Woking in England (Lopez and Bouton, 2015; Lopez, 2016, 2018), Hammarby and Västra Hamnen in Sweden, the Marcus Garvey Village in Brooklyn and the Austrian districts of Voralberg and Güssing (Dobigny, 2009). Each of these examples – in different time frames and contexts that go beyond the framework of our analysis (Coutard and Lévy, 2010; Forest and Hamdouch, 2015) – have sought to shift the management of power in line with the goal of self-sufficiency, and many have succeeded. The idea that traditional energy infrastructures can play a minor supporting role in projects like these has made headway in the countries of the North as well as in the South (Jaglin, 2004).

Questions of appropriate scale are far from being resolved – and in any case they take different forms, but the structural foundations of a 'modern' energy system are clearly shifting in line with the following trends. With a diversification of productive energy resources and systems, small technical or individualised supply systems are emerging that overlap with existing large scale networks. Now situated in relation to each other in new eco-systemic configurations, service networks (water, waste, sanitation, electricity) are no longer considered as wholly separate arrangements, but are routinely interlinked and complementary. These kinds of energy transition involve innovative partnerships and new decision-making processes between energy managers, public authorities and civil society, all of which generate and reflect new social and economic issues concerning service management and governance.

From this point of view, being autonomous now means being disconnected from the large-scale normative historical model, and being able to build a utility system on and across other scales. Disconnection is not a matter of imagining energy provision without the network but is, rather, a matter of reinventing the network along with other modes and moments of connection. On one hand energy futures are envisaged as a continuation of the historical tradition of large-scale connection, on the other hand, and at the same time, the potential for decentralised and self-sufficient systems is still strongly defended. New questions bridge between these debates. For example, are there full and partial forms of self-sufficiency, and if so, what does this mean for the extent and depth of interconnection involved? Who ensures the management of these interlinked services? Who pays? Faced with the unpredictable cost of energy transitions over the next ten years, real dilemmas are emerging especially at city scale where there is a choice between investing in networks, or pursuing greater levels of autonomy on the scale of more and less extensive real estate projects.

Conclusion

In the last few decades, the large-scale technological visions and projects inherited from the nineteenth century have increasingly been challenged by movements that look toward alternative infrastructures, greater local autonomy and decentralisation. Revisiting infrastructure has not only been a technological effort but has also entailed new types of governance, along with new partnerships between civil society, public authorities and private sector.

Energy self-sufficiency projects originally oscillated between the extremes of archaic communitarianism and technological futurism. Since the 1980s, energy self-sufficiency has branched out from these niches into the mainstream of urban regeneration and now has a central place in debates about the energy transition. What remains controversial and what is still unclear is the scale on which self-sufficiency will establish itself. Although projects that are disconnected from the network have not increased in any uniform or linear direction, the idea of autonomy has maintained momentum through to the present. Today, the idea of self-sufficiency is an idea that is part of reinventing people's relationship to energy systems and that is also part of modifying economic structures and management processes so as to create experimental spaces in which to develop a new sense of shared everyday life.

References

Banham, R. (1969) *The Architecture of the Well-Tempered Environment*. London: The Architectural Press.

Castoriadis, C. and Cohn-Bendit, D. (1981) *De l'écologie à l'autonomie*. Paris: Seuil.

Coutard, O. (2010) 'Services urbains: la fin des grands réseaux?', in Coutard O. and Lévy, J.-P. (eds.), *Écologies urbaines*. Paris: Economica. pp. 102–129.

Coutard, O. and Lévy, J. P. (2010) *Écologies Urbaines*. Paris: Economica.

Coutard, O. and Rutherford, J. (2015) 'Villes «post-réseaux»: infrastructures, innovation sociotechnique et transition urbaine en Europe', in Forest, J. and Hamdouch, A. (eds.), *Quand l'innovation fait la ville durable*. Lausanne: Presses Polytechniques Universitaires Romandes. pp. 97–118.

Dobigny, L. (2009) 'L'autonomie énergétique: acteurs, processus et usages. De l'individuel au local en Allemagne, Autriche, France', in Dobré, M. and Juan, S. (eds.), *Consommer autrement. La réforme écologique des modes de vie*. Paris: L'Harmattan. pp. 245–252.

Dupuy, G. (1984) 'Villes, systèmes et réseaux : le rôle historique des techniques urbaines', *Réseaux. Communication - Technologie – Société*, 4: 3–23.

Games, S. (1973) 'Open House', *The New Statesman*, 3 January 1975.

Forest, J. and Hamdouch, A. (2015) *Quand l'innovation fait la ville durable*. Lausanne: Presses Polytechniques Universitaires Romandes.

Graham, S. and Marvin, S. (2001) *Splintering Urbanism. NetworkRed Infrastructures, Technological Mobilities and the Urban Condition*. London: Routledge.

Gras, A. (1993) *Grandeur et dépendance, sociologie des macro-systèmes techniques*. Paris: Puf.

Harper, P. and Boyle, G. (1976) *Radical Technology*. London: Wildwood House.

Harper, P. and Boyle, G. (1973) 'Autonomous house', *Architectural Design*, January 1976, p. 3.

Hughes, T. P. (1983) *Networks of Power. Electrification in Western Society, 1880–1930*, Baltimore, MD: Johns Hopkins University Press.

Jaglin, S. (2004) '*Être branché ou pas, Les entre-deux des villes du Sud*', 56: 4–12.

Joerges, B. (1988) 'Large technical systems: concepts and issues', in Hughes, T. and Mayntz, R. *The Development of Large Technical Systems*. Frankfurt: Campus Verlag. pp. 9–32.

Krausse, J. and Lichtenstein, C. (eds.) (1999) *Richard Buckminster Fuller: your private sky*, Baden: Lars Müller Publishers.

Lopez, F. (2009) 'L'autonomie énergétique ou le rêve d'une déconnexion', in Rouillard, D. (ed.) *Imaginaires d'infrastructures*. Paris: L'Harmattan. pp. 105–125.

Lopez, F. (2010) *Déterritorialisation énergétique 1970–1980, de la maison autonome à la cité-autoénergétique*. Ph.D. thesis, Université Paris I Panthéon-Sorbonne.

Lopez, F. (2011) 'L'utopie énergétique d'Alexander Pike', in Alonzo, E. and Marot, S. (eds.) *Marnes, documents d'architecture*. Paris: Éditions La Villette. pp. 133–167.

Lopez, F. (2014) *Le rêve d'une déconnexion, de la maison autonome à la cité auto-énergétique*. Paris: Éditions La Villette.

Lopez, F. (2016) 'Les monuments de la transition énergétique' in Beltran, A. (ed.) *Mondes électriques*. Frankfurt am Main: Peter Lang.

Lopez, F. (2018) 'Keep the lights on! La décentralisation énergétique à Londres', in Lepensant, G. (ed.) *L'autonomie énergétique en Europe*. Paris: Inalco.

Lopez, F. and Bouton, A. (2015) 'Les micro-systèmes techniques de la transition énergétique', Revue Urbanités, November. Available at: www.revue-urbanites.fr/6-les-micro-systemes-techniques-de-la-transition-energetique/ (Accessed 29.12.17).

Maniaque, C. (2011) *French Encounters with the American Counterculture, 1960–1980*, Aldershot: Ashgate Publishing.

New York Times (1912) 'Edison's latest marvel, the electric country house', *The New York Times*, September, 15: 9.

Pike, A. and Frazer, J. (1972) 'Simple societies and complex technologies', *RIBA Journal*, 9: 377–378.

Reynolds, M. (1990) *Earthship, Volume I: how to build your own*. Taos (NM): Solar Survival Press.

Scott, D. (1973) 'The Alexander Pike autonomous house', *Popular Science*, August 1973.

Tarr, J. and Dupuy, G. (1988) *Technology and the Rise of the Networked City in Europe and North America*. Philadelphia: Temple University Press.

PART III

Standards, planning, adaptation

The chapters in this section examine the relationship between infrastructures, 'standards' and interpretations of 'normal' practices. Parking spaces in a new town in England in the 1960s, district heating in Belgrade, the installation of lifts and toilets in office buildings, and the recent spread of wireless communication may appear an odd mix of cases. We have placed them deliberately alongside each other here because they all raise fundamental questions about the creation of 'normality'.

Central heating, Wi-Fi-spots and power sockets are now taken for granted by most readers in the developed world. We may not always find a vacant parking space near our house, but we certainly expect parking spaces to be a 'normal' feature of residential neighbourhoods. These chapters are reminders of how recent and contested these arrangements are. Only 60 years ago – a short time in the annals of history – the majority of Europeans did not live in homes with central heating. Facebook only started in 2004. At that time, wireless communication and social media and networking sites were not part of 'normal' communication. There was nothing inevitable or automatic about their rise and diffusion. Precisely how 'normal' ways of living and working have evolved in increasingly energy-intensive ways is a theme that runs through the chapters in this section.

By setting benchmarks, standards tend to ratchet up expectations of normal provision. But this is not always the case: the relation between standards and planning laws and regulations and infrastructures is complex. In the case of Stevenage, a new town built in England after the Second World War, town planners initially planned and built an environment intended for cyclists and pedestrians. They were not prepared for the spread of private car ownership, the new demands this made on people's mobility or the ambition of having a parking space next to one's home. In this case, infrastructures were adapted to keep pace with changing practices and expectations. In modern office buildings, by contrast, designers and planners have been actively involved in constructing future 'needs'. In a competitive race to raise rent and investment potential, builders and planners have constructed office buildings that are equipped to a 'higher' standard than their occupants generally require. Work practices consequently adapt to a physical building that is over-provisioned with cooling, 'small power' (electricity) and multiple toilets and showers.

The relation between 'normal' practices and infrastructures is not straightforward: it can hide within it several historical trajectories. As the story of central heating in Stocksbridge, an industrial town in the North of England, shows, ambitious plans to install central heating were aborted in the face of austerity and cuts after the Second World War: a reminder that processes of 'normalisation' are subject to stops, starts and moments of reversal. While central heating is now the norm, it became so through different routes. In Stevenage, central heating systems were based on gas warm air systems, but in London flats the first systems depended on electric underfloor heating.

Together these chapters show that demand is not something that is latent and simply waiting to be met by a new technological system or cheaper type of energy. Demands have to be built sometimes in the face of resistance – the tenants in London flats that were equipped with electric underfloor heating preferred the warm glow of the open fire – and sometimes carried along by a tide of changing practices – as is the case with wireless communication and the emergence of a whole new host of communicative practices that have made a Wi-Fi-spot in homes, trains and cafes a must.

The chapters in this section work with a rich and innovative variety of sources and methods, using these to make visible features and dynamics of infrastructures that are otherwise hidden. The authors employ house plans and urban planning files, tenants' complaints, building codes and regulations, social surveys and interviews, along with reports by car parking and garaging committees. They draw on historical methods, science and technology studies, political economy and practice theory.

In demonstrating how infrastructures and practices constitute each other they raise thorny yet critical questions about the possibility for intervention to alter the shape of what will be 'normal' in the future. Standards, for example, might not just be employed better to reflect actual work practices and needs. They could also be used to change how we work and live. At present, planning tends to reproduce practices with which we are familiar today. That is not the only option, though. All around us, we see practices on the move in new directions. Solo living is on the rise but so are new forms of co-living. If car sharing takes off, it is bound to change the demand on infrastructures and with it the need for a private parking space. Appreciating the relative autonomy of practices and their endlessly dynamic character opens the way for new strategies of envisioning, planning and adapting infrastructures now and in the future.

7

THE OFFICE

How standards define 'normal' design practices and work infrastructures

Noel Cass, James Faulconbridge and John Connaughton

Introduction

The post-industrial city is a complex assemblage of infrastructures. Some scholars have written about the pipes and cables buried beneath the roads and pathways of the city (Graham and Marvin, 2001), whilst others note that we only become aware of many of these infrastructures when they fail (Graham and Thrift, 2007). Here, we concern ourselves with a different manifestation of infrastructure: the office building.

In its post-industrial guise, the city in the developed economies of Western Europe and North America has come to be defined by office work ranging from finance, insurance and real estate (Sassen, 2011) to cultural industries such as advertising and architecture (Scott, 2000) along with the administration and sales work required by corporations (Scott, 1996). All these sectors and more call for offices. The office has consequently become a fundamental feature not only of cities, but of a vast range of working practices. Roughly a third of workers were found in offices in 1974, and almost half in 2005 (46%), according to the Multinational Time Use Survey (Gershuny et al., 2010).

The pipes and wires that allow flows of electricity and water into and out of the office, and the roads that bring workers from their homes, are all infrastructures that serve offices. In categorising office *buildings* as infrastructures, we follow Star and Lampland (2009), who define infrastructures in two ways. First, they define infrastructure as something 'invisible, part of the background of other kinds of work'. Second, they define infrastructures as relational. As they put it,

> one person's infrastructure is another's brick wall ... the teacher considers the blackboard as working infrastructure integral to giving a lesson. For the school architect and for the janitor, it is a variable in a spatial planning process or a target for cleaning.
>
> *(Star and Lampland, 2009: 17)*

In this sense, the office is clearly an infrastructure for those working within it. De Wit et al. (2002) describe offices as 'space[s] in which different sets of heterogeneous technologies are mobilised in support of social and economic activities', whilst Niezabitowska and

Winnicka-Jaslowska (2011) adopt a similar conceptualisation, emphasising the coevolution between technologies, work practices and offices. In such views, the office is a machine for working, an infrastructural nexus of space, technology and practices (Hui, Schatzki and Shove, 2017).

In this chapter, we ask how those developing new offices and refurbishing existing ones produce building infrastructures that service a particular form of 'normal' office work. In particular, we focus on how various *standards* shape the design of office infrastructures and their impact on related infrastructures of electricity provision. By standards, we mean agreed rules which coordinate the process of designing offices and which specify acceptable levels of provision (Bowker and Star, 2000; Timmermans and Epstein, 2010). We focus on how standards define 'normal' office infrastructures that are capable of servicing 'normal' work practices. Using examples from the speculatively developed office market in London, UK, in the years 2010–2015, we show then how complex interplays between different standards generate interlocking effects that tie 'normal' offices (at least in the context of an international financial centre) to specific levels of infrastructural provision which have become ubiquitous. Underlying this trend are particular assumptions about work practices which drive understandings of what is 'needed' in a 'normal' office. This has implications for ongoing office building design and for the potential to adapt to changes in office work, office technology and environmental concerns.

Offices and standards

The office is analysed in a variety of ways. For some it is an innovation junction, in which technologies facilitate work (de Wit et al., 2002). For others, it is a symbolic space, attached to the identity of the companies that occupy it (Black, 2000). It can be seen as a space defined by cultural circuits of knowledge which construct ideas about productive and desirable working environments (O'Neill and McGuirk, 2003) and organisational forms (Burrell and Dale, 2003). Meanwhile, a political economy perspective emphasises the role of property markets (D'Arcy and Keogh, 1997) and valuation of office space in a context of financial investment in which 'form follows finance' (Willis, 1995).

We consider instead how the above influences come to be represented in a series of standards that define what the 'normal' office should provide, as an infrastructure for office work. There is an extensive literature on standards in the social sciences (e.g., Schmidt and Werle, 1992; Allen and Sriram, 2000; Busch, 2000; Bowker and Star, 2000), which provides a compelling account of their power to coordinate design processes. In particular, it is suggested that standards coordinate by homogenising: defining what is standard and conversely, what is non-standard and thus to be avoided. There is also recognition that standards come in many forms. Timmermans and Epstein (2010: 72) differentiate between *design* standards that specify technical properties, *performance* standards that define operation, *terminological* standards that use labels and categories to classify and *procedural* standards that define steps to be taken in any process. In the case of UK offices, several of these types of standards have coordinating effects, explored below in a summary of regulatory and voluntary standards relating to office building design.

In the UK, the law governs building design primarily through building regulations which specify conditions that designers have to meet (Imrie, 2007). These regulations cover issues such as structure, safety and well-being, for example, dealing with the structural loading capacities of different materials and the insulating properties of walls and windows. Others apply to the provision of ventilation/fresh air (driven by historical concerns about 'sick buildings'), lifts and stairs (particularly for emergency evacuation, based on expected occupancy of the building) and toilets (again, relating to occupancy).

Since 2010, the energy efficiency *performance* of new non-domestic buildings including offices has been addressed in 'Part L2A of the Building Regulations', addressing the 'conservation of fuel and power' (HM Government, 2013). Part L requirements are set in terms of CO_2 emissions reductions, with the onus on developers and designers to demonstrate that the intended building is designed to have lower emissions than a reference model.[1] However, Part L does not define *how* developers and designers should ensure that their building performs better than the similarly sized and shaped 'reference' building created for comparison. Rather, it focuses on the modelled performance of the design. It is also important to note that compliance with Part L is assessed on the modelled performance of a building's main heating, ventilation, air conditioning (HVAC), lighting and other major systems, using only standardised assumptions about building occupancy. It does not take account of anticipated patterns of occupancy and use, including the energy use associated with computers and other plug-in equipment (van Dronkelaar et al., 2016).

Building regulations are not the only *performance* standards involved. New buildings require an Energy Performance Certificate (EPC) before they can be sold or let. EPCs label the energy efficiency of the building on an A–G rating scale similar to those used to indicate the energy efficiency of domestic appliances (Department for Communities and Local Government, 2012). They are calculated using a similar methodology to that used for demonstrating Part L compliance (i.e., a modelled estimate under standardised conditions, not an estimate of likely real energy consumption). This is fairly typical of the international situation, where to bring coherence to international 'energy standards' for buildings, the EU's Energy Performance of Buildings Directive (European Commission, 2003) only demanded building certificates be based on actual energy performance 'to the extent possible'. A more prescriptive approach based on real performance has been adopted by many EU countries (Economidou, 2012). In the UK, Display Energy Certificates (DECs) also record real performance but are only in use in the public sector. DECs were not extended to private sector buildings under the post-2010 coalition government, although voluntary energy audits undertaken as part of the ESOS (Energy Savings Opportunities Scheme) have similar functions (Cohen and Bordass, 2015).

Another part of the regulatory framework that applies to building design is planning law. Planning consents are granted based on numerous factors, including maximum height, visual 'bulk' and style, the 'rights to light' of surrounding properties and more. These restrictions on design, while framed by national planning policy, are open to local interpretation and are, in part, negotiable. They are also legally enforceable.

There is a substantial literature on how formal regulations have influenced office design (Hamza and Greenwood, 2009; Pan and Garmston, 2012; Goulden et al., 2015). Regulatory standards are, however, only the tip of the iceberg. There are also voluntary standards which prove to be especially significant in competitive property markets.

In the UK, voluntary standards include BREEAM (the Buildings Research Establishment Energy Assessment Method) and the British Council for Offices' (BCO) Guide to Specification. The BREEAM process provides an evaluation of the 'sustainability' or environmental *performance* of a building, with credits given for diverse features including low carbon energy, green roofs, biodiversity, building location and links to sustainable transport. Credits for specific aspects of a building's heating, cooling and other systems are also included, and combined to give an overall rating for the building as a whole. Compliance with BCO guidance is also expected within the speculative office development sector. The BCO Guide, updated every few years, was first published in the 1990s with the purpose of helping property developers navigate between over-provision – including unnecessarily expensive and wasteful specifications – and the risk of producing buildings deemed to be 'below standard' in terms of quality and infrastructural provision (Guy, 1998). Compliance with BCO guidelines is now seen as *sine qua non*. BCO guidelines address many of the features also covered by building regulations (toilets, lifts etc.) but add guidance on levels of comfort and provision, for example, for ventilation, cooling and the availability of electrical power ('small power').

A final set of 'quality standards' emerge from cultural understandings and models of what a good quality office looks and feels like. These relate to features such as the façade and the aesthetics and feel of office space, alongside service provision. Such cultural standards are somewhat hard to define but are taken for granted and shared amongst actors in office design, development and marketing, as well as by their 'customers', the eventual tenants. The term 'Grade A' is often used as shorthand for this diffuse notion of quality. Although 'quality' means different things to different people (Cass, 2017), informal standards have a powerful influence on design and construction, and in making the market for 'Grade A' office space.

Conceptualising the effects of standards on office infrastructures

Having described the standards that affect office design in the UK, the next task is to conceptualise their effects on the character of offices as infrastructures for work and on the technologies that are incorporated and that link office buildings to electricity infrastructures. We do so by drawing attention to the role of standards as structuring devices within design practices.

Design standards operate in different ways. We can, for example, differentiate between standards dictating provision or performance. The former define the level, number or amount of facilities that have to be provided in a building. Examples include building regulation requirements and BCO guidance on toilet provision calculated with reference to assumptions about occupational density, gender balance and absenteeism. Performance standards instead define outcomes in terms of a standard or an outcome to be achieved (or anticipated) when the building is in use. An example would be the goal of providing a temperature range of 24°C ± 2°C in summer, and 20°C ± 2°C in winter, as set out in the BCO guidance (Gardiner and Theobald, 2014). The numbers of days on which these goals might not be met are also specified (e.g., 'not to exceed 25°C for more than 5% of occupied hours'), but with no restrictions on how to achieve them. Standards in the office sector often straddle these and other categories in Timmermans and Epstein's (2010) typology. For instance, BCO guidance includes *design* and *performance* standards, and an office that is BCO compliant is one that meets the *terminological* standard of 'Grade A'. They also have complex effects on the 'agency' of the various actors involved. For example, whereas prescriptive standards remove design discretion, performance standards appear to offer designers more freedom, though it is often the case that required outcomes can only be achieved in a limited number of ways.

Standards also vary in how they are used and enforced. The mechanisms of enforcement can be distinguished using Scott's (2008) 'three pillars' perspective on institutions, which also reminds us that standards can be both formal and informal (Brunsson and Jacobsson, 2000), visible and invisible (Timmermans and Epstein, 2010). The three pillars position suggests that institutions rest on *regulatory*, *normative* and *cultural-cognitive* forms of legitimacy with corresponding sanctions for non-conformity.

The most formal standards (e.g., planning agreements and building regulations) fit Scott's (2008) *regulatory* pillar, being rules imposed by the state with the threat of punitive, that is, legal consequences. This differs from the *normative* pillar in which collectively shared understandings of what *ought* to be done underpin standards policed through social sanctions: those not following normative standards are perceived to be acting illegitimately. Guidance from an established and recognised institution such as the BCO fits this description. The *cultural-cognitive* pillar is closely related to the normative, but involves institutions and standards reflecting basic beliefs about reality and understandings rooted in culture, rather than norms of behaviour. In the case of office design, this is exemplified by beliefs about what a quality, let-table building looks and feels like (i.e., bright, white, cool, with lots of glass). There is no 'hard evidence' to support these beliefs. Indeed, the concept of evidence does not apply to such cultural constructs, but in a social field, they become recognised to the degree that anyone not acknowledging or reproducing such beliefs is viewed as an outcast.

Standards influence the design of office infrastructures in two important ways: by defining provision and performance and by structuring the practices of designers through regulative, normative and cultural forms of policing that constitute the institutional environment in which they operate. Our next step is to show how this structuring operates in practice, and what this means for office design and for office work.

Commercial offices in London

The following discussion draws on expert interviews with informants in the field of office building design and refurbishment conducted in 2014–2016. These interviews were semi-structured (Fylan, 2005) and conducted using a schedule of questions designed to draw out the different factors that determined a building's form, functional and symbolic spaces, and the use of particular systems of heating, cooling, lighting and information technology. We used ten buildings as case studies to provide a focus for interviews and to ground what otherwise would have been abstract discussions. Questions explored the justifications and rationales for specific decisions about the design and the forms of infrastructural provisioning involved.

The case study buildings were selected to reflect different categories of office buildings. They were all located in London, they varied significantly in size from 3,000 to 23,000m², and the selection of cases included new build projects (n=6), major structural refurbishments of 1980s (n=3) and 1960s buildings (n=1). The range of building sizes included in the sample is representative of office buildings in London – properties below 1,000m² are too small to be covered by some guidance. All of the case study buildings were developed speculatively (in the years 2010–2015), meaning that the identity of tenants was unknown in early design phases, although in one case an occupier was involved in design discussions. Buildings that are designed with specific owners/occupiers in mind tend to be more varied in terms of servicing (Manning, 1965) and one reason for focusing on speculative developments was to examine the role of standards and guidelines as proxies for 'real' occupants and to consider the emergence of 'generic' office provision.

Table 7.1 summarises key features of the buildings we studied. This table demonstrates the diversity of the sample, and the fact that almost all were ranked as 'BREEAM Excellent' or better (n=9).

TABLE 7.1 Characteristics of case study buildings (sourced from fieldwork)

Characteristics	Dominant type	Other types
Age	New build: n=6	60s: n=1
		80s: n=3
Developer type	Investment: n=6	Managing developer: n=4
Location/sub/market	City (3) and West End (3): n=6	Midtown (3) and South of River (1): n=4
BREEAM ratings	Excellent: n=7	Outstanding: n=1;
		Excellent (older): n=1
		Very good: n=1
Occupancy density designed to	1:10m²: n=6	1:8m²: n=3
		1:8-1:12m²: n=1
Heating, ventilation and cooling system	4 pipe fan coil air conditioning: n=4	Displacement ventilation: n=3
		Variable refrigerant flow: n=1
		Variable air volume: n=1
		Chilled ceilings and beams: n=1
Air flow rates	16l/s/person: n=4	No data
Small power base provision	25W/m² base: n=6	15W/m² base: n=3; 30W/m² base: n=1
Small power additional capacity	+10-15W/m²: n=4	+20-40W/m²: n=3; None: n=3

Standardising effects

The next section works with Scott's (2008) 'three pillars' analysis to explore how the different standards involved influenced, and in a sense 'standardised' office infrastructures.

Regulative and normative standards

The regulative/coercive pillar is exemplified by the legal requirements to comply with building regulations and secure planning permission. However office building designers have to satisfy a combination of regulative *and* normative standards:

> first of all ... they need to pass the building regs and the compliance side ... can we make sure that passes whether it's a BREEAM 'Excellent' or something like that?
>
> *(Building developer and manager)*

Determining how many toilets, stairwells etc. to provide is a matter of following simple standards of provision. In other areas, such as specifying heating, cooling or the speed of lifts, *performance* standards also apply. But in both cases, building regulations establish a bare minimum which almost every developer will exceed in order to achieve what is deemed to be acceptable in the market. For example:

> Building regs for fresh air is 10 litres a second, but BCO recommends 12 litres to 16 litres. At [building] the client said 16 litres plus 10%. And on cooling loads it was plus 10%.
>
> *(Architect)*

An EPC and a BREEAM rating are not legally required but they are normatively expected in prime commercial offices. Some of these ratings refer to each other. For example, BCO guidance treats a high BREEAM score as a measure of sustainability and it has become increasingly common for developers and planners to insert BREEAM ratings into contracts with design teams, and as conditions for planning permission. A building services consultant commented:

> Often it's a planning requirement.... the market's changed over the time ... [BREEAM] was seen as very much being optional ....Whereas now ... you need it for marketing and ... corporate social responsibility.
>
> *(Building services consultant)*

An architect said that

> Our market insists that we're BREEAM "Excellent" ... as a company ... it's also the standard that we have set for ourselves to achieve.
>
> *(Architect)*

In practice, compliance with the BCO Guide to Specification is probably the single most powerful normative standard affecting commercial offices. Individuals involved in early design meetings stated that:

> the BCO criteria is where we start.
>
> *(Architect)*

and

> design standards will be taken from ... BCO guides and so forth because why would you do any different?
>
> *(Building developer and manager)*

The expectation of adhering to BCO guidelines (which becomes a regulatory-normative obligation when written into contracts), means the design process is strongly shaped by these norms. As one architect puts it:

> most commercial offices buildings would be immediately compared to the BCO specification ... it's almost like a regulatory must have.
>
> *(Architect)*

An M&E engineer pointed out that with buildings developed for short-term profit: 'The ability to sell ... is of prime importance ... a lot of it is a tick box exercise of "does this building comply with BCO?"' (Building services engineer). Another interviewee noted that speculative developers rely on advice from letting agents who stress that 'what you'll need is BCO spec, BREEAM Excellence, other than that it's up to you' (Building developer and manager).

Even the most respected developers were said to 'benchmark all their jobs based on BCO standards' (Architect). But the question remains, *how* do such 'market standards' actually affect design? EPCs and BREEAM do not prescribe particular features of office design, but those we interviewed suggested there are standardised ways of achieving the expected scores in these two assessments. One strategy was to standardise the majority of design features in a building in order to meet the BCO guidelines and achieve BREEAM 'Excellent'. This affects the design process in that following 'standards' obviates the need for one-off calculations, judgements, and decisions and favours reliance on default assumptions and measures of provision and performance. To some extent, guidelines replace the expertise, judgement and autonomy of design professionals and result in 'off the shelf' optimal solutions. This produces spaces that are relatively predictable, uniform and comparable and it is in this sense that BCO guidance and other 'regulatory-normative' standards define the 'normal' office.

In generating shared understandings of what a 'normal, modern, office space' looks and feels like, standards like these function as a form of non-governmental steering through regulation, but not of a form that is enshrined in law. We explore this process further by considering how such governance operates in the context of office markets.

Market standards and cultural norms

Commercial office buildings are more than sites in which office work is undertaken. An office building is also an investment vehicle and a potentially risky capital outlay that must produce a return, provided by effective real estate management. As one interviewee summarised: 'these buildings are investment vehicles. They are all about providing a return for a pension or … insurance policy' (Architect). The financial imperatives of the market and the symbolic power of market-valued buildings (Guy, 1998; Cass, 2017) are therefore interwoven with changing ideas about how office buildings might be used. Meeting the normative standards associated with BREEAM and BCO, is part of this bridging process.

Critically, design standards can be adopted and followed without knowing exactly who will occupy the building or what work practices the office, as infrastructure, might need to enable. In terms of architecture, the 'Grade A' cultural model supposes that quality office space will be open, light and airy, and will provide a 'blank canvas' for occupiers. The following observations were typical: 'that's quite important … getting a more open, more airy… sense of openness' (Architect), and 'greater height and space … a feeling of space and volume … you're trying to maximise … floor to ceiling heights … It's a better feel within your floor plate' (Letting agent).

Developers claim that tenants demand such features. They argue that these demands are conveyed through letting agents, through the demands of tenant's representatives in letting negotiations, or through direct interaction between tenants and developer-managers. These exchanges inform the view that tenants want faster lift speeds, marble toilets and larger and more impressive lobbies, in addition to provision for high levels of occupancy, air flow, cooling, etc. However there is a question mark over whether such standards actually reflect common occupier 'needs' and/or whether these are required to enable office work practices. Letting agents were often blamed for proliferating the 'Grade A' standard, in a way that some think is increasingly disconnected from what people actually do in offices. For example, a building services engineer suggested that:

> they'll say to let it you've got to have all glass … you've got to have air conditioning … they say the market wants it … because it looks good … it's not what people really want, but it sells it.
>
> *(Buidling services engineer)*

Letting agents allegedly push for a quicker letting, 'plug-and-play', 'Cat(egory) A' fit-out, in which the whole of the building is equipped with standardised suspended ceilings, raised floors and pre-installed services. As an architect explained, a '"Cat A" fit out doesn't leave you too many options if you're going to do it efficiently … We're very frustrated that we have to incorporate it at all but the agents want it …' (Architects). Perhaps more accurately, 'Grade A' and other quality standards are designed to deliver offices capable of accommodating all potential tenants and flexible enough to handle changes in tenancies: they consequently deliver a generic infrastructure designed to encompass all possible forms of office work but are arguably not ideally suited to any.

All the case study buildings detailed in Table 7.1 are to slightly varying degrees exemplars of the standardised infrastructure that is the 'normal' office. These offices are expected to be rated BREEAM 'Excellent' and to have an EPC rating of B or above. Following BCO guide-lines, they are designed to accommodate one person per 8–10m^2 and to provide 16 litres of fresh air per second per person. They often have four pipe fan coil unit air conditioning, and they are assumed to need 25 Watts of heat-gain producing small power provision per square metre of floor, in some areas supplemented by another 10–15W. This level of provision results from assumptions embedded in the standards discussed above about what is acceptable and 'needed' in quality office space.

Lock in, ratcheting and standardisation

As we have shown, standards of various sorts – some requiring certain levels of provision, some specifying expected performance, and all resting on different forms of institutional legit-imacy – act together to structure and standardise the design of speculatively developed office buildings in London. Normative standards as represented in the guidelines and assessment procedures of a number of professional industry groups, including the BCO and BREEAM, help shape buildings around a uniform model of form and function. These influences on design and the design process reflect the need to meet and demonstrate industry standards of quality as a precondition for saleability/marketability. Far from being voluntary, the demands of the market bind developers to a very specific, cultural-cognitive model of what a 'Grade A' office building should look and feel like (Cass, 2017).

Standards also interlock in various ways. For example, standards of provision associated with occupational densities (the density at which the floor space will be occupied, measured in square metres per worker) or small power requirements (Watts per area of floor space) in the BCO Guide assume a uniform, spatially and temporally undifferentiated use of office space, and of office technologies. This leads to further assumptions about levels of heat gain (of the PCs, VDU screens and human bodies presumed to occupy space), which inform deci-sions about how much ventilation and cooling the building needs. At the same time, cultural expectations of 'Grade A' quality encourage high levels of glazing and suspended ceilings which have further implications for heat gain and airflow. Following both these 'standards' results in the 'need' for resource intensive systems and infrastructures, such as mechanical air conditioning (rather than forms of passive or mixed mode cooling and ventilation) (Shove, Walker and Brown, 2014).

The 'normal' office infrastructure is derived from the interlocking of standards. As illus-trated above, the apparent need for air conditioning in the 'normal' office does not result from any single standard or design decision, but is a cumulative effect of multiple standards on multiple design decisions. Since these processes are difficult to unravel, a building that is designed to avoid air conditioning is likely to transgress multiple other standards, and in the speculative office market, few developers are willing to run the risk of non-compliance. These and other interlocking processes sustain the upwards ratcheting of norms, expectations and levels of provision, with implications for energy demand and carbon emissions.

Such ratcheting is not new or unique to office buildings (Shove, 2003). However, the precise ways in which building modelling, redundancy and standardisation combine give this societal trend an endogenous boost. As represented here, this is an unintended consequence of the interlocking of technical and market standards. The 'iPhone mentality' (as one interviewee put it) transforms best practice into an expected minimum, such that:

> What was considered high-tech in one model is considered norm in the next … what was considered to be state of the art in one building, the next generation, well we've got to have it …
>
> *(Building management systems consultant)*

Standards are, then, both productive of, and a means to achieve, standardisation. Homogeneity and uniformity of provision across office buildings is produced by standards, disregarding variations in work practice in order to ensure that 'normal' levels of provision are maintained and that office space is saleable in a competitive market (Cass, 2017).

Conclusions

In cities around the world and particularly in their Central Business Districts where speculatively developed office buildings are chiefly located, the culturally legitimated extravagances of status-expressing, iconic and apparently unique architectural forms and façades hide a closely kept secret. Offices as infrastructures for work, and their forms, functions, spatial arrangements and levels of provisioning, reflect an increasingly homogenised model of 'normality'. We have shown here how the different types of standards that apply in office building design sustain such homogeneity. Regulations backed by forms of coercion, normative standards and guidelines that define acceptability and cultural-cognitive shared understandings of what constitutes a high-quality, lettable office lock together to drive design in certain directions. As a result infrastructures that purport to enable office work reflect reified ideas of 'normality' and are rarely configured to enable actual or changing working practices. Instead, and as we have shown, interlocking standards mean that the 'normal' office is structured around a common understanding of what is 'needed'. For the moment, 'needs' are constituted in such a way that quality offices offer bright, white, airy, air conditioned space equipped with facilities (for small power, etc.) that have come to represent the 'normal' office infrastructure. Such provision in turn requires particular systems of lighting, heating, cooling and ventilation, all of which link to the wider infrastructure of electricity provision, *and all of which* affect the energy demand and the carbon footprint of office work.

There is some evidence that this model of 'the office' is out of sync with the separately changing realities of office life. Research since the 1990s (Stanhope, 1992, 1993; Cook and English, 1997) and more recently (British Council for Offices, 2014) has highlighted that provision, for example of small power, is often of a level far greater than that required by the majority of office work. The British Council for Offices (2013) have also produced empirical analysis of the densities at which offices are actually occupied, which reveals that even with an unrealistically high level of employee 'utilisation'[2] of 70%, 96% of surveyed offices would still be occupied at a lower density than that assumed in the design brief. This means that 'normal' office infrastructure exceeds the levels of provision actually required in the vast majority of cases, most of the time.

This curious situation is, in part, a result of the fact that designers focus on meeting standards and guidelines, rather than on figuring out what office work entails. Ironically, the success of market standards is at the same time evidence of what some might see as market failure – leading, in this case, to buildings that are often over-specified, and that incur unnecessary financial costs for those developing and renting office space, and environmental costs when these forms of provision results in air conditioning and other energy-intensive systems.

Could design standards and guidelines better reflect the realities of office work? The trajectory over the past 20 years suggests we should not be overly optimistic. Over this period, office work practices have changed dramatically. Trends include an increasing move towards home and third-space work, hot-desking in work, the domestication of office space with the addition of catering and leisure facilities and a shift in focus towards tenant well-being (Cass, 2015). All of this has co-evolved with the rise of the internet (from wired to wireless forms) and the replacement of bulky desktops (first by laptops and more recently by tablets). One might expect that these and other developments in the character of office work would have also changed ideas about what a 'normal' office infrastructure should provide. If office designers were responding to these developments, the trend would be towards lower requirements for small power provision, light and thus cooling and air conditioning. Instead we have witnessed a tendency for standards to change in the opposite direction: ratcheting up such that offices provide more of the same. Why has this happened and what would it take for designers to respond to developments in what office work involves? In reflecting on these outstanding questions, it is obvious that we have more to learn about how standards mediate between infrastructural provision and the practicalities of office work.

Notes

1 'Energy conservation' is thus actually assessed as the CO_2 emissions arising from energy use rather than the energy use itself.
2 Utilisation is defined and calculated as 'workplace density divided by the maximum utilisation of workplaces, expressed as a percentage' (British Council for Offices, 2013: 12).

References

Allen, R. H. and Sriram, R. D. (2000) 'The role of standards in innovation', *Technological Forecasting and Social Change*, 64: 171–181.

Black, I. S. (2000) 'Spaces of capital: bank office building in the City of London, 1830–1870', *Journal of Historical Geography*, 26: 351–375.

Bowker, G. and Star, S. (2000) *Sorting Things Out: classification and its consequences*, Cambridge, MA: MIT press.

British Council for Offices (2013) *Occupier Density Study*. London: British Council for Offices.

British Council for Offices (2014). *Desk Power Load Monitoring*. London: British Council for Offices.

Brunsson, N. and Jacobsson, B. (2000) *A World of Standards*. Oxford: Oxford University Press.

Burrell, G. and Dale, K. (2003) 'Building better worlds? Architecture and critical management studies', in Alvesson, M. and Willmott, H. (eds.) *Studying Management Critically*. New York: Sage, pp. 177–196.

Busch, L. (2000) 'The moral economy of grades and standards', *Journal of Rural Studies*, 16: 273–283.

Cass, N. (2015) 'Office work futures: the impact of mobile and flexible working. Demand insight 10. Available at: www.demand.ac.uk/wp-content/uploads/2015/11/DEMAND-insight-10.pdf (Accessed 04.01.18).

Cass, N. (2017) 'Energy-related standards and UK speculative office development', *Building Research & Information*, 1–21.

Cohen, R. and Bordass, B. (2015) 'Mandating transparency about building energy performance in use', *Building Research & Information*, 43: 534–552.

Cook, S. J. and English, C. (1997) 'Overspecification of speculative UK commercial office building: an international comparison', in Stephenson, P. (ed.) *13th Annual ARCOM Conference*, King's College, Cambridge: Association of Researchers in Construction Management.

D'Arcy, E. and Keogh, G. (1997) 'Towards a property market paradigm of urban change', *Environment and Planning A*, 29: 685–706.

de Wit, O., Cornelis, J., van den Ende, M., Schot, J. and van Oost, E. (2002) 'Innovation junctions: office technologies in the Netherlands, 1880–1980', *Technology and Culture*, 43(1): 50–72.

Department for Communities and Local Government (2002) *Improving the Energy Efficiency of Our Buildings*. UK Gov: DCLG.

Economidou, M. (2012) 'Energy performance requirements for buildings in Europe', *REHVA Journal*, Istanbul, Turkey: TSY.

EC European Commission (2003) 'Council Directive 2002/91/EC of 16 December 2002 on the energy performance of buildings', *Official Journal of the European Communities*, 1: 65–71.

Fylan, F. (2005) 'Semi structured interviewing' in Miles, J. and Gilbert, P. (eds.) *A Handbook of Research Methods for Clinical and Health Psychology*. Oxford: Oxford University Press on Demand, pp. 65–78.

Gardiner and Theobald LLP (2014) 'BCO specification for offices quick guide to key criteria: 2009–2014 comparison. Available at: www.gardiner.com/publication-uploads/BCO-Specification-For-Offices.pdf (Accessed 04.01.18).

Gershuny, J., Fisher, K., Altintas, E., Borkosky, A., Bortnik, A., Dosman, D. and Lai, A. (2010) 'Multinational time use study, versions world 5.5. 3, 5.80 and 6.0'. University of Oxford, United Kingdom, Centre for Time Use Research. Available at: www.timeuse.org/mtus (Accessed 04.01.18).

Goulden, S., Erell, E., Garb, Y. and Pearlmutter, D. (2015) 'Green building standards as socio-technical actors in municipal environmental policy', *Building Research and Information*, 1–13.

Graham, S. and Marvin, S. (2001) *Splintering Urbanism: networked infrastructures, technological mobilities and the urban condition*. London: Routledge.

Graham, S. and Thrift, N. (2007) 'Out of order', *Theory, Culture & Society*, 24, 1–25.

Guy, S. (1998) 'Developing alteratives: energy, offices and the environment', *International Journal of Urban and Regional Research*, 22: 264–282.

Hamza, N. and Greenwood, D. (2009) 'Energy conservation regulations: impacts on design and procurement of low energy buildings', *Building and Environment*, 44: 929–936.

HM Government (2013) *Conservation of Fuel and Power - Approved Document L2A, L2A Conservation of Fuel and Power in New Buildings Other Than Dwellings*. London: HM Government.

Hui, A., Schatzki, T. and Shove, E. (2017). *The Nexus of Practices: connections, constellations, practitioners*. London: Routledge.

Imrie, R. (2007) 'The interrelationships between building regulations and architects' practices', *Environment and Planning B: Planning and Design*, 34: 925–943.

Manning, P. (1965) *Office Design: a study of environment*. Stanford: Community College Planning Center.

Niezabitowska, E. and Winnicka-Jasłowska, D. (2011) 'Evolution of the office building in the course of the 20th century: towards an intelligent building', *Intelligent Buildings International*, 3: 238–249.

O'Neill, P. and McGuirk, P. (2003) 'Reconfiguring the CBD: work and discourses of design in Sydney's office space', *Urban Studies*, 40: 1751–1767.

Pan, W. and Garmston, H. (2012) 'Building regulations in energy efficiency: compliance in England and Wales', *Energy Policy*, 45: 594–605.

Sassen, S. (2011) *Cities in a World Economy*. London: Sage.

Schmidt, S. and Werle, R. (1992) 'The development of compatibility standards in telecommunications: conceptual framework and theoretical perspective', in Dierkes, M. and Hoffmann, U. (eds.) *New Technology at the Outset: social forces in the shaping of technological innovations.* New York: Campus Verlag.

Scott, A. J. (2000) *The Cultural Economy of Cities: essays on the geography of image-producing industries,* London: Sage.

Scott, P. (1996) *The Property Masters: a history of the British commercial property sector.* London: E and F. N. Spon.

Scott, R. W. (2008) *Institutions and Organizations: ideas and interests:* London: Sage.

Shove, E. (2003) *Comfort, Cleanliness and Convenience: the social organization of normality.* Oxford: Berg.

Shove, E., Walker, G. and Brown, S. (2014) 'Material culture, room temperature and the social organisation of thermal energy', *Journal of Material Culture,* 19: 113–124.

Stanhope (1992) *An Assessment of the Imposed Loading Needs for Current Commercial Office Buildings in Great Britain.* London: Stanhope.

Stanhope (1993) 'An assessment of small power loads for commercial office buildings'. *Stanhope Position Paper.* London: Stanhope.

Star, S. and Lampland, M. (2009) 'Reckoning with standards', in Lampland, M. and Star, S. (eds.) *Standards and Their Stories. How Quantifying, Classifying, and Formalizing Practices Shape Everyday Life.* Ithaca: Cornell University Press. pp. 3–24.

Timmermans, S. and Epstein, S. (2010) 'A world of standards but not a standard world: toward a sociology of standards and standardization', *Annual review of Sociology,* 36: 69–89.

Van Dronkelaar, C., Dowson, M., Spataru, C. and Mumovic, M. (2016) 'A review of the regulatory energy performance gap and its underlying causes in non-domestic buildings', *Frontiers in Mechanical Engineering,* 1: 17.

Willis, C. (1995) *Form Follows Finance: skyscrapers and skylines in New York and Chicago.* Princeton: Architectural Press.

8

THE CONSTRUCTION OF CENTRAL HEATING IN BRITAIN

Anna Carlsson-Hyslop[1]

Introduction

Radical changes in how we heat our homes have taken place over the last 70 years, a process likely to continue as we adapt to climate change. During the Second World War, three quarters (74%) of British working-class households only heated their living room, usually with a coal fire (Heating and Ventilation (Reconstruction) Committee, 1945: 56–57). In 1964, only a tenth (11%) of households had central heating, three fifths (58%) of which used solid fuel (Woolf, 1967: 89). By 1970, a quarter of households had central heating, by 1990 four out of five and by 2011, nine out of ten, most now using gas (Palmer and Cooper, 2013: graph 6b). By now, central heating is defined as single-source heating of more than one room, usually the whole home.

Accounts of the adoption of central heating have focused on price, convenience, cleanliness and technological change as driving forces, especially in the case of gas. By contrast, this chapter uses detailed case studies to follow the introduction of central heating in different areas, in order to explore the multiple time scales and different routes that made full central heating 'normal'. It shows that there was more at stake than price and convenience.

Existing explanations of the rise of central heating focus heavily on fuel, particularly the decreased cost of natural gas following the conversion from town gas. This shift was significant, but also had other effects, for example, reducing the availability of coke, a by-product of town gas manufacture (Goodall, 1999). Other technological changes, such as the introduction of the small bore system (using narrow copper tubing and an electric pump) and the creation of new electric and gas heating systems, provided alternatives to the coal fire, but the existence of an alternative is not on its own enough to explain its uptake (Ravetz and Turkington, 1995: 128; Goodall, 1999).

The Clean Air Acts of 1956 and 1968 required the use of smokeless heating systems, making use of old-style coal grates unfeasible (Ravetz and Turkington, 1995: 125). However, the type of replacement heating system was not stipulated and gas and electric systems did not qualify for grants until 1964. Many households ceased using coal fires before the introduction of local smokeless zones, particularly in the non-coal mining South (Scarrow, 1972).

Standards were an additional factor. Recommendations by the government's Parker Morris Committee in the early 1960s are often seen as a turning point, increasing the adoption of central heating (Glendinning and Muthesius, 1994; Ravetz and Turkington, 1995). However, the standards they established for public housing did not require bedroom heating and the temperatures suggested were only marginally higher than those recommended by government committees since the late 1940s: the existence of recommendations does not necessarily lead to their adoption.

Other authors have emphasised different reasons for the shift from coal fires to gas central heating. For Alison Ravetz, new technology, the Clean Air Act, an increased desire for heat and the Parker Morris standards are all crucial, but she also draws attention to some of the problems caused by central heating systems and the symbolic significance of losing the open fire, a gap partly filled by imitation coal fires (Ravetz and Turkington, 1995). In Francis Goodall's narrative, rapidly decreasing gas prices following the introduction of new manufacturing methods and later natural gas, advertising and new technology together ushered in a 'higher standard of living, a new labour-saving way of life' (1999: 244), cleaner and more convenient gas central heating becoming a 'natural' winner. Ben Highmore (2014), by contrast, emphasises increases in home ownership and cultural changes in how the home has been used, and insists that central heating was not always seen as beneficial, especially as it removed a focal point. Glendinning and Muthesius focus on debates between experts proposing different heating systems, the experiences of experimentation on different estates and the importance of various government standards (Glendinning and Muthesius, 1994: 18–22).

In summary, existing narratives of this transition emphasise technological innovation and decreasing costs, in combination with the legal requirement to comply with the Clean Air Act and increased demands for heating inspired by the Parker Morris standards.

In this chapter I question these assumptions: government standards, technology and economics do not feature as prominently in the cases presented here as the authors above would suggest. By using archival sources to track debates, decisions and discourses surrounding the introduction of central heating by three councils in Stocksbridge, Stevenage and London, the alleged smoothness and – occasionally – the desirability of the transition is called into question.

An early but stop-start 'transition': the case of Stocksbridge

Stocksbridge is a small town outside Sheffield where the main employer was a steelworks. This works processed coal to produce coke and as a side-product town gas, used by some for light, cooking and heating, especially in the inter-war period. When Stocksbridge Council began housing construction in the 1920s it chose locally produced gas as a light source and supplied coal fires and ranges for heating and cooking, but usually also gave the option of gas for cooking.

Stocksbridge Council began providing central heating in the late 1940s, when expanding an existing estate, Spink Hall, with a further 80 houses. The Council committee that designed the houses suggested solid fuel smokeless central heating, with a stove and back boiler to provide hot water for radiators and household use. Councillors wanted to increase their tenants' comfort, especially for those who considered their houses cold. Though expensive in capital costs, this system was deemed the most cost-effective way of providing increased heat, enabling more of the house to be occupied during winter (SUDC, c. 1944). The system provided 'background heating', to be topped up with heat from a fixed gas fire in the living room and electricity points elsewhere. When the external temperature was 30 degrees F (-1.1°C), the system was supposed to heat hall, dining and living room to 63 degrees F (17.2°C) and bedrooms to 55 degrees F (12.8°C) (SUDC, 1946a).

This kind of system was unusual. The 1944 central government *Housing Manual* suggested Local Authorities install efficient (compared to pre-war fires) solid fuel openable fires in houses, but not a network of radiators (Ministry of Health and Ministry of Works, 1944). Heating and hot water from a central boiler would normally only be considered for blocks of flats. However, the Stockbridge standards were in line with those recommended in 1945 by the Heating and Ventilation Committee, appointed by the Building Research Board of the Department of Scientific and Industrial Research to investigate the economies and efficiencies of different heating systems, both for the individual and the nation. The resulting 'Egerton Report' suggested that to maintain the health and comfort of inhabitants and reduce condensation, heating systems should provide daytime temperatures of 62–66 degrees F (16.7–18.9°C) in living rooms, 60 degrees F (15.6°C) in kitchens and 50–55 degrees F (10–12.8°C) in halls and bedrooms, while keeping the whole house above 45 degrees F (7.2°C) continuously. This was to be achieved through solid fuel background heating topped up with various gas or electric appliances: it was suggested living rooms be background heated to 50 degrees F (10°C), and topped up to 65 degrees F (18.3°C) in the morning, midday and the evening (Heating and Ventilation (Reconstruction) Committee, 1945: 19, 63). The following year, these recommendations were repeated by the Fuel and Power Advisory Council in its report *Domestic Fuel Policy* (Ministry of Fuel and Power, 1946).

The 1949 'Housing Manual' also advocated this combination of background and topping up, to temperatures similar or slightly lower than those in the 'Egerton Report', and recommended that background heat be provided by a continuous burning solid fuel appliance, ideally providing both space and water heating. Electric or gas fires were recommended for 'intermittent and auxiliary services'. The whole-house heating up to 65 degrees F provided by Stocksbridge was still considered experimental (Ministry of Health, 1949: 94, 99), ensuring laborious negotiations between the Council and the Ministry of Health (Malpass and Murie, 1999).

Having eventually convinced the Ministry of the plans for Spink Hall (SUDC, 1946b), the Council also insisted on central heating for its next estate, Stubbin Farm, in 1949 (SUDC 1949a). However, by that time a number of Councillors had turned against the policy (SUDC, 1949b), and it was abandoned in May 1950, when central government asked the Council to redesign houses for this estate to comply with the 1949 *Housing Manual*. This shift was part of a larger exercise in cutting capital costs. In addition, some tenants found the central heating system expensive to run and had difficulties finding solid smokeless fuel. The Council consequently reverted to the typical British arrangement of a living room fire with a back boiler feeding one radiator, convection heating in two bedrooms (a system enabling warm air to rise more easily from the ground floor), plus an open fire in the main bedroom and electric points elsewhere (SUDC, 1950).

This proved to be a temporary 'reduction' in standards, and Stocksbridge Council returned to central heating for the East Whitwell estate a decade later. A 1960 poll found that 94 of the council tenants in centrally heated homes were in favour of this type of heating, with only 13 against (SUDC, 1960a). Heating systems varied across the different phases of this estate: in one it was not used at all, but others used either electric underfloor heating or gas warm air central heating, transported through ducts (SUDC, 1962; 1963).

In summary, Stocksbridge Council began installing whole-house central heating in the post-war period, following the lead of certain government-appointed experts, but somewhat exceeding both those experts' recommendations and central government standards. Due to costs and shortages of smokeless fuel the strategy was abandoned, but re-established before the Parker Morris Committee published its report. This suggests that while central government standards were influential, local authorities maintained some independence with regard to heating systems.

The Parker Morris standards and retrofitting: Stevenage New Town

Stevenage was the first New Town designated after the Second World War. This case study reveals tensions between costs and government standards, between fuel suppliers and councils and between building and retrofitting houses.

The Corporation which ran the New Town built a large number of homes, increasing the town population from 6,000 in the late 1940s to 75,000 by 1981. A district heating scheme was initially considered but decided against in 1948, partly for cost reasons but also because it would remove control of heating and expense from tenants (SDC, 1950). Central heating was installed in the first dwellings, a tall block of flats, as a central boiler cost less than the flues and coal storage required for open fires (SDC, 1948). However, the Corporation settled for efficient continuous burning fires with back boilers in houses, as suggested by the 1949 *Housing Manual* (SDC, 1952).

Heating standards in Stevenage slowly increased, with the back boiler attached to the fire heating enough water for general household use plus one radiator by 1953 (SDC, 1953). By 1956, some houses had two radiators and some had convection heating (SDC, 1956). In 1962, an estate for old age pensioners had central heating (SDC, 1962a) while tall blocks of flats used electric underfloor heating (SDC, 1962b).

A key recommendation of the 1961 'Parker Morris Report' was raising heating levels, which it was thought would enable increased use of spaces within the home, for example, the use of bedrooms as studies. Heating systems should provide 65 degrees F (18.3°C) in living areas and 55 F (12.8°C) in kitchens and circulation areas, similar levels to those recommended in the 1945 'Egerton Report'. This time councils and other house builders actually implemented the proposals, especially once the Labour government made Parker Morris standards mandatory for New Town corporations by 1967 and all local authorities by 1969, although the recommendations were centrally interpreted as a maximum standard, not the minimum originally intended (Burnett, 1991: 308–309). Many local authorities regarded the new standard as requiring only partial central heating: the report had suggested it should be easy to add bedroom heating, but did not make this mandatory.

After the publication of the 'Parker Morris Report', Stevenage Corporation began installing more extensive central heating in new homes. Large houses had central heating across the ground floor and sometimes other parts of the house from 1963, (SDC, 1963) and by the following year, most houses had partial central heating, whether solid fuel, electric underfloor heating or gas warm air (SDC, 1965a), though some continued to use open fires (SDC, 1965b). From 1966, most houses built in Stevenage had full central heating, usually gas warm air heating (SDC, 1966), but even by 1969, some small houses only had such heating on the ground floor (SDC, 1969a). The heating system chosen for flats varied, with some having gas fires and an electric storage heater (SDC, 1968), others electric warm air heating

(SDC, 1970a) and yet others oil-fired heating from a central boiler (SDC, 1970b). When the Corporation adopted Parker Morris standards in 1965, it chose mainly gas warm air heating.

Central heating changed the relative significance of different fuels within the home, with heating becoming a major use of either gas or electricity. Thus the Parker Morris standard had the unintended consequence of disrupting a working formula agreed in 1956 between the Local Authority Association and the Electricity and Gas Boards. According to this agreement, the Boards would not ask for a 'capital contribution' providing certain conditions were met: 'the principal condition is that the tenants or purchasers of the houses are given freedom to choose the fuel for their main domestic use' (SDC, 1970e). When the agreement was made, the choice related mainly to fuel for cooking.

With the installation of gas warm air central heating in Stevenage, and water heating also typically reliant on gas, tenants no longer had a choice of fuel for these services. The Electricity Board asked the Corporation for a high 'capital contribution' to pay for electric mains installation. In the end, the Gas Board agreed to pay the Electricity Board's charges for installing electric mains, in exchange for the Corporation's use of gas warm air heating (SDC, 1970c).

Houses initially built without central heating were retrofitted to bring them up to 'standard', as well as to solve problems caused by condensation. Complaints about condensation in the C5 house type built in Bedwell, one of the first neighbourhoods constructed in Stevenage, led to the introduction in 1964 of a scheme for retrofitting insulation and installing a new solid fuel heating system capable of producing more heat (SDC, 1964). This scheme had been taken up by 476 tenants by 1969 (SDC, 1969b), when another scheme was also in operation, whereby tenants in older neighbourhoods could ask to have central heating installed, paying for it through increased rent (SDC, 1967).

Between 1967 and 1970, the vast majority of tenants using this scheme chose a solid fuel system (2,318 tenants), with only a few opting for electric (114) or gas (163) (SDC, 1970d). By 1978, 6,000 dwellings had full central heating. As there was no government funding for this work, the Corporation leased the heating systems from the supply Boards, which covered the capital expenditure (Balchin and Stevenage Development Corporation, 1980: 180).

Stevenage thus followed central government standards on heating, first concentrating on solid fuel fires and beginning to provide single-source central heating in houses with the shift to Parker Morris standards. In taking this to be a 'standard for all' the Corporation found ways round certain central government restrictions on capital expenditure, in order to retrofit central heating. In addition, the Stevenage experience reveals how the arrival of central heating initiated complex interactions between different fuel suppliers and local authorities.

Experiments and responses: experiences and expectations in London

This final case study illustrates the many technological and financial choices made en route to central heating in London council housing and the role tenants' opinions had in these decisions. The London County Council (LCC) was established in 1889 as a regional level local authority, with the Greater London Council (GLC) taking over in 1964 with responsibility for a larger area (Jackson, 1965; Clifton, 1989).

The LCC's approach to central heating in the pre- and post-war period reflects a mixture of generic innovations (in technology, in ideas about homes and heating) and more specific challenges such as those associated with heating blocks of flats. In London, perhaps more than elsewhere, tenants' views were systematically recorded, and the results of tenant surveys influenced decisions to provide, or abandon, specific systems.

The LCC experimented with central heating before the Second World War, for example on its Ossulston Estate, of about 480 flats near St Pancras. The first part of this estate, built in the late 1920s, was equipped with radiators heated by a central boiler that also provided hot water. The flats had coal fires in the living room and one bedroom, in part because solid fuel appliances were required for central government funding. These flats had no gas but used electricity for lighting and cooking and had several power points. However, as the resulting rents were too high for local people this provision was later downgraded, with the Southern block being built without the combined central heating and hot water system (LCC, 1931: 74, 78; Pepper, 1981).

After the Second World War the LCC began a major housing programme, building tens of thousands of houses and flats (LCC, 1949: 7), most adopting the type and standard of heating suggested by the Housing Manuals. These dwellings had an efficient (compared to pre-war appliances) solid fuel heating system that could burn smokeless fuels, but were not provided with a Stocksbridge-style central heating system capable of warming several rooms. Instead, the main solid fuel fire was designed to be topped up with gas or electric fires. Hot water was provided through a back boiler attached to the solid fuel fire, usually complemented by an electric immersion heater or gas water heater for when the fire was not in use (LCC, 1949; 1956; 1960).

This policy was reviewed and confirmed in 1961. Surveys of tenants showed they still preferred and used solid fuel fires, in particular because the back boiler provided hot water seemingly for free. One survey showed that 90% of tenants in flats with open fires with back boilers used the system daily in winter. Over three quarters (77%) of these tenants stated a preference for an open fire, with the most common reasons being that it also heated water, was 'cheerful' and provided good warmth (GLC, 1961).

The policy finally changed in early 1963, when the Housing Committee decided that only about 10% of new dwellings were to use solid fuel appliances with back boilers, now of a type that could heat two radiators as recommended by the Parker Morris Committee. As in Stevenage, the 'Parker Morris Report' was an important trigger in the LCC's changing policy and, again, the Council implemented the standards before they became mandatory. Whereas Councillors favoured higher standards of temperature (in keeping with the Parker Morris recommendations) and the increased flexibility and reduced work involved in keeping warm with central heating, officers of the Council were concerned whether tenants could afford to run these systems (GLC, 1963a). In the end, the decision to use forced warm air heating, directly heated by individual gas units or indirectly heated by hot water from a central boiler house and circulated through ducts by a fan, was justified on the grounds that it provided flexibility, convenience and higher heating standards (GLC, 1963b).

Tall blocks of flats were not built by the LCC until the mid-1950s, by which time government funding and land constraints favoured their development. Solid fuel heating was generally impractical in blocks of more than six storeys since too many flues were required: alternative systems were therefore adopted from the start. The number of flues was critical: if only every second storey had fire places with flues, as in blocks of maisonettes where bedrooms had gas or electric fires only, traditional heating systems could be used in blocks of ten storeys.

The first tall blocks of flats usually had heating and hot water provided from a central boiler on the ground floor. The cost of this was cited as an important factor in deciding whether to build a tall block or some other form of dwelling (LCC, 1956: Flats, point block and Maisonettes). These systems were designed to produce a set temperature of 65 degrees F (18.3°C) and all tenants incurred a fixed charge, meaning costs and temperatures were out of their control. The LCC's Housing Committee was keen to develop systems whereby tenants could choose a lower standard (GLC, 1963c).

In 1957, the LCC's Housing Committee decided, on the recommendation of Council officers, that electric floor warming should be used in most of the tall blocks then being planned. This shift was triggered in part by the London Electricity Board providing a more economic off-peak rate, a strategy which helped the Board avoid increasing peak load whilst making electric heating more competitive for tenants (GLC, 1957). Capital costs would also be lower than for a central boiler system and tenants would be able to control the heat in their own flat.

This policy continued until 1963, when Council officers recommended the adoption of warm air recirculating units, with the air heated by gas or oil-fired rooftop boilers. This change in policy was made for several reasons: many tenants disliked electric underfloor heating, the capital costs of installing other systems had fallen in comparison and new technologies gave tenants greater control. Finally, the Parker Morris Committee had recommended a higher standard of heating than the underfloor system was capable of providing (GLC, 1963c). As for houses and low blocks, forced warm air heating was seen as a flexible solution capable of meeting higher standards and remained in use throughout the 1960s (GLC, 1963d).

In 1968, the housing department's sociologist, Joyce Fairman, sampled the opinions of tenants with different heating systems: blown warm air systems (heated by central gas or oil boilers or individual gas units), electric underfloor warming and hot-water radiators (heated by either oil or solid fuel central boilers). The warm air system was disliked because it was prone to breakdowns, it was noisy, it produced a dry and stuffy atmosphere, it generated lots of dust, and provided insufficient heat. Electric underfloor warming was less used than other systems and disliked because it failed to deliver what tenants considered sufficient heat, produced a dry or stuffy atmosphere and cost too much to run. Radiators linked to a central boiler were accused of providing insufficient heat, creating dirt and dust, failing to provide direct heat in the bedrooms (if these did not have a radiator) and being difficult to control (GLC, 1970a).

Many LCC tenants therefore found 'central heating' of whatever type inadequate, topping up the basic system with the fixed panel fire or fires of their own, usually electric, sometimes oil fuelled. The 1968 survey showed that while most of those with warm air systems or radiators deemed the system satisfactory, only half with warm air or a quarter with underfloor heating or radiators found the living room warm enough in severe weather (GLC, 1970a).

Surveys like this highlight the problems people experienced in adjusting to central heating of all forms and to the move away from solid fuel. These changes called for new ways of inhabiting the home. For example, residents often rearranged the furniture in their living rooms as they no longer had an open fire as a 'natural' focus. Over half (57%) of tenants with underfloor heating used the electric panel fire as a central feature. The TV was also becoming a focus for some: 26% of those with radiators and 17% of those with warm air or electric underfloor heating said they 'focused' on the TV. These figures suggest a gradual change in how the space of the living room was organised and strengthens the idea that the TV did not automatically replace the open fire as a focus (GLC, 1970a; Highmore, 2014).

The GLC continued to provide gas warm air heating, either from a central boiler or individual warm air units in dwellings, until 1970. In some cases it also provided electric warm air units, along with electric block storage heaters, an invention that took off in the early 1960s. Storage heaters were widely used in large panel system flats after the 1968 Ronan Point disaster, when a gas explosion led to four deaths in the partial collapse of a tower block. The disaster led to gas being abruptly turned off in large panel system blocks across the country (Ravetz and Turkington, 1995: 56–57).

In 1970, the GLC's heating policy changed again, this time in favour of radiator systems heated either by a central boiler or individual boilers in each flat. The change had little to do with those factors usually mentioned as leading to the adoption of gas-fuelled radiator-based central heating: the conversion to natural gas, smoke abatement or the Parker Morris standards were not explicitly mentioned in the debates. Instead archival evidence points to the following four factors: (1) changes in fire safety regulations increasing costs for warm air systems; (2) complaints by tenants, especially older people, about lack of heat; (3) high maintenance costs of warm air systems and; (4) problems with condensation in dwellings heated with gas warm air, which involved rapid changes in temperature. The Council also increased heating standards to 70 degrees F (21.1°C) in the living room and 65F in all other rooms (18.3°C) (GLC, 1976).

The case of the LCC thus provides a clear example of radiator-based heating systems being adopted for reasons not usually featured in the 'standard' story of the increase in central heating. Instead, we see this large Council choosing a string of different systems for a range of reasons relating to technological developments, capital, running and maintenance costs, concerns with safety and condensation, but also relating to tenants' opinions and their ability to control the system. In addition, the surveys by the LCC illustrate the extent of tenant dissatisfaction with central heating and that, much as coal fires had been, such systems continued to be topped up with additional heaters.

Discussion

Pathways towards gas central heating have been many and varied. During the period studied here, definitions of central heating have themselves evolved, making it often hard to tell whether the term refers to the area that is heated (full or partial central heating) or the manner in which heat is provided (by one source rather than by many), or even more broadly the idea that homes should be uniformly heated to a certain temperature. These ambiguities are part of the story. For example, electric underfloor heating, being provided by one invisible source, was deemed to be 'central heating' by some LCC tenants, while LCC officials insisted it was not, having not been designed to be used on its own (GLC, 1964).

It is unlikely the late 1940s system in Stocksbridge would count as central heating today, though it was defined as such at the time. Standards and definitions of appropriate temperature levels have changed in the past and will change again: the level of heating suggested for the majority of the population by British public health officials was recently reduced from 21°C to 18°C (Walker, 2014).

As we have seen, official standards, as represented in Housing Manuals and the Parker Morris standards, have been influential in slowing down or encouraging shifts towards central heating in council housing. The Housing Manuals of 1944 and 1949 appear to have restricted attempts to introduce central heating in houses (as opposed to high-rise flats), but did not completely stop the process. Stocksbridge was eventually able to obtain government approval to provide 'central heating' in the late 1940s and after a lapse of about a decade, the Council reintroduced central heating before the Parker Morris standard was widely adopted.

Equally, the 'Parker Morris Report' clearly inspired a much more general uptake of central heating in local authority housing, though the recommended level of heating was not considerably higher than that proposed in 1945 by the Egerton committee. The implementation of the Parker Morris standard in council housing had unexpected consequences for energy suppliers selling gas or electricity. In most cases, the fuel used for central heating was also used for heating water and often for cooking. This had knock-on effects on agreements between fuel suppliers and local authorities regarding the cost of developing and installing gas and electricity infrastructures for new housing.

Other somewhat different processes and considerations were at stake when retrofitting central heating into existing properties. In the cases studied, central heating was at times introduced as part of a Council-instigated improvement scheme, or, as in Stevenage, could be an outcome of tenants choosing to take part in schemes organised by the Council but paid for through increased rent. As experiences in Stevenage also illustrate, many tenants who took part in these schemes initially opted for solid fuel central heating, not gas. This indicates that whilst there are obvious relationships between fuels and heating systems, the introduction and adoption of the concept of central heating (or whole-home heating) did not depend on gas.

In combination, these points suggest that the shift to central heating was made up of multiple transitions to different types of central heating systems, using different fuels, introduced through different routes (building new housing, retrofitting existing housing) and under different funding regimes. Some of these transitions were widespread and rapid. For example, following the Ronan Point disaster, gas heating in large panel system flats was swiftly replaced, usually by electric storage heaters. Less dramatically, the first central heating systems have been subject to an ongoing process of replacement, substitution and reconfiguration. As part of this, solid fuel central heating has often been replaced by what are now 'normal' gas-heated radiator systems. However, there were and still are many other forms of 'central' heating, with diverse lifespans and trajectories. For example, electric night storage heaters were often added when underfloor heating failed. Similarly, electric fires were used in place of those gas fires that could not be replaced after the conversion to natural gas in London (GLC, 1972).

In terms of daily life, experiences of heating standards do not always 'progress' in a seamless fashion: more commonly, people move between properties and back and forth between homes that are equipped in different ways. In addition, the fact that a property has 'full' central heating capable of delivering a consistent 21°C does not mean that such a system will be used in this way. The use of coexisting appliances – including gas and electric fires – remains significant. Even today, 63% of households in England have some type of 'secondary heating', with 3% using this as their main heating system in winter (Department for Communities and Local Government, 2015). In addition, the multiple changes that have, in aggregation, constituted a move toward central heating have not been smooth, but geographically and socially disparate. Not all council tenants, for example, were able to afford to take part in retrofitting schemes or run central heating systems once installed.

Similarly, there were many and varied causes for the shift to gas-fuelled central heating. Shortages of coke, in part due to the closure of town gas plants after the conversion to natural gas, have played a role: tenants in Stocksbridge already struggled to ensure a steady supply of coke in the late 1940s and this was again an issue in London after the introduction of natural gas. In 1970, the LCC was told that the Coal Board could only supply half of the previous year's supply of coke, which triggered discussions about the conversion of central boilers to other smokeless fuels (GLC, 1970b). Since the Clean Air Act prohibited the use of coal in smokeless zones, LCC tenants were worried about coke supplies (GLC, 1970b). This was also a national concern, with central government officials suggesting local authorities should be able to apply for the suspension of smokeless zones, enabling use of coal if necessary (Ministry of Housing and Local Government, 1970).

The availability of new heating technologies was clearly necessary for these changes, but the existence of new systems does not dictate their uptake. For example, in the inter-war period, the open fire continued to be used in Britain long after other European countries had adopted more efficient fires. Similarly, council provision in terms of technological infrastructure did influence practices, tenants usually used the system provided, at least for background heating. However, the technology, whether a fireplace or a boiler, did not necessarily determine what tenants did with it: the 'main' system was often supplemented with gas and electric fires. 'New' technologies have not necessarily been welcomed by users. As we have seen, there was much dissatisfaction with the levels and forms of heat provided by systems installed by the LCC in the late 1960s: central heating was not necessarily something to be desired.

In this chapter I have explored council records and accounts of the heating systems provided in three urban cases. These materials present a detailed picture of shifting arguments, rationales and discourses, leading to the adoption of different types of central heating at different points in time. I have emphasised that the decision to change to a certain type of central heating was taken for many different reasons: capital, maintenance and running costs were only part of these decisions. Similarly, government standards and technological innovation (changing the range of systems on offer) played a role, but did not necessarily determine the outcome. Instead, council records, along with tenant surveys and reports, draw attention to local contingencies in the decision-making process, revealing the role of different political, technological, financial, legal and cultural considerations and their combination in different locations and at different moments. The picture is of a complex, shifting 'patchwork' of steps, not of a steady or uniform transition to central heating. Whilst councils no longer have anything like the same role in shaping domestic infrastructure, this account gives a sense of the sheer complexity of heating provision, a complexity which remains.

Note

1   I would like to thank the DEMAND Centre, the Sustainable Consumption Institute and Joanna Baines for support and help with this work.

References

Balchin, J. and Stevenage Development Corporation (1980) *First New Town: an autobiography of the Stevenage Development Corporation 1946–1980.* Stevenage: Stevenage Development Corporation.

Burnett, J. (1991) *A Social History of Housing, 1815–1985.* London: Routledge.

Clifton, G. (1989) 'Members and officers of the LCC, 1889–1965', in Saint, A. (ed.) *Politics and the People of London: the London County Council, 1889–1965.* London: Hambledon, pp. 1–26.

Department for Communities and Local Government (2015) 'English housing survey 2013: energy efficiency of English housing' [online]. Available at: www.gov.uk/government/statistics/english-housing-survey-2013-energy-efficiency-of-english-housing-report (Accessed 25.11.2017).

Greater London Council (GLC) (1957) *Chief Engineer to Vice Chairman, 'Electric Floor Warming', 28/11/57.* GLC/ME/D/01/029, Electric Floor Heating. London: London Metropolitan Archive (LMA).

GLC (1961) *Report by the Chief Engineer, 12/4/61, 'Housing Estates – Use of Fires by Tenants', Housing Development and Management Sub-Committee.* GLC/HG/HHM/10/L055, Part 2 Development & Construction Heating & Hot Water Services, 1945 onwards. London: LMA.

GLC (1963a) *Housing Estates – Heating of Low Blocks, Order 27/2/63; Note to Mr Fishlock 28/2/63; Joint Report 12/2/63; Notes of Housing Committee Meeting 27/2/63*. GLC/HG/HHM/03/A224, Heating, 1962–1965. London: LMA.

GLC (1963b) *Information Notes, London County Council Architect's Department, 'Heating, Housing in Low Blocks', 17/7(?)/63*. GLC/HG/HHM/03/A224 (1), Heating, 1962–1965. London: LMA.

GLC (1963c) *Joint Report 24/6/63, 'Heating of Tall Blocks'*. GLC/HG/HHM/03/A224 (1), Heating, 1962–1965. London: LMA.

GLC (1963d) *Information Notes, LCC Architect's Department, 'Heating, Housing in Tall Blocks', 5/11/63*. GLC/HG/HHM/03/A224 (1), Heating, 1962–1965. London: LMA.

GLC (1964) *Herbert Bennett to the LCC Director of Housing, 11/8/64*. GLC/HG/HHM/L247, part 3. London: LMA.

GLC (1970a) *'Heating Survey'*, manuscript by Joyce Fairman. GLC/HG/HHM/1, Surveys of Seaside Bungalows and Central Heating. London: LMA.

GLC (1970b) *Report of Director of Supplies, to Finance and Supplies Committee, 'Coke Shortage – Conversion of Boilers', 28/4/70, District Officer, St Helier District, to Senior Assistant Director 'H', Coke shortage, 30/4/70*. GLC/HG/HHM/05/C041 Smokeless Fuel Grates, 1958–1974. London: LMA.

GLC (1972) *Conversion to Natural Gas, e.g. Barking Consumer Advisory Council to the Chairman of the LCC, 22/3/72*. GLC/HG/HHM/10/L068. London: LMA.

GLC (1976) *Report, 7/10/76, 'Method of Water and Space Heating With Relative Costs, Including a Review of 'Pool' Charges' Housing Management Committee*. GLC/ME/D/01/029 Electric Floor Heating. London: LMA.

Glendinning, M. and Muthesius, S. (1994) *Tower Block: modern public housing in England, Scotland, Wales and Northern Ireland*. London: Yale University Press for the Paul Mellon Centre for Studies in British Art.

Goodall, F. (1999) *Burning to Serve: selling gas in competitive markets*. Ashbourne: Landmark Publishing.

Heating and Ventilation (Reconstruction) Committee (1945) *Heating and Ventilation of Dwellings: post-war building studies report no. 19 of the Building Research Board of the Department of Scientific and Industrial Research*. London: H.M.S.O. for the Ministry of Works.

Highmore, B. (2014) *The Great Indoors: at home in the modern British house*. London: Profile Books.

Jackson, W. E. (1965) *Achievement. A Short History of the London County Council*. London: Longmans.

LCC (1931) *Housing, 1928–1930*. London: London County Council.

LCC. (1949) *A Survey of the Post-war Housing of the London County Council 1945–1949*. London: London County Council.

LCC (1956) *Housing Type Plans*. London: London County Council.

LCC (1960) *Housing Type Plans, enlarged edition*. London: London County Council.

Malpass, P. and Murie, A. (1999) *Housing Policy and Practice*. Basingstoke: Macmillan.

Ministry of Fuel and Power (1946) *Domestic Fuel Policy: report by the Fuel and Power Advisory Council* (Cmd. 6762). London: HMSO.

Ministry of Health and Ministry of Works (1944) *Housing Manual, 1944*. London: HMSO.

Ministry of Health (1949) *Housing Manual, 1949*. London: HMSO.

Ministry of Housing and Local Government. (1970) *Domestic Smoke Control and the Supply of Solid Smokeless Fuel*. HLG 120/1418, The National Archives.

Palmer, J. and Cooper, I. (2013) *United Kingdom Housing Energy Fact File 2013*. London: Department of Energy and Climate Change.

Pepper, S. (1981) 'Ossulston Street: early LCC experiments in high-rise housing, 1925–1929', *The London Journal*, 7(1): 45–64.

Ravetz, A. and Turkington, R. (1995) *The Place of Home: English domestic environments, 1914–2000*. London: E & FN Spon.

Scarrow, H. A. (1972) 'The impact of British domestic air pollution legislation', *British Journal of Political Science*, 2(3): 261–282.

SDC (1950) *Agenda and Reports Feb-Sept 1950, Meeting 14/3/50*. CNT/ST/1/2/2/1, Box 2, HALS.

SDC (1952) *District Heating, Vincent to Tickner, 14/8/52*. CNT/ST/4/1/D1 Vol 2, Box 88, HALS.

SDC (1953) *Agenda 12/5/53*. CNT/ST/1/2/5/2, HALS.

SDC (1956) *Minute Book 24/7/56.* CNT/ST/1/1/1/13 1956, HALS.

SDC (1962a) *Agenda and Reports Jan 62, Meeting 13/2/62.* CNT/ST/1/2/2/24, Box 7, HALS.

SDC (1962b) *Agenda and Reports Jul 62, Meeting 10/7/62.* CNT/ST/1/2/2/25, Box 7, HALS.

SDC (1963) *Agenda and Reports Jan 63, Meeting 25/6/63.* CNT/ST/1/2/2/26, Box 7, HALS.

SDC (1964) *Minute Book, Meeting 12/3/63.* CNT/ST/1/1/1/21 and *Agenda and Reports Jan-Jun 64, Meeting 17/3/64.* CNT/ST/1/2/2/28, Box 8, HALS.

SDC (1965a) *Agenda and Reports Jan 65, Meeting 19/1/65.* CNT/ST/1/2/2/30, Box 8, HALS.

SDC (1965b) *Agenda and Reports Jul 65, Meeting 20/7/65.* CNT/ST/1/2/2/31, Box 8, HALS.

SDC (1966) *Agenda and Reports Jul 66, Meeting 12/7/66.* CNT/ST/1/2/2/33, Box 8, HALS.

SDC (1967) *Minute Book.* CNT/ST/1/1/1 and *Agenda and Reports Jul 67, Meeting 11/7/67.* CNT/ST/1/2/2/35, Box 9, HALS.

SDC (1968) *Agenda and Reports Jul 68, Meeting 20/9/68.* CNT/ST/1/2/2/37, Box 9, HALS.

SDC (1969a) *Agenda and Reports Jan 69, Meeting 14/1/69.* CNT/ST/1/2/2/38, Box 9, HALS.

SDC (1969b) *Agenda and Reports Jan 69, Meeting 9/12/69.* CNT/ST/1/2/2/38, Box 9, HALS.

SDC (1970a) *Agenda and Reports Jan-Jun 1970, Meeting, 17/3/70.* CNT/ST/1/2/2/39, Box 10, HALS.

SDC (1970b) *Agenda and Reports Jul 1970, Meeting 13/10/70.* CNT/ST/1/2/2/40, Box 10, HALS.

SDC (1970c) *Minute on Capital Contributions to the Electricity Board, p 5, Minutes of 369th MC, 8/12/70, and Capital Contributions to the Electricity Board, General Manager's Report, in Agenda and Reports, Jul 1970.* CNT/ST/1/2/2/40, Box 10, HALS.

SDC (1970d) *Agenda and Reports Jan-Jun 1970, Meeting 14/4/70, General Manager's Report.* CNT/ST/1/2/2/39 Box 10, HALS.

SDC (1970e) *Capital Contributions to the Eastern Electricity Board for House Connections, Appendix A:2 to Finance Committee Minutes 26/2/70, Minute Book, Meeting 17/3/70.* CNT/ST/1/1/1/27, HALS.

Stevenage Development Corporation (SDC). (1948) *Architects Department, Meeting Reports, 7/12/48 and 21/12/48.* CNT/ST/1/2/1/AP/C12/3, Hertfordshire Archives and Local Studies (HALS).

Stocksbridge Urban District Council (SUDC). (ca 1944) *Report on Proposed Houses, Spink Hall Estate, p 3, CA 96/6 Corr and Papers with Details of Types and Lay-out of Houses.* Collection of Stocksbridge Local Board of Health and Urban District Council (CSLBH), Sheffield Archives (SA).

SUDC (1946a) *Specification, Hot Water Central Heating, CA 96/7 Specification, Tenders and Contracts.* CSLBH, SA.

SUDC (1946b) *Housing Generally, 19 Sep 1946, CA61/3 Extracts from Council and Committee Minutes (arranged by subject), 1927–1947, volume Jan 1942–Dec 1946.* CSLBH, SA.

SUDC (1949a) *Housing Committee, 18/1/49, p 252, CA 60/23 Stocksbridge Urban District Council Minute Book (SUDCMB) Apr 1948–May 1949.* CSLBH, SA.

SUDC (1949b) *Housing Committee 29/3/49, p 324 & 329, CA 60/23 SUDCMB Apr 1948–May 49.* CSLBH, SA.

SUDC (1950) *Housing Committee 31/5/50, p 8, CA 60/25 SUDCMB May 1950–May 1951.* CSLBH, SA.

SUDC. (1960a) *Housing Committee 19/1/60, p 228, CA 60/34 SUDCMB May 1959–May 1960.* CSLBH, SA.

SUDC (1962) *Finance Committee 19/4/62 p 344, and Housing Committee 9/7/63 p70, CA 60/34 SUDCMB 1962–1963.* CSLBH, SA.

SUDC (1963) *Housing Committee 19/11/63 p. 207–208. CA 60/34 SUDCMB 1963–1964.* CSLBH, SA.

Walker, G. (2014) '*Why room temperature needed to be taken down a notch*'. *DEMAND Centre blog* [online]. Available at: www.demand.ac.uk/05/11/2014/why-room-temperature-needed-to-be-taken-down-a-notch-the-conversation-4-november-2014/ (Accessed 27/9/2015).

Woolf, M. (1967) *The Housing Survey in England and Wales 1964.* London: HMSO.

9

DISTRICT HEATING IN BELGRADE

The politics of provision

Charlotte Johnson

Introduction

The evolution of Milorad Branković's[1] central heating system is a good place to start thinking about the politics that are created through urban energy infrastructure. In 2011, at the time of research, heating was an issue in Belgrade. The government had identified electric heating as a source of waste and pollution and aimed to switch people on to the city heating network, Milorad's neighbourhood had been identified as an area for new connection. Milorad is an entrepreneur in his late thirties who runs his business out of the relatively large Belgrade town house that his great-grandfather built in 1928. At the time of construction, the area was on the edge of Belgrade and served by the electricity grid, but heating was an individual's affair. Milorad's house had been built with a wood-fuelled boiler in the basement, which provided the house with central heating. This system was no longer functioning. Milorad's great-grandmother had dismantled it in 1941 at the time of the German occupation of Belgrade, as a tactic to make the house less attractive to the occupying forces. The strategy did not work, 'so we got our German officer who was living right here, in this room and that one', Milorad said, gesturing to the office in which we were sitting and the neighbouring room which housed the top of the range printing machines that were the basis of his current successful business. The central heating system had never been restored, because, with the Communist Party taking power, his family's fortunes changed. '[A]fter the war, my great-grandfather was an enemy of the state and we didn't have money. It's as simple as that', explained Milorad. Despite the shift in fortunes of his bourgeois family, they had managed to keep ownership of their home, and today, in addition to Milorad's printing firm, two branches of his extended family were housed in apartments above. Now they heat the house with electricity and use individual radiators to heat the rooms as required.

Central heating can create a domestic environment that differentiates between social groups, as Milorad's great-grandmother was aware. In the early twentieth century, it signified membership of an affluent elite which did not have to stoke open fires to keep warm. By the middle of the century, with the rise of mass consumerism, this form of technology-enabled comfort was within the reach of a much wider population. Shove's (2003) work on comfort has shown that managing heat in the home cannot be interpreted as purely a matter of individual taste and rising affluence. It is driven by much broader dynamics including medical understandings of human physiology and technical innovations in managing internal environments, both of which contribute to normative understandings of what conditions a home should provide. With optimum internal conditions defined, the market can both create and meet demand for these conditions. Shove points to the gradual international harmonisation of indoor living conditions around 22°C as evidence of how standardised needs are socially created and met.

Under the socialist system, the uptake of central heating was driven not by the market, but by the state. Central heating was recognised as a living standard that a modern industrial society should be able to provide for its urban citizens. In common with other socialist states, Yugoslavia[2] invested in large-scale district heating systems in its cities in order to optimise efficient resource distribution through centrally planned urban development and produce modern, healthy homes for the labour force (The Heating and Ventilating Research Association, 1967). These networks of pipes and pumps delivered heat generated at power plants into the central heating systems of the city's buildings. The networks were overtly political, as they were used to promote socialism's ability to provide comfortable living conditions, and to reward certain groups through allocation of the flats connected to the system. They have been described by critics as 'implementation tool[s] for the political ideologies and development policies of communist states' (Poputoaia and Bouzarovski, 2010: 3820). As the heating network extended through Belgrade, it created a territory in which specific roles and responsibilities were created, casting the city as provider and its residents as beneficiaries of the socialist political economy. Access to these standardised domestic environments was secured through people's connections with the socialist state and their contribution to the socialist economy. Those falling foul of it, such as Milorad's family, were less able to achieve these conditions. However, for those within the network, the municipal technology shaped social practices and created norms of sharing and of negotiating personal comfort within a wider social group.

These values and practises are being exposed today, as the district heating system is subject to upgrades and reforms. District heating is again being pursued as the optimal way to manage urban energy (Connolly et al., 2014), recognised as a low carbon way to heat city homes (Lund et al., 2014). Achieving this vision in Belgrade means retrofitting capitalist relations into the socialist designed systems, which challenges the previous political logics of distribution, changes the roles and responsibilities of actors within the system and unsettles the values and practices of residents.

The aim of this chapter is to understand these politics and to show how they affect the way heating happens in Belgrade today. To do this, I bring together two areas of research: science and technology studies' (STS) critiques of neo-liberal reform of infrastructure and practice theory approaches to energy and comfort. The first body of literature helps understand how urban infrastructures create institutional forms and social differentiation by analysing technical arrangements and the relationships of scale, ownership and power they create (Graham and Marvin, 2001; Gandy, 2004; Bouzarovski, 2010). The second body of literature focuses on the lived experiences of these infrastructural arrangements and in particular how habits and social values form part of these systems (Lutzenhiser, 1993; Shove, 2003; Shove, Walker and Brown, 2014). In this chapter, I make use of both strategies to analyse how Belgrade's district heating network created a set of social values and institutional forms which continue to be experienced in the home. I then use this framework to show how the proposed technical upgrade and economic liberalisation of the heating infrastructure is creating new roles and social relations. I conclude that the proposed reform involves creating new scales of responsibility and new categories of financial risk, which undermine the ability to mobilise social and infrastructural relations to improve the efficiency of the system.

Shaping institutions and practices through territory and technology

Belgrade's district heating system is intimately tied to the development of Yugoslav socialism and the city's fluctuating fortunes as the capital first of the Yugoslav federation of socialist states, and then of Serbia. In the early days of Yugoslav socialism, Belgrade's development served a number of key symbolic purposes from promoting socialist economic progress, to accommodating the different nations of the federation. Belgrade needed housing urgently after the war, and the mass housing projects of the 1960s and 1970s not only fulfilled this need, but were used to demonstrate the high standard of living that the socialist political economy provided for its citizens and the rewards it offered to loyal socialist citizens and workers who were allocated the right to use them (Blagojević, 2007; Kulić, 2014). Heating infrastructure was part of this demonstration, since central heating indicated a high standard of convenient and comfortable modern urban living (Johnson, 2018).

District heating was the modern and efficient way to provide such a standard at scale. On the tabula rasa sites of new socialist housing developments, heating plants were sized and built to pump heat into the planned homes. These homes were spaces that needed to be kept above a certain temperature for certain times of the day and certain parts of the year. When temperatures fell, the heating was switched on and stayed on until spring. Heating pipes ran vertically through apartments linking bedroom to bedroom and sitting room to sitting room as they rose up through the building. Flats on these networks did not have individual controls and residents could not control the amount of heat from their radiators, nor when they came on or went off during the day, or the year. There was no space for individual preferences. Instead, the occupant's notional role was to labour for the socialist economy by day and enjoy the cosy rewards of this economic development by night. The heating infrastructure created and reproduced standardised interpretations of health, comfort and modernity, materially linking residents to their neighbours, their city and their state in these terms.

At first, this style of living was provided in new neighbourhoods on the edge of the city, where district heating systems could be built to supply new housing. The year 1970 marked a conceptual reorganisation of Belgrade's heating with the foundation of a 'workers' heating utility, Beogradske Elektrane. This brought all shared heating systems including individual small-scale coal and heavy oil boilers used in older apartment blocks under the same management, conceptually linking physically separate systems and technologies. The city boundaries were changed to give the municipality control over a nearby coal field. Belgraders thus had their own fuel source and large scale networks could extend through the city channelling heat from thermal plants into both new and existing housing. Such reorganisation followed broader political reforms in Yugoslavia at the time, which increased state control over development and supported Yugoslavia's form of self-management by creating governance structures that could integrate local supply with local demand (Estrin, 1991: 189). Guided by a principal of self-management of resources, the municipal firm was responsible for delivering equal services to the people of Belgrade and for providing 'comfortable' conditions indoors regardless of such fluctuating externalities as the weather or the price and availability of different types of fuel. Through the

1980s the network extended into older pre-socialist neighbourhoods, removing polluting oil boilers and coal fires from existing housing and integrating them into the network.

The 1990s marked another conceptual shift. With the end of socialist Yugoslavia, Beogradske Elektrane stopped being a workers' organisation and instead became a public utility company (javno kumunalno preduzeće). It now began to reconsider its service as something that needed to pay for itself, rather than something that was provided by the state as a universal standard of living. Nonetheless, the new firm's aim was 'not to maximise profits, but to deliver thermal energy to the city's population and economy' argues a book produced by the utility celebrating its 45 year history (JKP Beogradske Elektrane, 2010: 77).[3] This decade of war and sanctions not only produced internal challenges to the logic of heating provision, but external ones too. Coward (2009) has argued that the bombing of Belgrade explicitly targeted urban infrastructure in order to make life unliveable, disrupt the social contract and undermine the government's support. Making Belgrade go cold was a way of demonstrating military power.

The end of the Milošević regime in 2001 saw Serbia rejoin international energy and finance markets, a move which has seen a new form of infrastructural politics of development loans and liberalisation. The system faces major problems with old pipework, outdated generating facilities, badly maintained pumping stations and a lack of end user controls. The firm is targeting these issues through a modernisation programme aided by loans and international consultants (JKP Beogradske Elektrane, 2010: 112).

The firm currently services 40% of the city's households, but is continuing to expand. Pipes are now being extended into the oldest parts of the city through neighbourhoods like Milorad's under a mandate to reduce the highly polluting electricity being used to heat homes. Milorad's household was offered the option to connect, but he has been emphatically against it. The district heating utility is still owned by the city and he was sceptical of the company's role in maintaining socialist-era patronage and dependencies. Not only that, his house is above the maximum distance from the nearest substation and in order to connect he would have had to pay for a new one to be put in his basement. This was not something he would consider:

> I really can't understand why I should give 20,000 euros for a pipe this big. And to give one room in the basement for something that they need. … Because by the contract that you are making with them, it's their room in your house! I don't want to do that. I really don't. It's my house.
>
> *(Milorad, 2011, interview)*

In his account, installing a heating substation seems an imposition almost like the billeting of an enemy officer. It allows a discredited municipal body to take up residence in his home and extort money. In his eyes, the network extension is simply the municipal firm's strategy to trap more and more residents into paying for a bloated and leaky state organ. For Milorad, the district heating system still connotes a socialist middle class which is 'well connected' and which earns these privileges by allowing the state into its private sphere. Others, who supported or directly benefitted from the socialist political economy, view the infrastructure differently.

Shared heating and shared practices

In Belgrade, flats are advertised according to their radiator types and fuel sources. Those connected to the city's district heating system are currently able to earn a premium on the rental market. This suggests the system still appeals. Jana, a professional in her late forties, lives in a flat built in the mid 1970s that had been allocated to her husband's family. It's connected to the city heating which she likes because it removes the inconvenience of dealing with solid fuel boilers. She explained,

> it's much more satisfactory because there aren't stable market conditions. One year it's better to heat with electricity and the next year wood and the third on coal, but you can't change your boiler every year to electricity, coal, wood.
>
> *(Jana, 2011, Interview)*

Her comment captures the difference between those whose homes fall within the 'heated territory' of the city and benefit from standardised provision and those who have to work harder to keep their own home warm and are more exposed to market fluctuations. Such awareness also comes through in a conversation with Ognjen, a pensioner in his 70s, who lives in a 1930s building which predates the socialist era. Close to Milorad's neighbourhood, the building's residents also had the option to connect and Ognjen explained why opting in had been a good option for him. The new central heating replaced his electric storage heaters and now he no longer had to choose which parts of his flat to heat or wait for the cheaper electricity tariff. With the city heating, he said,

> we don't think at all about… whether it will heat there or not.
>
> *(Ognjen, 2011, interview)*

Being connected to the system is an acceptance of the state's role in managing resource distribution and in Ognjen's account suggests a continuation of a socialist vision of abundance; the completion of a work in progress that had been abandoned in the 1990s, leaving many on the waiting list for a lifestyle they had been contributing to through their role as socialist citizens. For both Jana and Ognjen, the standardised system mitigates market uncertainty and maintains consumer comfort. For others, this standardisation is problematic. It is an ideal type that is confounded in reality by things like pipes breaking down, conditions in apartments varying as they're exposed to northerly winds or south-facing warmth and the differences in people's tastes and perceptions of comfort.

In this context, a malfunctioning radiator symbolises different kinds of failure. For some, it represents an anachronistic remnant of the misplaced socialist faith in progress which has shackled the present administration to a legacy of unachievable ideals and unrecoverable expenses. For others, however, it is evidence of the state reneging on its contract to provide the population with the basic standards of a 'normal' standard of living. The unreachable ideal of universal provision is such that diverse strategies are privately employed to alter the home environment. For example, larger radiators are added to the pipes to boost heat levels or additional technologies are used to extend heating beyond the prescribed periods. These additions turn the system into a site of ongoing negotiation organised around the goal of maintaining a reliably heated home. These are not just technical negotiations about how comfortable conditions might be achieved, they also involve conceptions of civic duties and responsibilities. The two pipe system means that individual flats cannot be cut off for non-payment and therefore the decision to pay, reflects a household's evaluation of the service provided and of the wider state of the political economy. For example, when I asked one public sector employee whether she paid her bills regularly, she replied that when the state does not enable her to earn a living wage, she does not pay the state either.

The infrastructure also situates residents in relation to one another. Alterations made to the system can disrupt the supply to other residents' homes and such interventions are interpreted as being unfair and un–civic-minded. Conversations with residents who had altered parts of the network in their homes revealed this awareness. Irena, a journalist in her fifties, had recently added thermostatic valves to her radiators to adjust the heat they emitted. She found her flat too hot and due to her health condition it was particularly problematic. She used defensive language about having altered the system in her home, aware that altering the system in one's own flat has a knock on effect for others connected to the system. She explained that a Beogradske Elektrane engineer had come to investigate a major problem with the whole building's supply pipe and while he had been working in the building, Irena had asked him for help:

> They sent someone really responsible from the service, who understood my problem and who wanted to help. He said, 'ok that is something that you have to pay yourself. That is not included in our service'. And I'm sure he didn't lie to me. ... [H]e has put three valves in three radiators here. And I am very grateful for that. .... If it is too hot we turn it down. ...[H]e did it... and we paid for it.
>
> *(Irena, 2011, interview)*

Irena felt the need to justify both his and her actions:

> First of all it was strictly out of his working hours. Strictly, that's something that he told me that I should be aware [of]. ... My logic was that he's the guy that has been working at that place for 30 years. He's responsible and he knows how to do things. Why should I go and look for some person I cannot trust at all instead of asking this guy to be kind enough to do me a favour?
>
> *(Irena, 2011, interview)*

Irena's account indicates the relationships created through the infrastructure that link her domestic space to the city and state; as described, this situation creates a tension between her role as citizen within a system and as occupant with individual tastes and requirements. She recognises the infrastructure in her private sphere as belonging to a broader system that requires both users and suppliers to play fair in order to make it work. In adding controls, she is going beyond the normal role of a citizen and feels that it is her responsibility to pay for the valves and the labour to install them. But she is also concerned that through this private investment, she does not damage the broader system: it is in these terms that she justifies her use of a moonlighting state employee to help create conditions that she will find comfortable within her own home. Because of his experience, he can be trusted to make sure that the wider system continues to distribute heat equally and to perpetuate the equality of the service.

Irena uses a framework of trustworthiness and responsibility to work within the system, distinguishing between those who do and don't play fair. Earlier in our interview she had been sceptical about the previous socialist state and was very cynical about the subsequent administrations, which she felt continued to be corrupt and ineffective. Even so, she was committed to the universalist principle of the heating system and accepted that there was a collective need to manage resources and protect social equity. This is not unique, ethnographic studies of post-socialist life have shown how the social values of previous regimes remain engrained in the habits and materialities of everyday life. Alexander (2007) and Humphrey (2007) have demonstrated the disconcerting experience people have as they negotiate their roles as citizens in a new political economy equipped with established infrastructure and its associated practices and values. Residents experienced a sense of 'social upheaval' or 'moral loss' at the removal of standardised provision when services were privatised or manipulated by political elites (Humphrey, 2003: 92). However, Irena's experience brings a new aspect to this; she is intervening in the infrastructure to get the kind of service she wants, but in way that aligns with her interpretation of the values embedded in that system. Given the new technology that now exists to control heating in her home, she is investing her own resources to 'upgrade' the standardised equipment. By opting to put in thermostatic radiator valves rather than leave her windows open to let the heat out, she is not only acting according to her understanding of the moral economy of the heating system, but also in a way that aligns with policy recommendations to improve the efficiency of the system (see OECD/IEA, 2004).

Research into the problems of post-socialist cities' district heating identify overheating and limited control over the amount of heat used in the home as two sources of system inefficiency. They also identify the difficulties of mobilising the capital needed to add controls and improve performance (Rezessy et al., 2006). Technical appraisals call for the utility to be liberalised, unbundled and privatised to overcome these difficulties. These calls follow the broader trend apparent in the management of urban infrastructure, which has seen a shift from social welfare models of service provision paid through rates to a liberal model of prices charged per unit consumed. This shift is accompanied by the 'unbundling' of publically-owned and vertically-integrated utilities into separate generation, distribution and customer-facing activities which can be privatised. Graham and Marvin (2001) describe this shift as replacing 'the modern infrastructural ideal' with a splintered urbanism which forgoes the ideal of universal provision. This is key feature in post-socialist economic reforms, particularly in energy infrastructure (Bouzarovski, 2010). Reforms rework the social and material characteristics of the network and open up what Collier (2012) has called a 'problem space' in which explicit debates over technical and economic improvements contain implicit assumptions about the forms of social relationships and institutions that should exist. This 'problem space' is explored in the following section.

Liberalisation: creating autonomy and locating risk

Arguments in favour of liberalising Belgrade's district heating system and replacing state distribution with the market highlight problems with the present system. First, Belgrade's district heating system is extensive and loses large amounts of energy through its distribution network. Second, it relies on expensive imported natural gas or highly polluting heavy fuel oil and coal, raising environmental concerns about the carbon intensity of the heat supplied and economic concerns about the burden it places on state and municipal budgets (Karam and Palmreuther, 2012). Third, high-quality fuels are used in heat-only boilers: a more efficient strategy would be to use these fuels for electricity production or other industrial processes and use the low-grade heat produced as a by-product to heat homes (Karam and Palmreuther, 2012; UNDP, 2004). Finally, the present system sends heat out according to predetermined criteria such as the external temperature and floor space, charging a flat rate for this, rather than supplying the amount of heat wanted by the residents and charging them for what they consume (Kavgic et al., 2012). This flat rate is subsidised by the city and therefore perpetuates the inequality created through the socialist housing allocation system, which rewarded the middle class, who continue to benefit from living in these higher quality and warmer buildings. The UNDP have argued that subsidised 'district heating services and maintenance [can be interpreted as] rent on accumulated social capital' (UNDP, 2004: 76). Whereas under socialism the district heating system was a standard to which society was progressing, now it is seen by some as a mis-targeted subsidy that has been hijacked by the middle class and an inefficient waste of resources which is indebting both the city and its citizens.

As a result of these problems, reforming the district heating system is a priority for the city (City of Belgrade, 2008). Although the difficulties listed above are located in different parts of the system, one over-riding theme is the need to liberalise the service and charge consumers the market cost of the thermal energy they consume. Just as the heating utility's history book described the consolidation of territory and technologies to provide a standardised service, these arguments for reform rest on the shared belief that this territory must be broken up through metering technology in order to expose the 'real' amount of energy being used in different parts of the system and identify who should take responsibility for the cost and efficient management of the heat.

The first step, as advised in the technical literature, is to split the heating system into two types of networks: a primary one which connects power stations, generating plants and substations through city pipes and secondary ones which run between substations and residential blocks or small groups of buildings (OECD/IEA, 2004; Euroheat and Power, 201122). This allows for two areas of improvements to be made: more efficient generation in the primary network from new, low carbon heat generating technologies and more efficient use of heat within homes.

These primary and secondary pipe networks exist, but heat has historically flowed unmonitored between them. Meters are therefore needed to create a boundary between these parts of the system by producing data on how much heat is being sent to and from substations. In creating this data, meters help delineate a jurisdiction in which residents can become active subjects of the new system and take control of their heat consumption at home. To date, residents have been recipients of heat with a limited ability to influence the amount they use. The system needs to enable residents' agency to turn them into active heat consumers. This is done by replacing the rates system of billing with a two-tier tariff system composed of fixed and flexible costs. The fixed costs refer to the capital sunk into the network in the form of pipes, energy plants, control room technologies and staff who manage the production and distribution of the heat. The flexible costs relate to the energy used. These costs are flexible because the price of fuel fluctuates, but also because the amount of heating fluctuates in response to such unpredictable variables such as residents' preferences and the weather. These flexible costs are the ones that the residents notionally have the ability to control. This seemingly benign admission of the state of uncertainty within an energy network simultaneously situates the problem as one that is located in the secondary network. This means the financial challenge of managing fluctuating fuel prices and demand can be shifted down the pipes out of the city-utility's jurisdiction and into homes. The logic is that flexible costs can be passed on to the 'consumer', because this new subject has the power to alter them.

This image of the active consumer exists in energy efficiency policies, but actually achieving this subject position is technically problematic. First, due to the lack of radiator valves, many residents do not have the ability to reduce the amount of heat that comes into their home. They would need to add the valves if they wanted to do this. Second, due to the pipe layout which links radiators vertically between flats rather than horizontally within them, it is not possible to know how much heat is being consumed within any one home. To find out how much heat an individual household is using, all residents need to fit heat cost allocators on each radiator to sense the amount of heat being emitted, then, the total amount of metered energy entering the building can be attributed proportionally to each radiator, giving an idea of how much each flat has used. Third, it is hard to know exactly why residents are consuming the amount of heat they are. If one building uses a lot of heat, this could be because the residents are keeping their flats at very high temperatures, or because the building is poorly insulated or the central heating systems are poorly installed or badly maintained. It is therefore not clear how residents can manage their energy consumption while maintaining a warm home. And there is a final difficulty which remains: for residents to turn their homes into these bounded sites of individual consumption within the network, they will to invest collectively in the infrastructure itself, buying heat cost allocators to know how much of the substation's heat is being emitted by their own radiators. The investments needed to individualise consumption are framed as vehicles for releasing consumer sovereignty and the promise is that the costs involved will be recouped through reduced energy bills (Živković, Todorović and Vasiljević, 2006; Fankhauser and Tepic, 2007). If this is to happen, residents will have to work together to manage their shared thermal energy and invest in the infrastructure.

In addition to the technical issues that undermine this rescaling and reallocation of responsibility, there is another reason why this is a problematic proposition. It is based on the idea that people's primary motivation will be financial. However, as we have seen above, what people do reflects different interpretations of comfort as well as of their responsibility towards the system as a whole and the impact of their actions on their family, their neighbours, the city or the state. In fact, a field trial of meters and radiator valves found that those who had the capacity to adjust their heating did so despite having no economic incentive. Monitored over two winters, Belgraders in two 'test' buildings used between 10.5% and 15% less heat, despite being charged the same flat rate (Živković, Todorović and Vasiljević, 2006: 81). Other studies have had similar results, for example, a study of communal energy use in the US found that

> even where lack of concern for energy use is endemic, cultural practice and collective restraint can produce both highly variegated and lower-than-expected consumption levels among households who, by economic reasoning, might be considered likely to exploit common property resources.
>
> *(Lutzenhiser, 1993: 258)*

However, an upgrading programme that relies on cultural practice and collective restraint defies the logic of the current infrastructural politics which only recognises privatisation and individualisation as the route to system upgrade.

The liberalisation of Belgrade's heating system depends on turning the home into a bounded site of energy consumption and financial responsibility. This involves positioning anxieties about rising fuel costs within the domestic sphere and at the same time supposing that households have the ability to control their consumption. It prioritises the ability of an individual to act on his/her own consumption, rather than attempting to achieve system level gains through a collective response. Although the plans for improving the efficiency of the heating system involve a reworking of relationships between citizen and municipality and reconceiving the processes through which heat is consumed, these plans clash with the material arrangements and values embedded in the existing system.

At the time of research (2010–2011), Serbia's second largest city Novi Sad was progressing further towards the liberalisation of its heating firm. This generated press coverage of the new metering system being implemented. One article discussed the cost of installing meters, saying that it would amount to 50 euros per radiator. This provoked a flow of comments, two of which illustrate different perspectives on this topic.

> The meters need to be introduced urgently. Why do we pay for heating according to an apartment's floor space? Where else still has that?. … I will switch off the radiator when I don't need it … and I will not pay for heating I haven't used. … Is there anything fairer than a man paying for what he's used? I don't think there is.
>
> *(Petrović, 2010)*

This reader's comment reveals his frustration with the wastefulness of the municipal system and his outrage at having to cover the cost of this wastefulness. However, another reader presents a different perspective:

> [W]hy would I pay 50 euros for that meter and finance the heating firm? The ultimate hypocrisy is that the firm says that they will 'meet the citizens halfway' and the citizens can buy those devices on credit. That sounds like our public enterprise, i.e. the state, making loans... [t]o buy and install the meters, so that the firm can then be sold off more easily.
>
> *(Petrović, 2010)*

In this account, heating is a social asset which should be protected. Instead, the state is attempting to use the creditworthiness of its citizens to upgrade the network in preparation for privatisation. In this interpretation, heat generation and distribution assets are being separated from the home, which becomes a disconnected space of financial risk, rather than a reliably warm dwelling.

These comments exemplify some of the themes discussed in this chapter, including scepticism towards the motivations of those in power, anxiety about the market encroaching into areas that should be protected and a sense that daily life is affected as infrastructure and its managers reshape related roles and responsibilities. The debate suggests that people have a sense of the political value of warmth in the home. For some, a warm home ensures health benefits and the luxury of not engaging with the market; for others it means wasteful oversupply and limited consumer sovereignty. The reforms, driven by a different interpretation of the kinds of relationships that should be created, and of the infrastructural changes involved (more metering), do not capitalise on this sense of participation and responsibility towards the heating network.

Conclusion

This analysis of Belgrade's district heating has demonstrated how the system has shaped social norms and affected practices over time. It created a heated territory based on normative values about residents' rights and responsibilities and the sort of conditions the state should provide. When framed in these terms, warmth in the home came to be associated with politics, both the everyday politics of connections between neighbours and the formal politics of the state. The conversations I had with residents whose buildings were connected to the network revealed a range of responses to the politics surrounding and created through this infrastructure. They discussed private strategies employed to improve the warmth of the flat, using electric heaters to top up the heating or adding thermostatic valves to reduce the warmth. Some hankered for a more straightforward 'consumer' role and were frustrated by the wastefulness of the system. Others accepted the porosity of the border between their domestic sphere and the shared spaces and systems of the building, arguing neighbours had to collectively contribute to the upkeep of these shared systems in order to benefit from them.

Reforms have the potential to produce technical, financial and legal boundaries between residents and provide them with limited control over their domestic space, but these boundaries will also weaken residents' connection with broader issues that govern the price and reliability of home heating. I have suggested that concerns with these issues remain and that the political value of warmth is still attached to the design and operation of the technical system, and understood by residents. District heating connotes an idealised standard of living that the state should be able to provide, but the reality of living with these systems reveals the difficulty of achieving this ideal. In response, some argue for continued participation and for actively working towards this goal, others feel exposed to abuse and exploitation and would prefer a different way to achieve warmth in the home. Within these debates, the radiator valve has a central role: it is rhetorically constructed as the instrument through which to produce material and social arrangements of the kind that are in demand in Belgrade today. Residents are eager to be rid of political corruption and to sever links with neighbours who do not play fair, but despite its technical promise, the valve fails to produce these purified forms and is persistently undermined by an obdurate material network of pipes.

I have developed this argument by looking at how power relations flow through the socio-technical assemblage that makes up Belgrade's district heating system. I have also paid attention to how people respond to the technologies of home heating. This has helped me articulate the values that are inscribed in the system and describe how practices of keeping warm are interpreted. Bringing these two aspects together highlights the tension that appears when technical upgrades and economic reforms clash with existing social relationships supported by an established heating infrastructure. These tensions define the 'problem space' created by the liberalisation of the system. I have argued that assumptions associated with this project constrain opportunities for improving the system's efficiency by promoting individual agency over and against the collective action that is required to manage heat consumption and reduce demand. I have also noted that proposed solutions do not align with the materiality of the existing network nor with the social practices this materiality supports and that it is not obvious that new understandings of scale, individualism and agency can be retrofitted at will.

Notes

1   Pseudonyms are used for all interlocutors.
2   Belgrade was the capital of the socialist Federal Republic of Yugoslavia from 1945 and has been the capital of Serbia since the end of Yugoslavia in the 1990s.
3   All translations are mine.

References

Alexander, C. (2007) 'Soviet and Post-Soviet planning in Almaty, Kazakhstan', *Critique of Anthropology*, 27(2): 165–181.

Blagojević, L. (2007) *Novi Beograd: ospereni modernizam*. Beograd: Zavod za udzbenike.

Bouzarovski, S. (2010) 'Post-socialist energy reforms in critical perspective: entangled boundaries, scales and trajectories of change', *European Urban and Regional Studies*, 17(2): 167–182.

City of Belgrade (2008) 'City of Belgrade development strategy: goals, concept and strategic priorities of sustainable development'. Belgrade.

Collier, S. J. (2012) *Post-Soviet Social: Neoliberalism, Social Modernity, Biopolitics*. Princeton: Princeton University Press.

Connolly, D., Lund, H., Mathiesen, B. V., Werner, S., Möller, B., Persson, U., Boermans, T., Trier, D., Østergaard, P. a. and Nielsen, S. (2014) 'Heat roadmap Europe: combining district heating with heat savings to decarbonise the EU energy system', *Energy Policy*, 65: 475–489.

Coward, M. (2009) 'Network-centric violence, critical infrastructure and the urbanization of security', *Security Dialogue*, 40(4–5): 399–418.

Estrin, S. (1991) 'Yugoslavia: the case of self-managing market socialism', 5(4): 187–194.

Euroheat and Power (2011) 'District heating in buildings', *Optimization*.

Fankhauser, S. and Tepic, S. (2007) 'Can poor consumers pay for energy and water? An affordability analysis for transition countries', *Energy Policy*, 35(2): 1038–1049.

Gandy, M. (2004) 'Rethinking urban metabolism: water, space and the modern city', *City*, 8(3): 363–379.

Graham, S. and Marvin, S. (2001) *Splintering Urbanism: networked infrastructures, technological mobilities and the urban condition*. London & New York: Routledge.

Humphrey, C. (2003) 'Rethinking infrastructure: Siberian cities and the great freeze of 2001', in Schneider, J. and Susser, I. (eds.) *Wounded Cities: destruction and reconstruction in a globalized world*. Oxford: Berg. pp. 91–107.

Humphrey, C. (2007) 'New subjects and situated interdependence: after privatisation in Ulan-Ude', in Alexander, C., Buchli, V. and Humphrey, C. (eds.) *Urban Life in Post-Soviet Asia*. Abingdon, Oxon and New York: UCL Press. pp. 175–207.

JKP Beogradske Elektrane (2010) *Beogradske Elektrane 1965–2010*. Belgrade: JKP Beogradske Elektrane.

Johnson, C. (2018) 'The moral economy of comfortable living: negotiating individualism and collectivism through housing in Belgrade', *Critique of Anthropology*, 38(3).

Karam, S. and Palmreuther, S. (2012) 'Improving energy efficiency in Belgrade, Serbia: TRACE study' Europe and Central Asia Sustainable Cities Initiative (ECA SCI), Washington DC, (December). Available at: https://esmap.org/sites/esmap.org/files/DocumentLibrary/TRACE_Belgrade%20Final_Optimized.pdf.

Kavgic, M., Summerfield, A., Mumovic, D., Stevanovic, Z. M., Turanjanin, V. and Stevanovic, Z. Z. (2012) 'Characteristics of indoor temperatures over winter for Belgrade urban dwellings: indications of thermal comfort and space heating energy demand', *Energy and Buildings*, 47: 506–514.

Kulić, V. (2014) 'New Belgrade and Socialist Yugoslavia's three globalisations', *International Journal for History, Culture and Modernity*, 2(2): 125–154.

Lund, H., Werner, S., Wiltshire, R., Svendsen, S., Thorsen, J. E., Hvelplund, F. and Mathiesen, B.V. (2014) '4th generation district heating (4GDH)', *Energy*, 68: 1–11.

Lutzenhiser, L. (1993) 'Social and behavioral aspects of energy use', *Annual Review of Energy and the Environment*, 18: 247–289.

OECD/IEA (2004) *Coming In From the Cold: improving district heating policy in transition economies*. Paris: OECD/IEA.

Petrović, L. (2010) 'Grejanje jeftinije uz naplatu po utrošku? [Heating cheaper with payment by consumption?]', *Blic*, October.

Poputoaia, D. and Bouzarovski, S. (2010) 'Regulating district heating in Romania: legislative challenges and energy efficiency barriers', *Energy Policy*, 38: 3820–3829.

Rezessy, S., Dimitrov, K., Ürge-vorsatz, D. and Baruch, S. (2006) 'Municipalities and energy efficiency in countries in transition', *Energy Policy*, 34: 223–237.

Shove, E. (2003) *Comfort, Cleanliness and Convenience: the social organisation of normality*. Oxford & New York: Berg.

Shove, E., Walker, G. and Brown, S. (2014) 'Material culture, room temperature and the social organisation of thermal energy', *Journal of Material Culture*, 19(2): 113–124.

The Heating and Ventilating Research Association (1967) *District Heating: a survey of practice in Europe and America*. London: National Coal Board.

UNDP (2004) *Stuck In the Past: energy, environment and poverty in Serbia and Montenegro*. Belgrade: UNDP Country Office in Serbia and Montenegro.

Živković, B., Todorović, M. and Vasiljević, P. (2006) 'Energy savings for residential heating in two pairs of buildings achieved by implementation of actually consumed energy measuring', *Thermal Science*, 10(4): 79–88.

10

UNLEASHING THE INTERNET

The normalisation of wireless connectivity

Janine Morley

The internet is a remarkable, complex and evolving infrastructure. As a physical network, it has expanded massively to connect and conduct data between billions of computers, servers, data centres and the computational circuits embedded in a huge range of devices, appliances and environments throughout the world. The services this provides and the practices it supports are also changing and expanding in range and number. Whilst the 'consequences' of these developments are many, varied and debated, this chapter focuses instead on an aspect of this expanding infrastructure that is often overlooked: wireless connectivity as provided by Wi-Fi networks. Over the last 15 or so years, wireless devices such as laptops, smartphones and tablets have become the most common and preferred way of accessing the internet (Ofcom, 2017) and over half of all internet traffic (52%[1]) is now carried via Wi-Fi (Cisco, 2017a). In combination with the connectivity provided by mobile networks, the internet – as it is experienced, used and operates today – is to a large extent wireless. The nature of this 'wirelessness' (Mackenzie, 2010) and the role it plays in mediating relationships between the physical infrastructure of the internet, the services it provides and the practices it supports is fundamental to how the internet is developing over time as an infrastructure-in-use (Shove, Watson and Spurling, 2015).

By focusing specifically on Wi-Fi and its role in an evolving internet, this chapter pursues several aims. First, it asks exactly how Wi-Fi is implicated in the growth of this infrastructure. Since this also entails a growth in energy consumption (Van Heddeghem et al., 2012; Andrae and Edler, 2015), a better understanding of this process is relevant to efforts to reduce global energy demand. Second, the chapter aims to develop ideas about how infrastructures become 'normal' and 'necessary'. Today, it is easy to take the 'usefulness' of the internet for granted, but the nature of internet use has changed radically over time. The processes by which new infrastructures become 'useful', and thereby more or less obdurate, are complex and deserve further scholarly attention. In showing how Wi-Fi has been progressively implicated in the co-evolution of broadband infrastructures, mobile computing devices and a range of practices, the chapter describes a process of dynamic and ongoing 'normalisation' (Hand and Shove, 2007) in which certain of these elements have, thus far, become increasingly interdependent. In particular, it proposes that as with innovation in the design of information technologies (de Wit et al., 2002), some sites are more important than others for the co-evolution of infrastructures, devices and practices. These can be thought of as 'normalisation junctions'.

By situating Wi-Fi as an important *part* of the wireless internet-in-use, the chapter develops a distinctive account of the development and expansion of Wi-Fi that contrasts with much of the previous literature on the subject. Scholarly attention has tended to focus either on the design of wireless technologies and the process by which, as a standard, Wi-Fi emerged, was agreed and adopted (Lemstra, Hayes and Groenewegen, 2011) or on Wi-Fi as a potential infrastructure in its own right, for example: its conformity to sequenced stages of infrastructural development (Sawhney, 2003), the successes, failures, politics and modes of development in community and municipal initiatives to provide city-wide networks (Sandvig, 2004; Mackenzie, 2005; Powell, 2008) and the spatial and socio-economic implications of public hotspot distribution (Grubesic and Murray, 2004; Torrens, 2008). Here, my interest is not so much in Wi-Fi as a separate or alternative communications infrastructure but rather how its integration with the wider, wired internet (to produce a wireless internet) makes possible certain kinds of relationships with everyday practices, and how these change together over time.

The chapter draws on a range of secondary materials from consumer surveys and academic literature. It begins by introducing the scale and rapidity by which Wi-Fi has expanded globally. It then discusses how this process of expansion and normalisation might be understood, which leads on to an account of the shifting assemblies that have come together in UK households as Wi-Fi has come into use. This shows that the home is a key site at which configurations, expectations and experiences of wireless connectivity are established. The chapter concludes with reflections on what this case contributes to understanding the processes by which infrastructures and practices change together.

The growth of Wi-Fi

Wi-Fi is a registered trademark that represents a certified protocol for interoperable wireless communication technologies to join or provide a local area network over short distances (tens of meters). This family of international standards (technically known as 802.11) is agreed by the Institute of Electrical and Electronics Engineers (IEEE) and continues to evolve to provide higher speed connectivity. These standards are widely integrated into mobile and digital devices as well as access points that connect, via routers, to the internet. As measured by the numbers of each, the trend is clear: Wi-Fi has expanded significantly and rapidly since its first incorporation in a mass market product (the Apple AirPort system) in 1999. By 2017, the Wi-Fi Alliance had certified over 35,000 compatible kinds of products (Wi-Fi Alliance, 2017). In the same year, the estimated number of 'hotspots' worldwide reached 262.3 million, up from 26.5 million in 2013 (iPass, 2017).

More broadly, the internet was used by 48% of the global population in 2017, with 84% of households in developed countries having access at home (ITU, 2017). In the UK, almost all of the 82% of households with a fixed internet connection also have Wi-Fi (Ofcom, 2015b; 2017). And whilst Wi-Fi is not the only way to access the internet and the services it provides, it does carry the largest portion of internet traffic in the UK: in 2016 57.6% of traffic travelled over Wi-Fi networks compared to 40% for fixed connections and 3.5% for mobile networks (Cisco, 2017b). Not surprisingly, then, to many people Wi-Fi is an inextricable part of what internet access means. This is playfully illustrated by an image that circulated on social media in 2012 depicting 'Wi-Fi' crayoned in at the base of Maslow's hierarchy of needs (Weknowmemes, 2013).

As an example of technological innovation and diffusion, Wi-Fi is considered to be a global 'success' (Lemstra, Hayes and Groenewegen, 2011). Yet narratives of diffusion and of the construction of large technical systems, such as Hughes' (1983) account of electricity networks, often make assumptions about demand, either concluding that it follows unproblematically from the provision of technologies or infrastructures or that it was already latent and unmet (Shove, 2016). But it is evident that the attractions and expectations associated with using the internet today, wirelessly or otherwise, were not the same in 1999 when the Wi-Fi standard was first included in a mass market product. So how can accounts of infrastructural change be more sensitive to the multiple ways in which infrastructures are used and 'demanded' at different times and in different locations? How do new infrastructures, and aspects of them, come to be so widely used and essential, in ways that are almost unimaginable when they first emerge? In other words, what are the processes of 'normalisation' by which new 'uses' and 'needs' for infrastructures arise and become established?

Normalisation junctions

These questions can be approached by thinking about how infrastructures feature within and relate to past, current and planned sets of practices (Shove, Watson and Spurling, 2015; Shove, 2016). Within consumption studies, theories of practice have been influential in emphasising and conceptualising the ordinary and ongoing use of goods and services (Warde, 2005; 2015). For instance, Røpke and Christensen (2012; 2013) note how extensively internet-connected technologies have been integrated into diverse everyday practices. It is this position, of being part of practices that defines how technologies are used and the extent to which they are felt to be necessary. Wants and needs do not emerge from individual desires, but 'emanate' from practices: 'the practice is the conduit and raison d'être for the gratifications which arise from its component moments of consumption' (Warde, 2005: 142). Therefore, as (Hand and Shove, 2007) argue in the case of freezers, the status of being ordinary and necessary is not an inherent or singular characteristic of the object itself but of the pivotal roles it occupies in what people do: not just single practices but in inter-connecting systems of practices; and not just in a single, universal way but as 'simultaneously embedded in strikingly different configurations of "ordinary" practice' (2007, p.95). In other words, products become necessary over time by co-constituting the practices in which they are used, and how these hang together with other practices in ways that only such products can allow (Shove and Southerton, 2000).

Importantly, this outcome of being normal and necessary is not fixed or final, even for technologically stable products, like freezers, which are widely owned and have been in use for many years. Whilst the normalisation of new technologies may be understood as processes of diffusion or domestication which ultimately draw to a close, (Hand and Shove, 2007) argue that normalisation is best thought of as an 'ongoing achievement'. They suggest there is a 'persistent instability' in the positioning and status of freezers precisely because they are 'multiply anchored within diverse and themselves dynamic systems' and in simultaneously multiple ways (Hand and Shove, 2007). As these practices and their inter-relations are reproduced, so too is the normal and necessary status of the objects on which they depend.

If infrastructures are similarly conceptualised through their relationships to practices (Shove, Watson and Spurling, 2015; Shove, 2016), we can expect that the roles, functions and meanings of 'infrastructures-in-use' are also dynamic and heterogeneous, even as their material basis stays fixed and obdurate (and plausibly vice versa). But the relationships between practices and infrastructures are more complex than those with single products. As Shove (2016) suggests, infrastructures are conjoined, directly and indirectly, with multiple practices that are often codependent on other infrastructures, and in multiply articulated webs of relationships, such that changes can take place simultaneously at different rates and in different directions. Infrastructures are also spatially extended, and studies often emphasise dynamics that emerge through the challenges of geographical expansion (de Wit et al., 2002). This is not necessarily a helpful approach for Wi-Fi, whose geographical expansion is a case of 'second-order', bolting on to wired networks and building into billions of access devices. Nor is it necessarily a helpful approach for analysing the ongoing development of infrastructures-in-use, since use occurs in specific places, as part of specific practices.

An alternative approach to studying the ongoing normalisation of infrastructures-in-use is to focus on particular locations. Drawing on Cowan (1987/2012) who described the household as 'the consumption junction' at which consumers decide between competing technologies and thereby significantly shape their diffusion, de Wit et al. (2002) propose the concept of 'innovation junctions'. These are sites at which multiple technologies coexist and are used, resulting in 'interactions and exchanges [that] lead to location-specific innovation patterns' in the design of technologies (de Wit et al., 2002, p.51). Similarly, I suggest that investigating the interactions and connections that form between various devices, infrastructures and practices – at what might be called 'normalisation junctions' – enables us to analyse the processes by which infrastructures become necessary and normal. After all, relationships between infrastructures and practices are mediated by appliances or other interfaces (Shove, 2016), and are likely to be concentrated in particular locations.

Thus, to analyse Wi-Fi as part of an evolving wireless internet-in-use, it makes sense to start by asking: where and how is Wi-Fi used? As the rest of the chapter shows, the home is an important 'normalisation junction' for the wireless internet, a key site in the process by which wireless connectivity has become the most normal way to access the internet *and* where internet use itself has become so necessary to everyday life.

Wi-Fi at home: shifting wireless internet assemblies in UK households

Even though it has not received much attention in previous research into Wi-Fi development, the home is an exceptionally important site both for the initial uptake of Wi-Fi and for its ongoing use. For a start, most Wi-Fi hotspots are domestic: of an estimated 262.3 million worldwide hotspots in 2017, 242 million are located in homes (iPass, 2017). The following discussion focuses on UK homes, reflecting the availability of a series of annual surveys conducted by the national telecommunications regulator, Ofcom, which show high levels of home Wi-Fi ownership. By 2015 (the last year that Ofcom separately reported on the uptake of Wi-Fi routers) this applied to the majority of UK households (75%), encompassing almost all households with fixed broadband internet access (78%) (Ofcom, 2015b). In 2014, the survey also asked about the use of Wi-Fi inside and outside the home: more respondents reported using Wi-Fi at home (79%) than anywhere else, such as when abroad (28%), at a place of work or study (15%), while travelling (14%) or in a public place (11%) (Ofcom, 2014). This section explores the shifting assemblies of devices, infrastructures, services and practices that have formed, with and through Wi-Fi, at this most significant site of use.

The wireless laptop

The early commercial development of wireless local area networks (WLANS) in the 1980s was not focused on the home. Instead, one of the leading 'application(s) in which customer demand was recognised' was in wirelessly connecting cash registers in large American department stores (Lemstra, Hayes and Groenewegen, 2011): as these systems were computerised, stores faced costly rewiring whenever sales floors were reconfigured. Other notable deployments took place in universities (e.g., Carnegie Mellon's Wireless Andrew initiative). Yet by the time the first standard for WLANs was adopted as IEEE 802.11 (a and b) in 1999, later to become known as Wi-Fi, interest in domestic applications had grown as home computing took off in the 1990s. In fact, in 1997 a group of major companies including Intel, Microsoft, HP and IBM started work on a competing standard called HomeRF, which for various reasons was not ultimately adopted. Nevertheless, the very first application of the IEEE 802.11 standard brought the technology directly into homes: the Apple iBook laptop launched in 1999 (Lemstra, Hayes and Groenewegen, 2011).

The iBook was the first Apple laptop aimed at domestic and educational markets and included the 802.11 standard, under the branded name of AirPort, as an optional extra consisting of a plug-in card and an access point for the home. Over the next few years most laptop manufacturers rapidly followed suit and made their new products compatible with the Wi-Fi standard, embedding it into hardware, processing chips and software. Sales of laptops grew steadily through the following decade: from an estimated 1.5 million units in UK households in 2000 to 17.3 million in 2010 (BEIS, 2017). But unlike the name suggests, this 'diffusion' was not a physical process of dispersion. What lies behind such figures is the fact that laptops were becoming useful. But how precisely did standardised wireless connectivity play a role?

Wireless connectivity was certainly integral to Apple's vision for their portable home computers and it was also central to how the company presented and marketed the iBook: positioning it as both technologically cutting-edge and as a useful addition to the home. This was in two ways: first, this wireless laptop was said to offer a new kind of freedom from 'doggone wires' and the 'liberating experience to surf the internet from your iBook while freely moving about your home or classroom – without any power or networking cables to tie you down' (Steve Jobs, quoted at the 1999 MacWorld launch (Thinkingbricks, 2009) and in a press release (Apple, 1999)). Second, 'AirPort lets everyone surf at the same time' (Apple, 2001): a claim illustrated by a schematic image of a home with an iBook and two other Apple desktop computers, each in different rooms, each wirelessly connected to the AirPort. In this way, wireless connectivity helped establish the iBook as an *addition* to the desktop PCs that target customers may already have had. From this it is evident how Wi-Fi facilitates the presence of multiple connected computers in the home and supports the concept of *personal* devices that can be used in various private spaces including bedrooms.

Empirical research has demonstrated just how important wirelessness is to the 'place' that laptops have 'found' within homes; not just in terms of where they are used, but also what they are used for. Based on qualitative interviews with new laptop owners in 2009, (Spinney et al., 2012) argue that laptops are woven into home life, both aesthetically and in terms of the temporal and spatial organisation of domestic activities in a way that desktop PCs are not. Without unsightly wires and with physical dimensions that fit to the body reclined on a sofa, laptops have made themselves at home in the living room. This allows couples to spend more time together in the same room whilst engaging in different activities (some online,

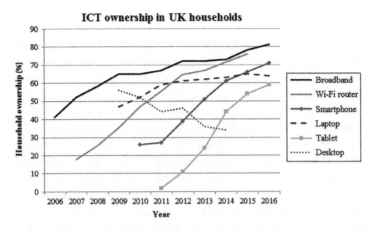

FIGURE 10.1 Household ownership of internet-related technologies in UK households.

some not). Just as important, the mobility of the laptop means that conflicting activities can be disentangled and taken to different rooms (such as teenagers playing games when particular TV programmes are on). In other words, wireless connectivity is essential to the way that laptops have come into use as additional to and different from desktop computers that may already have been in use. At first, some PCs may have continued to be used alongside laptops but in more specialist roles (Røpke, Christensen and Jensen, 2010); over time, however, ownership of desktop computers has declined as that of laptops has increased (see Figure 10.1).

The 'wireless-laptop assemblage' (Spinney et al., 2012) that is stitched together within homes, does not simply reflect the coupling of wireless connectivity to a particular kind of computer, nor of how that combination then fits within domestic routines and spaces, but also speaks to the use (or not) of other devices, like the non-wireless PC. Moreover, concepts like assemblage, ensemble or (my preference here) assembly are important in emphasising the mutual constitution of collectivities of infrastructures, devices, practices and places through which discrete objects like laptops or routers are used and 'together constitute the collective conventions of everyday life' (Shove, 2003). Yet within this wireless internet assembly, the roles of laptops or routers are far from fixed: they may characterise one configuration but the advent of other wireless devices, such as smartphones and tablets bring reconfigurations. I consider this in a moment. But first, there is another significant and prior part of this wireless internet assembly worth highlighting: broadband.

The broadband connection

Broadband refers to a type of communication protocol that allows for an always-on connection to the internet in which telephone calls and internet traffic can simultaneously coexist on the same, existing telephone line. Yet in the early 2000s, at the time when Wi-Fi was becoming increasingly standard in laptop design, not many UK households had broadband access (only a quarter did in 2004 (Ofcom, 2005)). Ownership increased throughout the following decade, preceding Wi-Fi take-up, which did not catch up until around 2014 (see Fig 10.1). In other words, broadband ownership appears to have preconditioned wider Wi-Fi ownership, and this makes sense: it is possible but not very practical to use Wi-Fi with a dial-up connection. Moreover, Wi-Fi helps to realise the benefits of broadband – without the need for extra wires throughout the house. Perhaps reflecting this symbiosis, Wi-Fi routers were increasingly included as part of broadband marketing. For instance, BT, the primary incumbent telecommunications company in the UK, first included their Home Hub router in a broadband package in 2004. By 2011, Ofcom commented that such packages had become the norm (Ofcom, 2011). Thus, just as Wi-Fi was integrated into laptop design, so too was it integrated into the provision of broadband.

These two key aspects of Wi-Fi connectivity, as embedded into laptops and broadband provision, were distributed and arrived in homes by very different channels and at somewhat different times; yet they were nevertheless assembled at this 'junction' as laptops were used wirelessly via routers connected to broadband networks. Importantly, it seems that the relationships between these parts are mutually reinforcing: the take-up of laptops benefited from, but also reinforced and perhaps further facilitated the earlier uptake of broadband.

However, that earlier uptake of broadband was itself closely connected with desktop PCs, and not laptops. Numbers of desktop PCs actually increased until 2007, and would not be matched by laptop ownership rates until around 2010 (Fig. 10.1). In other words, at least one of the key parts of the wireless-laptop assembly first came into use in quite a different assembly: one of 'fixed point internet access'. Similarly, even though laptops first helped to establish wireless means of using internet services, they are no longer the sole, or even primary, device for this: smartphones and tablets are increasingly important.

Smartphones and tablets

Smartphones began to be marketed from around 2005 onward, and the Nokia 6136, launched in 2006, was the first with Wi-Fi (Ofcom, 2006). Prior to this, it was too energy-intensive for mobile phone batteries to sustain a Wi-Fi connection (The Economist, 2004). The first iPhone, one of the most popular smartphones, was released in 2007, and the first successful tablet, the iPad, in 2011. Uptake of both smartphones and tablets has been rapid in the UK, and to some extent seems to be predicated upon, and facilitated by, the availability of home Wi-Fi networks. Almost half of households had Wi-Fi routers in 2010 (Fig. 10.1); meaning that for many a key infrastructural requirement for these newer generations of wireless device was already in place.

Over the last ten years, smartphones have become the most widely owned internet-connected device: in 2017 76% of UK adults owned one and 42% of internet users felt they were the most important device for accessing the internet; greater than for laptops (26%), tablets (16%) or desktops (11%) (Ofcom, 2017). Indeed, of the average 83 hours per month per person 'spent online', 89% is spent on a smartphone (as measured in March 2017; Ofcom, 2017). Moreover, a survey in 2015 suggests that much of this occurs at home: only 9% of those who use internet services on a smartphone reported doing so *only or mainly away* from home, with others reporting an equal share of internet use on their smartphones at home and elsewhere (63%), or mainly or always at home (27%) (Ofcom, 2015b). Thus, despite the fact that many people will not leave the house without their smartphones, the home is still a major site where they are used as part of a wireless internet assembly.

Much of the internet access that occurs over smartphones and tablets is via Wi-Fi. This is clearest for tablets, which are often not fitted with the data-SIM cards needed to access mobile phone networks (Lord et al., 2015). But even for people with fast mobile network connectivity (4G) from their smartphones, monitoring surveys suggest that the majority of internet access (69% of connections) occurs via Wi-Fi rather than mobile networks (Ofcom, 2017). This is likely to be because mobile phone data contracts are often capped, whilst those for fixed broadband–Wi-Fi connections are usually 'unlimited'. In addition, the actual speeds experienced are higher over Wi-Fi networks than 4G (Ofcom, 2017).

In sum, the home is a key site where newer generations of wireless (and largely Wi-Fi) devices have come into use, further underpinning the 'need' for broadband Wi-Fi provision. It is at this 'junction' of broadband, Wi-Fi routers and multiple devices where reliable, quick and cheap access to a wide range of internet services is experienced, and is being integrated into an increasing range of practices. Since the changing wireless internet assembly is knitted together actively and on an ongoing basis *through* practices, it is important to now turn and consider them more directly.

Services and practices

In describing the sequential layering of parts in this shifting wireless internet assembly, it is easy to take the use of the internet itself for granted. Yet this is something that has also changed over time alongside the increasingly wireless and multiple ways of accessing internet services. Indeed, the attractions of wireless connectivity and the practices that constitute wireless internet assemblies in the home are not be the same in 2017 as in 2001, when Apple marketed their wireless AirPort system with the strapline 'put a 10,000-volume library on your bedside table with a wireless iBook' (Apple, 2001). Now that the web is populated by YouTube, Facebook, Snapchat, video streaming services, shopping websites and so on, the wireless ability to read digitised books in bed is perhaps not the first attraction we would think of today.

Surveys suggest that levels of participation in internet-related practices and the time spent doing them have increased significantly over the last 15 years (Ofcom, 2015a; 2017). Whilst general browsing and emailing have always been the most common activities, the internet has become a more plural 'place' for entertainment, shopping, social networking, video calling, banking, paying bills and much more (Ofcom, 2017). The diversity of these activities suggests that the internet is embedded in very many different configurations of practice. It is therefore challenging to explore how practices have co-evolved along with the wireless internet assembly. Undoubtedly, Wi-Fi has been instrumental in facilitating multi-computer households where most, if not all, members access internet services throughout the house on their 'own' devices. In principle, this facilitates greater participation in internet-based practices, both broadening and deepening their role in everyday life. But in more specific terms how has this happened? How has the wirelessness of internet access at home helped shape the very practices for which it has become a necessary part, and vice versa? I do not have the space here to offer a full answer. But we can usefully begin to consider this question by examining the role of wireless connectivity in specific internet services.

YouTube is a platform that hosts millions of videos, and is one of the most visited sites on the web (about 42 million people in the UK visited YouTube in March 2017 (Ofcom, 2017)). It is most commonly accessed on laptops or PCs (by 71% of respondents) but smartphones are also frequently used (52%); and in this case 'people typically wait until they are connected to the internet via Wi-Fi' (Ofcom, 2017). A monitoring app installed on over 4,000 android smartphones found that compared to wireless connectivity over mobile phone networks, 76% of YouTube sessions took place over a Wi-Fi connection, taking longer than those carried out over 4G and 3G connections, and using even more data (83% of the total data by that app) (Ofcom, 2017). In other words, Wi-Fi connectivity, in contrast to other forms of wireless connection, is especially important for one of the most popular of all internet services. The popularity of YouTube itself no doubt reflects the diversity of practices in which it is used: from streaming music to accompany work or leisure activities, to watching TV programmes and funny videos, to instructional and information videos relating to a huge range of other practices, like learning a musical instrument or fixing a vacuum cleaner. Speculatively, the wirelessly-enabled ability to watch such videos anywhere in the house, and even in the garage or garden, may also be part of why YouTube is so widely used.

Video calls provide another example of a predominantly Wi-Fi-dependent internet service. Voice and video calls are offered by a range of Voice over IP (VoIP) platforms (such as Skype and Facebook) and are usually free to use. Though not as widely accessed as YouTube, VoIP services are still well used (by 44% of internet users in the UK in 2017 (Ofcom, 2017)). Surveys from 2015 suggest that smartphones were the most frequently used device for accessing VoIP services (61% of respondents), with declining use of laptops (42%) and desktop computers (24%), and growing use of tablets (39%) (Ofcom, 2015b). Across all devices, most VoIP calls in 2015 seem to have been made over Wi-Fi networks at home (mentioned by 75% of those who use a laptop, 73% with a tablet, and 46% with a smartphone) (Ofcom, 2015b).

This example shows how in the case of communication-related practices, specific combinations of infrastructures, devices and services are more or less common at any one time. Making 'a call' used to be the sole domain of telephones (fixed line or mobile), and making a video call used to be something that required a desktop PC or laptop. As the practice of 'calling' evolves in the context of wireless internet connectivity, possibly also facilitating this development, so too does wirelessness become increasingly necessary in order to engage in this relatively common and valued form of practice. And whilst people may have become accustomed to activities like video calling, watching videos, emailing, browsing the web and using social media primarily at home these practices and the expectations they carry are not limited to the home. For instance, in a campaign for free Wi-Fi to be provided in UK hospitals, it was argued that 'in the modern world, where we are used to communicating all the time, not being connected makes you feel incredibly cut off from the real world' (John Popham quote, in Scott, 2013).

Wireless assemblies: moving 'out of home'

Whilst most people in the UK still use the internet at home more than anywhere else, an increasing proportion are also using internet services when away from home; this has been attributed to 'increased smartphone take-up and the increased availability of Wi-Fi' (Ofcom, 2015b). Indeed, Wi-Fi networks are now provided in diverse 'public' locations including hotels, cafes, restaurants, shops, workplaces, buses, airplanes, trains, on city streets and, of course, hospitals. In 2015, the NHS adopted a target to provide free Wi-Fi in all its buildings by 2020 (The Guardian, 2015). The traffic carried by 'public' networks is also growing (from 45 GB on average for each of 33,851 hotspots in 2013 to 73 GB across each of 44,804 hotspots in 2015 (Ofcom, 2015c)); so it seems they are being used, perhaps for very similar practices that take place at home.

The volume of traffic carried over mobile phone networks is also growing, and more rapidly than Wi-Fi traffic (Cisco, 2017a). With the take-up of 4G, higher-speed mobile connectivity can increasingly play a similar role to Wi-Fi in wireless internet assemblies.

Yet rather than competing, these alternative forms of wireless connectivity appear to facilitate each other. Wi-Fi at home has helped to promote increasingly widespread forms of communication, entertainment and other activities that now 'depend' on wireless connectivity, however that is achieved. In many ways, this has helped to make faster (4G) mobile networks more useful. Thus the home appears to be an important 'normalisation junction' not just for Wi-Fi but for wireless connectivity more generally.

At the same time, the capacity of mobile networks remains limited; and mobile services are increasingly being designed to work alongside Wi-Fi networks to 'off-load' traffic on to them wherever they can. The same is true for many smartphone and tablet apps, which are now designed to switch to Wi-Fi wherever available, or otherwise tailor their operations. For instance, Snapchat is an incredibly popular app for sharing images and videos but it was also notorious for eating up mobile network data allowances; so a data-saving mode was introduced for non-Wi-Fi connections (Plummer, 2015). In sum, default Wi-Fi connectivity is being designed into smartphone apps and operating systems to provide higher quality services and a more seamless transition between Wi-Fi and mobile networks.

Conclusion

There can be little doubt that wireless connectivity, in the form of Wi-Fi, has been important to the development of the internet as an infrastructure-in-use. It has shaped commonly-used devices and services and thereby the very 'usefulness' of the internet itself. The chapter also shows how Wi-Fi plays a key role in the expansion of the internet: in the number of connections, the volume of traffic, the time spent online and the range of practices that have come to depend on it. Whilst the vision of a multi-computer household has already been realised through laptops, smartphones and tablets, Wi-Fi is increasingly being built into other kinds of everyday devices and appliances, from e-readers, TVs and games consoles to thermostats, cars and kettles. Thus, thanks to Wi-Fi, the number of internet-connected devices continues to grow, from an average of 5.7 devices per capita in the UK in 2016, to a forecast figure of 9.4 by 2021 (Cisco, 2017b). This further entrenches the need for Wi-Fi. Moreover, this ongoing extension of wireless internet assemblies arguably represents 'a transition in the wrong direction' as far as energy demand is concerned (Røpke and Christensen, 2013). Understanding, and perhaps seeking to shape, the ongoing normalisation of Wi-Fi is therefore relevant to efforts to manage and reduce energy demand.

In following co-evolving assemblies of wired infrastructures, wireless technologies, computing devices, internet services and practices, this chapter provides some insight into processes of sequential, path-dependent layering associated with rapidly changing and yet increasingly normal and taken-for-granted arrangements. In facilitating the uptake of laptops, smartphones and tablets, in shaping the design and use of internet services like YouTube, Skype and Snapchat, and in prefiguring faster mobile phone connectivity, Wi-Fi has become twisted into these arrangements. Thus, the assemblies that Wi-Fi makes possible simultaneously hold it in place as an ordinary and necessary infrastructure for everyday life. Yet, it is not just Wi-Fi that has become more embedded amongst other technologies, systems and practices but also, seemingly, the whole assembly of wireless internet use which is becoming (more thoroughly) embedded at sites like homes, hospitals and public transport.

Across the board, a sense of the institutional obduracy of Wi-Fi, and more generally of wireless connectivity, is emerging based on a gradual building up of heterogeneous 'layers' that assume wireless connections: in the design of devices, apps, even homes and the configurations of practice. Opportunities for physical internet connections are increasingly absent, favouring a wirelessness that stands in contrast to the assumed material obduracy of large networked infrastructures, but that may be just as enduring. To many, the multiple embeddedness of wirelessness goes a long way to explain its apparent obduracy and irreversibility (see Hommels, 2005). But in building on (Hand and Shove, 2007), it can also be argued that the richness of embedding within multiple configurations of practices is a source of flux, as well as obduracy. For instance, the embedding of wireless-laptop assemblies eventually marginalised the role of desktop computers, and helped to facilitate that of smartphones and tablets, which in turn led to changes in the roles of laptops. Importantly, these changes have sustained wireless connectivity. So whilst this chapter presents evidence of 'co-existing forms of adaptation and obduracy' as might be expected when studying infrastructures-in-use (Shove, 2016) it also suggests that these are not necessarily opposing; that is, the obduracy of particular arrangements may depend on ongoing adaptations.

I refer to this process as dynamic normalisation. Whilst this includes technological and design adaptations, such as the launch of smartphones and the progressive development of Wi-Fi standards, it is not a process of innovation or diffusion that concerns just one product. Instead, dynamic normalisation refers to technologies-in-use: a conceptualisation which positions technologies within the wider assemblies in which they are used. A core assumption of this chapter has been that such assemblies are rooted in practices. Yet, in giving an historical account of shifting wireless internet assemblies, it has been difficult to single out particular practices, and easier to focus on proxy changes in device, router and broadband ownership, and the use and design of particular internet services. Other kinds of adaptations, including within particular practices, are surely possible, and likely to be more evident to research methods that are less heavily dependent on secondary material.

Nevertheless, the strategy of studying the interactions and relationships between infrastructures, devices, services and practices at a specific site, or 'normalisation junction', has proved useful. The chapter shows how the distinctive intermingling that takes place in homes has been endemic to the making of wireless internet use, even beyond the home; and this looks set to continue. Thus, when studying other infrastructures-in-use, methods that investigate site-specific relationships, be it in the home or elsewhere, may be equally valuable.

Note

1   This figure excludes IP traffic on managed networks (such as cable TV networks).

References

Andrae, A. and Edler, T. (2015) 'On global electricity usage of communication technology: trends to 2030', *Challenges*, 6: 117.

Apple (1999) 'Apple introduces AirPort wireless networking'. Available at: http://web.archive.org/web/20001206005100/http://www.apple.com/pr/library/1999/jul/21lucent.html (Accessed 28.11.17).

Apple (2001) 'Put a 10,000 volume library on your bedside table with a wireless iBook'. Available at: http://web.archive.org/web/20010214001019/http://www.apple.com/ibook/wireless.html (Accessed 28.11.17).

BEIS (2017) 'Energy consumption in the UK (ECUK) 2017 data tables'. Available at: www.gov.uk/government/statistics/energy-consumption-in-the-uk.

Cisco (2017a) 'VNI forecast highlights tool'. Available at: www.cisco.com/c/m/en_us/solutions/service-provider/vni-forecast-highlights.html (Accessed 28.11.17).

Cisco (2017b) 'The zettabyte era: trends and analysis'. Available at: www.cisco.com/c/en/us/solutions/collateral/service-provider/visual-networking-index-vni/complete-white-paper-c11-481360.html (Accessed 2.7.18).

Cowan, R. S. (1987/2012) 'The consumption junction: a proposal for research strategies in the sociology of technology', in Bijker, W. E., Pinch, T. J. and Hughes, T. P. (eds.) *The Social Construction of Technological Systems: new directions in the sociology and history of technology.* Cambridge, MA: MIT Press.

de Wit, O., van den Ende, J. C. M., Schot, J. and van Oost, E. (2002) 'Innovation junctions: office technologies in the Netherlands, 1880–1980', *Technology and Culture*, 43: 50–72.

Grubesic, T. and Murray, A. (2004) ' "Where" matters: location and Wi-Fi access', *Journal of Urban Technology*, 11: 1–28.

Hand, M. and Shove, E. (2007) 'Condensing practices: ways of living with a freezer', *Journal of Consumer Culture*, 7: 79–104.

Hommels, A. (2005) 'Studying obduracy in the city: toward a productive fusion between technology studies and urban studies', *Science, Technology & Human Values*, 30: 323–351.

Hughes, T. P. (1983) *Networks of Power: electrification in Western society, 1880–1930*. Baltimore: Johns Hopkins University Press.

iPass. (2017) 'Wi-Fi growth map'. Available at: www.ipass.com/wifi-growth-map/ (Accessed 28.11.17).

ITU (2017) 'ICT facts and figures 2017. Available at: www.itu.int/en/ITU-D/Statistics/Pages/facts/default.aspx (Accessed 2.7.18).

Lemstra, W., Hayes, V. and Groenewegen, J. (2011) *The Innovation Journey of Wi-Fi: the road to global success*, Cambridge: Cambridge University Press.

Lord, C., Hazas, M., Clear, A. K., Bates, O., Whittam, R., Morley, J. and Friday, A. (2015) 'Demand in my pocket: mobile devices and the data connectivity marshalled in support of everyday practice', *Proceedings of the 33rd Annual ACM Conference on Human Factors in Computing Systems*, 2729–2738.

Mackenzie, A. (2005) 'Untangling the unwired: Wi-Fi and the cultural inversion of infrastructure', *Space and Culture*, 8: 269–285.

Mackenzie, A. (2010) *Wirelessness: radical empiricism in network cultures*. Cambridge, MA: MIT Press.

Ofcom (2005) 'The communications market 2005'. Available at: http://webarchive.nationalarchives.gov.uk/20160703015033/http://stakeholders.ofcom.org.uk/market-data-research/market-data/communications-market-reports/cm05/ (Accessed 13.7.18)

Ofcom (2006) 'The communications market 2006'. Available at: http://webarchive.nationalarchives.gov.uk/20160703015014/http://stakeholders.ofcom.org.uk/market-data-research/market-data/communications-market-reports/cm06/ (Accessed 13.7.18).

Ofcom (2011) 'Communications market report: UK. Available at: https://www.ofcom.org.uk/research-and-data/multi-sector-research/cmr/cmr11 (Accessed 13.7.18)..

Ofcom (2014) 'Communications market report'. Available at: https://www.ofcom.org.uk/research-and-data/multi-sector-research/cmr/cmr14 (Accessed 13.7.18).

Ofcom (2015a) 'Adults' media use and attitudes: report 2015'. Available at: https://www.ofcom.org.uk/research-and-data/media-literacy-research/adults/adults-media-use-and-attitudes (Accessed 13.7.18).

Ofcom (2015b) 'Communications market report'. Available at: http://stakeholders.ofcom.org.uk/market-data-research/market-data/communications-market-reports/cmr15/downloads/ (Accessed 2.7.18).

Ofcom (2015c) 'Connected nations report'. Available at: http://stakeholders.ofcom.org.uk/market-data-research/market-data/infrastructure/connected-nations-2015/ (Accessed 2.7.18).

Ofcom (2017) 'Communications market report: United Kingdom'. Available at: www.ofcom.org.uk/research-and-data/multi-sector-research/cmr/cmr-2017/uk (Accessed 2.7.18).

Plummer, Q. (2015) 'Latest Snapchat update introduces data-saving travel mode'. *Tech Times*. Available at: www.techtimes.com/articles/75653/20150812/latest-snapchat-update-introduces-data-saving-travel-mode.htm (Accessed 28.11./7).

Powell, A. (2008) 'WIFI PUBLICS: producing community and technology', *Information, Communication & Society*, 11: 1068–1088.

Røpke, I. and Christensen, T. H. (2012) 'Energy impacts of ICT – insights from an everyday life perspective', *Telematics and Informatics*, 29: 348–361.

Røpke, I. and Christensen, T. H. (2013) 'Transitions in the wrong direction? Digital technologies and daily life', in Shove, E. and Spurling, N. (eds.) *Sustainable Practices: social theory and climate change*. London: Routledge. pp. 49–68.

Røpke, I., Christensen, T. H. and Jensen, J. O. (2010) 'Information and communication technologies – a new round of household electrification', *Energy Policy*, 38: 1764–1773.

Sandvig, C. (2004) 'An initial assessment of cooperative action in Wi-Fi networking', *Telecommunications Policy*, 28: 579–602.

Sawhney, H. (2003) 'Wi-Fi networks and the rerun of the cycle', *Info*, 5: 25–33.

Scott, J. (2013) 'What is stopping the NHS rolling out Wi-Fi access?' *ComputerWeekly*. Available at: www.computerweekly.com/feature/What-is-stopping-the-NHS-rolling-out-Wi-Fi-access (Accessed 28.11.17).

Shove, E. (2003) *Comfort, Cleanliness and Convenience: the social organization of normality*. Oxford and New York: Berg.

Shove, E. (2016) 'Infrastructures and practices: networks beyond the city', in Coutard, O. and Rutherford, J. (eds.) *Beyond the Networked City: infrastructure reconfigurations and urban change in the North and South*. Abingdon, Oxon: Routledge, pp. 242–258.

Shove, E. and Southerton, D. (2000) 'Defrosting the freezer: from novelty to convenience: a narrative of normalization', *Journal of Material Culture*, 5: 301–319.

Shove, E., Watson, M. and Spurling, N. (2015) 'Conceptualizing connections: energy demand, infrastructures and social practices', *European Journal of Social Theory*, 18: 274–287.

Spinney, J., Green, N., Burningham, K., Cooper, G., and Uzzell, D. (2012) 'Are we sitting comfortably? Domestic imaginaries, laptop practices, and energy use', *Environment and Planning A*, 44: 2629–2645.

The Economist (2004) 'Case history: a brief history of Wi-Fi'. Available at: www.economist.com/node/2724397 (Accessed 28.11.17).

The Guardian (2015) 'Every NHS building to get free Wi-Fi'. *The Guardian*. Available at: www.theguardian.com/society/2015/dec/21/every-nhs-building-free-wifi-technology (Accessed 21.12.2015).

Thinkingbricks (2009) 'Steve Jobs introduces WiFi to the masses with hula hoop!' Available at: www.youtube.com/watch?v=HFngngjy4fk (Accessed 28.11.17).

Torrens, P. (2008) 'Wi-Fi geographies', *Annals of the Association of American Geographers*, 98: 59–84.

Van Heddeghem, W., Vereecken, W., Colle, D., Pickavet, M. and Demeester, P. (2012) 'Distributed computing for carbon footprint reduction by exploiting low-footprint energy availability', *Future Generation Computer Systems*, 28: 405–414.

Warde, A. (2005) 'Consumption and theories of practice', *Journal of Consumer Culture*, 5: 131–153.

Warde, A. (2015) 'The sociology of consumption: its recent development', *Annual Review of Sociology*, 41: 117–134.

Weknowmemes (2013) 'Maslow's hierachy of needs updated'. Available at: http://weknowmemes.com/2013/08/maslows-hierarchy-of-needs-updated/ (Accessed 28.11.17).

Wi-Fi Alliance (2017) 'Wi-Fi alliance. The worldwide network of companies that brings you Wi-Fi'. Available at: www.wi-fi.org/who-we-are (Accessed 28.11.17).

11

MAKING SPACE FOR THE CAR AT HOME

Planning, priorities and practices

Nicola Spurling

Introduction

In 2014, there were 28 million private cars in Great Britain. Given that the current standard for residential parking bays is 2.4m by 4.8m (HM Government, 2010) and estimating that every car has a space at its owner's home, that is 336 million square metres. Nearly all the Isle of Wight or placed in a straight line, a third of the distance to the moon. Residential parking space is a big topic, yet just 60 years ago, it was not part of neighbourhood plans at all. This chapter focuses on residential parking spaces and explores how they became a normal, legitimate and planned for aspect of everyday life.

Accounts of the embedding of automobility into everyday life have almost exclusively focused on cars in motion. Analysis has privileged the trips, distances and new living arrangements that automobility affords and the institutions and infrastructures that have made possible the emergence and stabilisation of car-dependent lifestyles (Urry, 2004; Geels, 2005). This focus on cars in motion is understandable. For example, in debates of sustainability it is car *use* which impacts greenhouse gas emissions; cars accounted for more than 50% of the UK transport sector's greenhouse gas emissions in 2015 (BEIS, 2015). Likewise, for those concerned with the impact of (auto)mobility on society, it is the transformative effects of *movement* which is the central concern (Sheller, 2003).

In contrast to these accounts, this chapter focuses on parked cars rather than cars in use, and explores how planning for stationary vehicles has helped to make automobility what it is today. To do so, it conceives of parking space as an interface of infrastructure and systems of practices, and draws on this framework to present archival work from Stevenage New Town, in the UK. Planned and built between the mid-1940s and 1970 to rehouse the residents of war-damaged areas of London, Stevenage was based on a utopian vision for the post-war working class. Importantly for this study, the original house plans did not include any parking spaces at all. This soon proved a problem as the building of Stevenage coincided with a massive rise in motorcar ownership in the UK, from 1.7 million private cars in 1945 to approximately ten million private cars in 1970 (DfT, 2015). The planners faced the challenge of providing space for the car from the moment that the first residents arrived. Given this interweaving of the history of Stevenage and the rise of the motorcar, it provides a pertinent case with which to explore how parking space became normal.

The chapter demonstrates a changing relationship between planning and everyday life across the period of study, namely 'envisioning', 'contestation and control', 'survey and provide' and 'predict and provide'. The following sections introduce the conceptual framework and present the Stevenage data to argue that the planning of parking space played an important part in making automobility what it is today. The conclusion reflects on the implications of the analysis for the present and future.

Infrastructure, practices and space

Forms of mobility, such as driving, can be usefully conceptualised as practices (Shove, Pantzar and Watson, 2012; Spurling and McMeekin, 2015). For example, Shove, Pantzar and Watson's three elements model (2012: 26) draws attention to driving as constituted of meanings, skills and materials. As noted by Aldred and Jungnickel (2013), the materials of mobility practices (and, in fact, of all practices) are 'at rest' in between performances. These resting objects make demands on space, including requirements of size and scale, location and connectivity (e.g., to the road infrastructure).

In itself, this is not a new problem. For example, in 1900, there were an estimated 50,000 horses in London providing horsepower for 11,000 hansom cabs, thousands of omnibuses and for moving freight in railway yards. When 'resting', this transport system required space for cabs, carriages and carts; stables for horses and systems to deal with the 15–35 pounds of manure produced by each horse every day (London Transport Museum, 2016). The Camden Railway Heritage Trust (2016) records that at its peak, Camden Goods Depot had 700 working horses, a demand for space that was met through several phases of development from stabling for 50 horses in 1839 to stabling for 427 horses in the revised plans of 1849 and subsequent additions of blocks, connected by horse tunnels, in the 1850s.

In recent decades, car parking space in towns and cities has posed similar challenges. The main focus for those concerned with these challenges has been the aesthetic and environmental consequences of hard surfaces, including the increased difficulty of dealing with rainwater and the reduction of green space in the urban environment (Ben-Joseph, 2012). In this framing, the problem is that parking space stands empty for much of the time and the solution is to make flexible spaces that might be more often in-use as public space. These forms of analysis and intervention focus on improving parking space itself, but without asking what driving is for or challenging the role of parking space in perpetuating private car dependence.

An alternative approach is to conceptualise parking space as an interface. Driving is a practice, but we can also conceive of it as an outcome of interlocking practices (Shove, Watson and Spurling, 2015; Spurling and McMeekin, 2015). This line of thought argues that journey patterns are an outcome of where and when activities take place. Across time, temporal and spatial patterns of practice are reflected – in material form – in the road network. Activities become car-dependent because the spatial geography of practice – where we work, live, exercise, take children to school, shop and so on – takes material form. As such places and patterns of practice are shaped and perpetuated by processes of land use, planning, the development of road networks and the use of cars.

Pushing this conceptual scheme a step further, the current chapter argues that parking spaces and parked cars form the interfaces of the road network and the systems of social practices which driving makes possible. The chapter focuses on one particular interface, between the road network and people's homes. It explores how the provision of space for private cars, as close to the home as possible, became a normal aspect of planning and everyday life. To conclude, the chapter explores the potential of parking to perpetuate or reduce car-use in the present and future.

Exploring histories of parking space

The data presented was collected in June 2014 and 2015 from The Stevenage Development Corporation Archives. Stevenage was the first of 14 post-war new towns in Britain, established under the 1946 New Towns Act (HM Government, 1946) and planned in the late-1940s. These were new centres of housing and employment outside of major conurbations, in this case London. The small country town of Stevenage, which had circa 6,000 inhabitants, was planned as a new town for 60,000 people with a town centre, industrial area and six neighbourhoods providing homes, schools, community centres and churches.

The governance of New Towns was unique. Rather than being assigned to local authorities, new Development Corporations were established by Act of Parliament (Black, 1951: 43). Although similar to Local Authorities in that they prepared plans and provided services, there were many differences too. For example, they had much greater upward influence and were exempt from standards that applied in other places. They purchased land, which gave them control over development, and as landowners they were concerned with balancing construction costs and rents charged. They were (initially) dependent on the National Exchequer for all their funds, but knew this would be time-limited. They were therefore concerned with their own attractiveness to residents and industrialists (Black, 1951: 44). Their geographic jurisdiction cut across existing district boundaries (three district councils in the case of Stevenage), and the relations of the Corporations and Councils were fraught with tension because of these overlapping jurisdictions (Black, 1951: 46). The Development Corporations were wound up in 1981 (HM Government, New Towns Act, 1981) at which point all responsibilities were ceded to the Stevenage Borough Council.

As the first post-war new town in the UK, Stevenage's history is well documented. This is one reason Stevenage was chosen for this study of parking space in residential areas. The second reason is the coincidence of the planning and building of Stevenage (approximately 1945–1970) with the rise of the motorcar in Britain.

The materials reviewed for this chapter include books of house plans (1951–1969), administrative files on car parking and housing areas (1950–1975), Development Corporation Annual Reports (1948–1979), files of the Social Relations Officer (1960–1971), the Car Parking and Garaging Committee (1960–1971), several folders of reports and surveys (1946–1971) and the plans and files from Bedwell (1948–1977), the first new neighbourhood. The analysis that follows reveals a shifting relationship between planning and everyday life across the period, namely: envisioning; contestation and control; survey and provide and predict and provide.

Making space for the car in residential neighbourhoods

Envisioning everyday life and the car 1946–1953

In the initial phases the planners were in an unusual position: they had a large amount of freedom to design an entire town on a green field site. As such, they envisioned future ways of life that might 'put right' some of the social problems of the pre-war period and create a 'land fit for heroes' returning from war (Talking New Towns, 2015). This involved the creation of an alternative to overcrowded cities, smog, pollution and long commutes, and a focus on green 'garden' cities and fresh country air in which all families would have their own home, a job and time to engage in leisure activities, all of which would be provided for in the town itself. Although radical in the sense of being a nationalised effort to create a better life, many aspects of social structure inherent of the era remained unchallenged. Specifically, envisioned futures centred on providing for the nuclear family (Aldridge, 1996), on the young and growing family (Ledeboer, 1947) and contained implicit assumptions about gender, in particular that the husband would be employed and earn a family wage (Aldridge, 1996: 30).

The town was designed with a system of cycle ways and pedestrian walkways that were segregated from the roads. This provision was viewed as vital if workers and school children were to experience fresh country air and safer commutes. The Government cartoon *Charley in New Town* (Central Office of Information, 1948) provides a pertinent example depicting the 'everyman' Charley and his scenic bicycle ride to work. This vision not only underpinned the construction of the cycle way infrastructure, but also influenced land use planning with the creation of zones for different kinds of activity, and a focus on locational relationships, such that most journeys could be cycled or walked (Bunker, 1967: 216). Issues of road safety also played their part, especially in arguing for segregation of different modes. For example, Eric Claxton, who designed and advocated the cycle way system recalled in 1986 that 'beyond all this was my experience of the terrible carnage of wartime… if I could possibly help it, nobody should ever be injured again' (Talking New Towns, 2015).

The centrality of cyclists and cycling should not detract from the otherwise modernist vision of the motorcar upon which the town was based. The segregation of traffic was as much designed to facilitate the fast, smooth movement of cars as to facilitate cyclists and pedestrians. For example, a 1949 technical report on The Road System in the New Town recommended that 'main roads be designed and constructed for vehicular traffic only, excluding cyclists and pedestrians. No footway being provided but a strip of grass verge being left for the stranded motorist or other exceptional user' (SDC, 1949). The Great North Road, which ran through Stevenage's centre, was to be replaced with a road of motorway standard skirting the New Town (Bunker, 1967). Moreover, pride was taken in making the town centre the first in England to properly accommodate the motorcar via road access and car parking (Vincent, 1960). There were therefore multiple futures envisioned in the plans. On the one hand, Stevenage was a modernist town built for the motorcar, on the other hand, the envisioned life of the Stevenage 'everyman' was associated with walking and velomobility.

These envisioned futures had implications for the planning of parking space for houses and neighbourhood areas. Bedwell was the first new neighbourhood, built in 1950. Developed in the period following The Dudley Report (The Dudley Committee, 1944), car parking did not feature in national house design standards, nor in Bedwell. It is not only because there was no national standard that parking was not planned, but also because automobility was not part of the envisioned way of life for future residents.

For example, an early report for the SDC (Ledeboer, 1947) stated:

> There will be a great number of bicycles and a great deal of gardening at Stevenage. It cannot be sufficiently stressed that adequate provision is necessary… the shed should be large enough to contain a bicycle.
>
> *(Ledeboer, 1947: 18)*

This report gave particular consideration to terraced houses and how to 'avoid dirtying the house with the traffic of children, dustbins and bicycles'. The report suggested that the location of the shed should be changed, so that instead of being at the back of the house, it should be brought to the front with access to the street. This suggestion was taken up in the Bedwell C5 house design, in which terraced houses had two doors on the front of the house, a front door and a door providing access to the store.

Parking space was not completely absent in Bedwell: one parking space was provided for every eight households (Stevenage Borough Council, 2004), though it is unclear if this was driveways, garages or on-street parking. It is also unclear how the planners arrived at this level of provision, but one hypothesis is that it derived from the proportions of housing for different income groups. A principle of mixed housing in neighbourhoods was adopted by the New Town planners (The Dudley Committee, 1944), and given the anticipated population of skilled and semi-skilled workers (Ledeboer, 1947; Willmott, 1964) it is possible that one in eight homes was expected to be middle class and to therefore own a car.

Landscape was also a crucial part of the new town vision. Edwards (1956: 45) notes that consultant landscape architects were involved in both the initial Master Planning and throughout the building process. This work included detailed planning of neighbourhoods, open space, parks and allotments and the design and execution of landscape schemes and their maintenance. In Bedwell, the majority of houses had front gardens and in some cases, grass verges between the garden and the road. There was at least one area of allotments, woodland (Whomerley Wood), a park and several smaller play areas for children. Such provision was viewed as vital to the realisation of the 'garden city'. However, as we will see, such spaces were threatened once car ownership increased.

Between 1946 and 1953, multiple futures were envisioned. On the one hand, Stevenage was built with the future of the car in view. On the other hand, the future daily lives of the majority of its residents were characterised as lives lived locally, with cycling and walking as the main modes of transport. This is reflected in the design of homes and the provision of parking spaces in the first neighbourhood. The first residents moved into Bedwell in 1952 and the newly built infrastructure became part of everyday practices, which did not entirely reflect the plan.

Contestation and control 1954–1959

Car parking in residential neighbourhoods emerges as a topic in the SDC archives from 1954 onwards (SDC, 1954–1959). We know from national car ownership statistics that private car ownership in Britain more than doubled in the 1950s, from circa two million in 1950 to approximately five million in 1960 (DfT, 2015). By 1960, approximately 22% of British households had access to a car (Leibling, 2008). Willmott (1964) quotes national statistics from 1960 that of those households owning a car, 52% were middle class and 22% were working class. It is highly probable that car ownership in Stevenage was higher than the planners' estimates from the moment that the first residents moved in.

A small survey of 380 Stevenage residents by Willmott (1964) shows that by 1960, car ownership in Stevenage was way above the national average, with 59% of non-manual and 40% of manual households owning a car – an average of around 50%. This is also supported by Osborn and Whittick (1963) who note of Stevenage that 'the people have had well-paid regular jobs in the factories and this has… enabled them to furnish their homes well, to acquire televisions, cars and domestic gadgets' (1963: 24).

The SDC's Car Parking and Garaging Committee was established in 1954 and a memo from November that year notes that

> the Ministry of Housing and Local Government has only allowed the Corporation to build initially 8–14% of garages to dwellings, although recently it has been found that even the initial demand for garages from tenants of newly occupied dwellings has been as high as 16%.
>
> *(SDC, 1954)*

In 1956, just four years after the first residents had moved into Bedwell, the SDC Annual Report commented that: 'the problem of garage accommodation and parking space in the residential neighbourhoods is still acute, but the completion of additional garages, for which expenditure was approved during the year, will be of considerable help' (HMSO, 1956). This early attempt to meet the demands of residents contrasted with the events that followed.

The period 1957 to 1959 witnessed a marked shift in the planners' approach. They became focused on controlling the emergent practices of residents and on keeping to the original plan. They enforced that there would be no spaces on roads and verges for motorcars. For example, the SDC Annual Report in 1957 noted that 'the problem of cars parked overnight on roadways and grass verges is one which continues to exercise the Police, the local authority and the Corporation' (HMSO, 1957).

Bedwell was particularly problematic: not only was it built for a future without the car, but its development had coincided with funding cuts that had been achieved by reducing road widths and building higher density homes (SDC, 1971). Narrow roads meant that roadside parking caused congestion and as a result, tenants were leaving cars on front gardens and landscaped areas. As noted above, these green spaces were key tenets of the new town philosophy; moreover they were maintained by the SDC, and as such the planners fought to protect them.

A series of memos between the Corporation's Chief Estates Officer (CEO) and the Chief Architect (CA) reveals these tensions. On 18 November 1958, the CEO wrote how there were 'many tenants who insist on having their vehicle in the immediate vicinity of their houses…', that 'landscaped areas are being ruined' and that 'Harlow Development Corporation [a neighbouring new town] do not allow any vehicles to be parked on grassed areas' (SDC, 1958a). Another memo, from 1959, records a 'persistent offender… parking at night opposite number 30 Whormley Road… making a bad mess of the grass' (SDC, 1959a). The memo requested that the vehicle be removed.

These measures were accompanied by schemes that attempted to retrofit parking. A 1958 report (SDC, 1958a) on the initial Stevenage neighbourhoods listed land that could be used for garages and hard standings. This included: the temporary use of undeveloped land such as the site of the future nursery school, the rear of the telephone exchange, parts of children's play areas, parts of the gardens of houses and getting rid of pavements and grass verges (SDC, 1958b). Other options discussed included car stacking (i.e., multistorey car parking) (SDC, 1958c), though this was never implemented.

Alongside these concessions, the enforcement of parking became stronger. In 1959, the Urban District Council and SDC agreed to prosecute residents if they parked on a grass verge when hard standings or garages had been provided (SDC, 1959a). On 23 April 1959, the CA wrote to all tenants informing them that the Corporation was 'concerned at the number of cars being parked on grass verges… [their] very unsightly appearance… [that they are] causing damage' and warning tenants that 'the SDC would use all their powers to stop the practice' (SDC, 1959c). On 10 December 1959, 15 cars parked on landscaped areas in Bedwell were removed (SDC, 1959d).

These are just a few examples of how the residents' lived practices came into conflict with the planners' imagined futures and the planners' attempts to control activities. At the same time, these experiences provided an opportunity to more accurately plan the next areas to match the demands of future tenants.

Challenging the standards: survey and provide in new build areas 1957–1960

Rather than envisioning future daily lives and the transport that might be part of them, the planners began to focus on actual parking demands based on their experiences in the original neighbourhoods. This led the SDC to challenge the standard of 8–14% dwellings with parking space that the Ministry had previously set. In a letter to the car parking and garaging committee in 1955 (SDC, 1955a), the Chief Architect noted that 'under pressure from the Corporation the Ministry has now agreed to consider a larger provision'. In July 1955 (SDC, 1955b), these new standards were outlined as being at least one in four 'A' type dwellings (aimed at lower income groups) would have a garage and eventually one in two. 'B' and 'C' type dwellings (aimed at higher income groups) would have an allocated garage each. In Stevenage, these new standards were implemented immediately and the next tranche of contracts was modified so that from 1957, garages were built into the neighbourhoods (SDC, 1955b). For 'A' type dwellings, which were often terraces, these took the form of separate garage blocks. In 'B' and 'C' type dwellings, the garages were attached to the homes (SDC, 1955b).

This demonstrates a revised approach to the future on the part of the planners. They accepted that patterns of life were different to those they had envisioned. The planners learned from how tenants lived in the original areas and proposed new standards based on their observations. These were not so much forecasts or models as we know them today, but a view that lived experience provided the most useful estimate of the amount of provision required. For example, the SDC Annual Report in 1957 notes that

> surveys conducted during the year have revealed that although the initial demand for garages in areas of standard housing is generally between 20 per cent and 25 per cent, within three years this increases to an average of 35 per cent.
>
> *(SDC, 1957: 364)*

Under pressure from the SDC, the Ministry agreed to Stevenage applying these new standards and eventually adopted the standard nationally.

For the areas built in the late 1950s, the approach to the future was no longer one of envisioning daily life. Rather, it was about monitoring and keeping up with the rise of the motorcar. From the start of the 1960s, their approach began to shift again, as newly available statistics and forecasts led planners to anticipate and get ahead of the future, predicting demand and providing for it, even before it happened.

Predict and provide 1961–1970

Within National Housing standards, provision for the car first appeared in the Parker Morris report on housing space standards (1961). The context was one of growing concern that housing standards had declined across the 1950s because of spending cuts and a focus on quantity over quality. The recommendation on parking space within this report was a response to a Road Research Laboratory study in 1960, which estimated that by 1980, there would be an average of one car per household in Great Britain (Road Research Laboratory in Mackenzie, 1961). This Study was taken seriously at the SDC, where a *Daily Telegraph* article (Mackenzie, 1961) about it was discussed in the Car Parking Committee meeting. The Parker Morris report suggested that

> each of these ten and a half million extra cars will need about 250 square feet of scarce residential land or building space for overnight parking and for access to the place where it is kept.
>
> *(Mackenzie, 1961: 45)*

The report suggested that parking space should 'be provided as near as possible to the home' (1961: 45). Though the recommendations in the Parker Morris report were not compulsory, in 1961, the County Council advised the SDC to 'plan with the motor vehicle and not against it', because 'motor cars are a universal ideal' (SDC, 1961a).

These new guidelines influenced approaches in existing areas as well as areas yet to be built. For example, the enforcement of illegally parked cars in the original areas continued until the end of 1960 then, in 1961, the discourse changed. SDC discussions began to frame illegally parked cars as evidence for more and better parking provision. A memo from the CEO to the CA on 13 December 1961 (SDC, 1961b) requested the provision of additional parking: 'There is a lot of parking on forecourts every night with consequent damage to verges. Is there any possibility that a temporary parking area could be made available on the vacant land?' In this example, the CA responded by informing the CEO of multiple parking developments that were nearly complete in the area, including 65 new garages on the offending street (SDC, 1961c).

This new acceptance of retrofit was reiterated in the 1961 SDC Annual Report (HMSO, 1961), which recorded that the demand for garages showed 'no sign of slackening' and reported that the Corporation had prepared schemes for 600 more garages to be provided by 1963. Further, the SDC responded positively to tenant demands. For example, in 1962, a petition signed by residents of King George's Close on the edge of Bedwell was sent to the SDC (SDC, 1962a), requesting that the grass verge at the top of the cul-de-sac be converted into parking spaces. After some quibbling over responsibilities between the SDC and the Stevenage Urban District Council (SDC, 1962b; 1962c), the change was included in the SDC's minor improvement works in 1963 (SDC, 1963). The progress and impact of retrofit schemes was carefully monitored. In 1965 alone the SDC undertook ten surveys that noted details of parked cars at different times of day and across the days of the week at specific locations, many of which were in Bedwell.

The 1960s saw a shift away from the emphasis on garages that had been the solution up to that point. Gardens and landscaped areas were conceded for the creation of drive-ins (which we now call drives or driveways) and parking bays (hard standings on the grass verges between the front garden and the road). New estimates suggested that 150% provision (i.e., 1.5 parking spaces per dwelling) was possible in even the oldest neighbourhoods to meet the Parker Morris recommendations.

The Car Parking and Garaging Committee discussed how the retrofit of parking spaces should be organised, as some tenants did not want to pay the additional rent. The SDC decided to build drive-ins and garages whenever a change of tenancy occurred (SDC, 1965a). There was therefore a full commitment to retrofitting based on predict and provide and a sense of urgency underpinned the whole endeavour. This is captured in a 1965 Report which stated that provision 'should be made at the best pace possible…' (SDC, 1965b).

The SDC embraced this approach in relation to new build areas too. The SDC Annual Report in 1961 (HMSO, 1961) recorded that land was being reserved for 100% garage provision (i.e., a garage for every dwelling) in all new developments. In 1966, this was updated to 2.3 parking spaces per dwelling irrespective of size or type: 'the minimum provision must be about 2.3 car spaces per unit if we are going to cater properly in the future for keeping the cars off the highway' (SDC, 1966). These spaces were provided in front or adjacent to the property, with additional spaces for casual parking.

The SDC Annual Report in 1973 (HMSO, 1973) noted that the new standard of 2.3 parking spaces per dwelling was being retrofitted into the original areas to keep up with demand. This was achieved by building more drive-ins and parking bays and the development of 'car tracks' (hard standing tracks which ran through rear gardens) (HMSO, 1976). Allotments were another source of space in this swathe of development and in an Allotment Survey (SDC, 1970), the usage of the 20 allotment areas in Stevenage was evaluated and proposals were made about the proportion of each that could be reallocated for parking cars.

Conclusion

This chapter argues that planning for stationary cars has helped to make automobility what it is today. It has offered an account of how parking for ever-increasing numbers of vehicles became a normal and legitimate aspect of housing and neighbourhood design. The archive material demonstrates that between 1946 and 1970, planning practices were variously shaped by and helped shape the practices of residents through processes of envisioning, enforcing, surveying, predicting and providing. By tracing parking space over time, the chapter illustrates that predicting and providing for car use – and parking – is not the only possible approach. It reminds us that parking standards (and thus assumptions about car use and car dependence) are currently embedded in a range of planning domains – for example within house design and neighbourhood planning. Finally, the study demonstrates that approaches to parking are inseparable from ideas and visions of (auto)mobility and its anticipated future.

Given these findings, I wish to conclude by reflecting on how the historical work might contribute to analyses of the present and future, and in particular to futures with less car travel and fewer cars. To do so I briefly consider near futures of parking and automobility reflected in the most recent Stevenage Parking Strategy, and reflect on them in the context of broader discourses of city and transport futures.

Within the most recent Stevenage Parking Strategy (Stevenage Borough Council, 2004) parking space is woven into several anticipated futures, with different approaches contained in each, namely survey and provide; intervening to reduce car use; and, creating new forms of car use. How do these multiple, conflicting approaches come to coexist alongside each other?

Survey and provide: The discussion of parking on residential streets is reminiscent of that in the historical material: 'many of our residential streets suffer chronic parking congestion causing safety hazards and environmental damage to verges' (2004: foreword). Although the document notes that providing ever more parking space into the future is not a viable option, the strategy illustrates a shortage of alternatives. As such there is a focus on increasing provision to cope with demand, for example, through surveying the types of vehicle parked and offering new kinds of parking for certain categories (e.g., separate secure parking areas for work vans). Rather than challenging patterns of car and vehicle use, such strategies reproduce the existing system and its associated problems.

Intervening to reduce car use: There is a different approach on new build developments where the ratios of parking space per home have been lowered. Such maximum (rather than minimum) parking standards have been included in a number of new build developments nationally over the past five to ten years with the aim that new residents will take up car-free (or reduced car) living. What such interventions mean for car ownership and use (and for the practices to which car use interconnects) is an empirical question. However, the historical findings of this chapter suggest that such interventions in car use are likely to be most successful if the intervention is part of a broader series of developments that make car-free living practically possible. The conflicting approaches within the parking strategy suggest that such synergies have not yet been achieved in this case.

Creating new forms of car use: Third, the Stevenage Parking Strategy describes parking space as an important prerequisite to Stevenage's future as a commuter town for London, a vision that contrasts with the regionalised economic strategy that underpinned the town's original development. Improving the railway commute to central London and accommodating an increased number of 'park and ride' commuters is deemed essential. Here, national standards beyond the control of the local council come into play, inadvertently tying the car into Stevenage's future. To explain, the Stevenage Railway Station finds itself in competition with a proposed Parkway station, the standards of which require large amounts of parking space. Parkway stations are generally located in out-of-town developments – next to stadiums or shopping centres – where such space is easy to come by. In this case, the proposed Parkway Station would replace Stevenage as the local stopping station on the London Mainline, posing a major threat to Stevenage's envisaged economic future. The town centre station must therefore demonstrate that it can meet Parkway station standards to survive.

These examples highlight a central challenge that planners face in their day-to-day work: balancing visions of long-term futures of lower car use (often developed elsewhere) with the more pressing challenges of the here and now. As such the current transport infrastructure developments in the town (which emphasise car-use for London commutes) are at odds with the lower parking provision in new residential developments (which emphasise reducing car use). Such challenges are not simple to resolve, however, identifying the issue and reflecting on how and why current strategies pull in opposite directions is a useful initial step.

The model of maximum parking standards in new build housing has developed within contexts of dense urban living and future (liveable) cities. In these locations the provision of less parking is a controversial issue, and its impact on car use an empirical question. However, at least in these contexts the idea makes logical sense. This is because there are multiple social, built environments and technological developments occurring within urban centres, with altered patterns of car use and car dependence emerging.

These include recent reductions in car-based travel for 18–30 year olds (a cohort who also make up a sizeable proportion of urban dwellers); changes in shopping and working patterns because of online shopping and working at home or in third spaces; new forms of traffic and parking in the form of light goods vehicles (to deliver online shopping), which require areas for waiting whilst deliveries are made; and finally, a recent emphasis away from private vehicle ownership to the provision of mobility as a service (Demand, 2017). As such, lower parking provision at home, or the separation of home rental or ownership from parking space rental or ownership (unbundling) might support such shifts. Importing one element of this broad swathe of visions and innovations into the Stevenage context makes little sense.

In the late 1940s and early 1950s the future belonged to Stevenage. Whole ways of life for the post-war working class were envisioned, planned and built into the town. The situation today is quite different. Large urban centres are the focus of envisioned futures and infrastructural innovation. Urban futures is the theme of the day, as reflected in the titles of research centres, conference themes and special issues of journals. Futures of other places – towns and small cities – and reflections on what ambitions for the future (and specifically for reducing car use) are practically possible for them, is unchartered terrain. The implications of these alternative pasts, presents and futures, for (auto)mobility and for parking, is therefore ripe for further research. This chapter forms a first step in that direction.

References

Aldred, R. & Jungnickel, K. (2013) 'Matter in or out of place? Bicycle parking strategies and their effects on people, practices and places', *Social and Cultural Geography*, 14: 604–624.

Aldridge, M. (1996) 'Only demi-paradise? Women in garden cities and new towns', *Planning Perspectives*, 11: 23–29.

(BEIS) Business, Energy and Industrial Strategy (Department for) (2015) '2015 UK greenhouse gas emissions: final figures - data tables' [online]. Available at: www.gov.uk/government/statistics/final-uk-greenhouse-gas-emissions-national-statistics-1990-2015 (Accessed: 13.02.18).

Ben-Joseph, E. (2012) *Rethinking a Lot*. Cambridge, MA and London: MIT Press.

Black, R. B. (1951) 'The British new towns: a case study of Stevenage', *Land Economics*, 27: 41–48.

Bunker, R. (1967) 'Travel in Stevenage', *The Town Planning Review*, 38: 215–232.

Camden Railway Heritage Trust (2016) 'Camden goods depot' [Online]. Available at: www.crht1837.org/history/camdengoodsdepot (Accessed: 14.02.18).

Central Office of Information (1948) 'Charley in New Town' [Online]. Available at: www.talking newtowns.org.uk/content/resources/films-new-towns. (Accessed: 14.02.18).

Demand (2017) 'Commission on travel'. Avaliable at: www.demand.ac.uk/commission-on-travel-demand/ (Accessed: 14.02.18).

(DfT) Department for Transport (2015) 'Vehicle licensing statistics' [Online]. Available at: www.gov.uk/government/collections/vehicles-statistics (Accessed: 14.02.18).

Edwards, P. (1956) 'Landscape at Stevenage', *The Town Planning Review*, 27: 45–48.

Geels, F. W. (2005) *Technological Transitions and System Innovations*. Cheltenham, UK and Northampton, MA, USA: Edward Elgar.

HM Government (1946) The New Towns Act.

HM Government (1981) The New Towns Act.

HM Government (2010) *The Building Regulations 2010 Part M: Access to and Use of Buildings*. London: HMSO.

HMSO (1956) *Reports of the Development Corporations*, CNT/ST/17/6/1-32, HALS (Hertfordshire Archives and Local Studies) Box 596–599.

HMSO (1957) *Reports of the Development Corporation*, CNT/ST/17/6/1-32, HALS Box 596–599.

HMSO (1961) *Reports of the Development Corporations*, CNT/ST/17/6/1-32, HALS Box 596–599.

HMSO (1973) *Reports of the Development Corporations*, CNT/ST/17/6/1-32, HALS Box 596–599.

HMSO (1976) *Reports of the Development Corporations*, CNT/ST/17/6/1-32, HALS Box 596–599.

Ledeboer, J. G. (1947) *Stevenage Development Corporation (SDC) Report on Housing Requirements and Standards*. HALS (Hertfordshire Archives and Local Studies) Box 585.

Leibling, D. (2008) *Car Ownership in Great Britain*. London: RAC.

London Transport Museum (2016) Public Transport in Victorian London: Part One: Overground. Available at: www.ltmuseum.co.uk/ (Acccessed 3.7.18).

Mackenzie, W. A. (1961) 'More than 9M vehicles now on the roads', *Daily Telegraph* in: Car Parking and Garaging (CPG) Vol 2, CNT/ST/5/1/AP/C37, HALS.

Osborn, F. J. & Whittick, A. (1963) *The New Towns. The Answer to Megalopolis*. London: McGraw-Hill.

Parker Morris Committee (1961) *Homes for Today and Tomorrow*. London: HMSO.

SDC (1949) *Road System in the New Town*, 22 July 1949, in CNT/ST/17/1/7, HALS, Box 582.

SDC (1954) *Memo to Chief Architect*, 4 November 1954, in CPG Vol. 1, CNT/ST/5/1/AP/C37, HALS, Box 148.

SDC (1954–1959) CPG Vol. 1. CNT/ST/5/1/AP/C37, HALS, Box 148.

SDC (1955a) *CA to Clerk of the Council*, 8 December 1955, in CPG Vol. 1, CNT/ST/5/1/AP/C37, HALS, BOX 148.

SDC (1955b) *CA to CPG Committee*, July 1955, in CPG Vol. 1, CNT/ST/5/1/AP/C37, HALS, BOX 148.

SDC (1958a) *C. G. Richards to R. G. Patterson*, 18 November 1958, in CPG Vol. 1, CNT/ST/5/1/AP/C37, HALS, BOX 148.

SDC (1958b) *Parking Proposals*, in CPG Vol. 1, CNT/ST/5/1/AP/C37, HALS, BOX 148.

SDC (1958c) *Meeting Minutes*, October 1958, in CPG Vol. 1, CNT/ST/5/1/AP/C37, HALS, BOX 148.

SDC (1959a) *CEO to CA 'Cars Parking on Grass*, 31 December 1959, in CPG Vol. 1, CNT/ST/5/1/AP/C37, HALS, BOX 148.

SDC (1959b) *Urban District Council to the SDC*, 4 April 1959, in CPG Vol. 1, CNT/ST/5/1/AP/C37, HALS, BOX 148.

SDC (1959c) *CLO to the General Manager*, 23 April 1959, in CPG Vol. 1, CNT/ST/5/1/AP/C37, HALS, BOX 148.

SDC (1959d) *CEO to CA*, 10 December 1959, in CPG Vol. 1, CNT/ST/5/1/AP/C37, HALS, BOX 148.

SDC (1961a) *Clerk of the County Council to SDC*, 24 March 1960, in CPG Vol. 2, CNT/ST/5/1/AP/C37, HALS, BOX 148.

SDC (1961b) *CEO to CA*, 13 December 1961, in CPG Vol. 2, CNT/ST/5/1/AP/C37, HALS, BOX 148.

SDC (1961c) *CA to CEO*, 20 December 1961, in CPG Vol. 2, CNT/ST/5/1/AP/C37, HALS, BOX 148.

SDC (1962a) *CEO to CA*, 29 October 1962, in CPG Vol. 3, CNT/ST/5/1/AP/C37, HALS, BOX 148.

SDC (1962b) *CEO to Mr Marshall*, 3 December 1962, in CPG Vol. 3, CNT/ST/5/1/AP/C37, HALS, BOX 148.

SDC (1962c) *Stevenage Urban District Council to Mr Vincent*, 13 December 1962, in CPG Vol. 3, CNT/ST/5/1/AP/C37, HALS, BOX 148.

SDC (1963) *Acting Chief Engineer to the CA*, 11 Feb 1963, in CPG, Vol. 3 Jan 1962–Mar 1966, CNT/ST/5/1/AP/C37, HALS, BOX 148.

SDC (1965a) *R. C. Edleston to CEO, CE, CFO, CEA*, 12 October 1965, in CPG Vol. 3, CNT/ST/5/1/AP/C37, HALS, BOX 148.

SDC (1965b) *Report on Additional Garages and Provision of Drive-Ins*, 12 October 1965 in CPG Vol. 3, CNT/ST/5/1/AP/C37, HALS, BOX 148.

SDC (1966) *B. T. Collins to CA*, 30 November 1966, in CPG Vol. 3, CNT/ST/5/1/AP/C37, HALS, BOX 148.

SDC (1970) *Draft Masterplan Working Paper No 1: Allotments Survey*, in Social Relations, CNT/ST/17/1/43, HALS, Box 585.

SDC (1971) *Social Indices in Stevenage*, CNT/ST/17/1/43, HALS, Box 585.

Sheller, M. (2003) 'Automotive emotions: feeling the car', *Theory, Culture and Society*, 21: 221–242.

Shove, E., Pantzar, M. & Watson, M. (2012) *The Dynamics of Social Practice: everyday life and how it changes.* London: Sage.

Shove, E., Watson, M. & Spurling, N. (2015) 'Conceptualising connections: energy demand, infrastructures and social practices', *European Journal of Social Theory*, 18: 274–287.

Spurling, N. & McMeekin, A. (2015) 'Interventions in practices: sustainable mobility policies in England', in Strengers, Y. and Maller, C. (eds.) *Social Practices, Interventions and Sustainability: beyond behaviour change.* London: Routledge.

Stevenage Borough Council (2004) *Stevenage Parking Strategy* (Full version). Available at: http://www.stevenage.gov.uk/parking/50427/ (Accessed 13/07/2018).

Talking New Towns (2015) 'Eric Claxton about creating a safe town' [Online]. Available at: www.talkingnewtowns.org.uk/content/category/towns/stevenage/eric-claxton-engineer (Accessed 3.7.18).

The Dudley Committee (1944) The Design of Dwellings, the Report of the Sub-Committee of the Central Housing Advisory Committee appointed by the Minister of Health, London: HMSO.

Urry, J. (2004) 'The "system" of automobility', *Theory, Culture and Society*, 21: 25–39.

Vincent, L. G. (1960) 'The town centre', *The Town Planning Review*, 31: 103–106.

Willmott, P. (1964) 'East Kilbride and Stevenage: some social characteristics of a Scottish and an English new town', *The Town Planning Review*, 34: 307–316.

PART IV

Drawing boundaries and managing networks

State, market and designers

As well as making connections between distant sites of consumption and provision, infrastructures reproduce divisions and boundaries – for example, between consumers and providers and between state and market actors. The chapters in this section show how technological interfaces and institutional roles and responsibilities shape each other.

For example, it is not yet clear exactly how electric vehicles, charging points and infrastructures will be integrated in the future: is the charging cable part of the car or part of the grid? As Grandclément et al. explain in Chapter 12, there is ongoing uncertainty about where the 'appliance' ends and the infrastructure begins. To complicate matters, there is a good chance that the status of things like cars might switch between 'appliance' (and consumer product) and being part of the 'infrastructure' (delivering battery power back to the grid).

The recent history of smart metering reveals shifts of a different nature. No longer simply recording resource consumption, digital meters turn electricity demand into a new object of circulation, management and control. In effect, power becomes data and data becomes power. Situated within a new regime of knowledge and data, consumers are expected to take an interest in how much electricity they use and when. Providers, for their part, are keen to use smart meter data to discipline the 'demand-base' and enable new business models and markets, including the introduction of real-time pricing. Here are signs of an emerging parallel network of commodification and knowledge management, layered on top of an established system of electricity provision.

How these relations work out is, in turn, bound up with changing interpretations of the role of the state and the market. For example, in France, as in the UK, smart meters are designed, justified and rolled out as devices that enable consumers to reduce and manage demand. In this they depend on a market logic of 'rational consumption' deployed in pursuit of collective goals like those of carbon reduction.

These details matter for how meters are embedded in regimes of investment, management and control. On one side there are people who operate call centres, manage supply in real time (see also Chapter 14 in this volume), organise 'back office' systems, invest in new hardware and operate with the tools and models of commercial business operations. On the other side, there are people who are going about their daily lives, selecting and shopping for appliances and plugging them in and out. These are clearly separate 'worlds' but also worlds that are intimately connected through the meter.

Detailed empirical studies of devices at the interface, involving interviews with professionals, managers, designers and households show how concepts of provision and consumption and ideas about the role of state and market are materialised and embodied in the fabric of the infrastructure itself. As in the early days of domestic electrification (see Chapter 3), the rate at which electric vehicles are, or are not, 'taken up' is of massive importance for the coordination of electricity supply at a national scale, and for the design and standardisation of 'small' devices like plugs and sockets.

Exactly how dilemmas regarding smart metering and electric vehicle charging pan out over the next few years remains to be seen. More and less likely scenarios – including smart home technologies; time of use tariffs, new interpretations of energy services, etc. – are linked to broader social and political concerns including national and international commitments to carbon reduction, to interoperability and standardisation (in the case of EVs), and to pervasive concepts of 'consumer' sovereignty and choice. But as the chapters in this section make abundantly clear, infrastructures are sites of restless change.

12

CONTENTIOUS INTERFACES

Exploring the junction between collective provision and individual consumption

Catherine Grandclément, Magali Pierre, Elizabeth Shove and Alain Nadaï

Introduction

This chapter takes a distinctive approach to the task of understanding relations between collective provision typically supplied by infrastructures, and individual consumption commonly enabled by appliances. It does so by investigating a selection of critical and contentious interfaces at which multiple interests and actors meet. The sites on which we focus – one being the plugging in of electric vehicles, the other being the design and positioning of smart metering systems – provide different but complementary insights into the ongoing 'making' of roles and categories around which infrastructures are organised. In taking this approach we show that such distinctions are reflected and also reproduced in the design and operation of the material objects and networks of which infrastructures are formed.

In most discussions of electricity supply and consumption, there is a clear separation between questions that pertain to infrastructures managed by large organisations, and those that relate to the world of consumption, characterised by the seemingly private choices of millions of individual customers. In emphasising the mutual dependence of infrastructures and appliances we show that collective provision and individual consumption are much more entangled than is commonly understood.

More specifically, we focus on objects positioned at the interface between infrastructures and appliances and their role in separating the realms of provision and consumption, the public and the private sphere, collective as distinct from individual consumption, the technical versus the domestic and the world of politics from that of the market. The work of distinguishing between these domains is work that is real in its effects, leading to the 'black boxing' of certain material, as well as organisational and institutional relations. In homing in on points of controversy and uncertainty in the design and initial diffusion of 'interface' devices, we follow a long-standing tradition of examining cases in which boundaries are not yet specified and in which different possibilities remain open and visible (Callon and Latour, 1981; MacKenzie, 1990). Discussion of these contested situations allows us to reveal the importance of devices that are simultaneously embedded in the fabric of everyday practice and central to the reproduction of responsibilities associated with categories such as those of supply and demand. Such analysis is crucial if we are to reconceptualise the material politics of energy demand.

The chapter is organised around two empirical examples. The first relates to the development of electric vehicles and the infrastructures associated with them. In this case it is the status of the wire that leads from the car to the charging point, and hence to the electricity grid that is in question. Is this properly understood as part of the car or is it part of the electricity infrastructure, and how and by whom should it be provided? These proved to be surprisingly important questions for new electric vehicle owners in France, not all of whom realised that depending on the model of the car they had bought they would have to spend several hundred euros to get a special charging point (a wall box) installed in their home. Whilst others were able to avoid this costly installation they still had to have the safety of their electric wiring checked out.

The second example concerns the status of smart meters and in-home displays of electricity consumption. Meters are almost always positioned at the interface of provision and consumption – but their role is changing. They are increasingly viewed not as inert recording devices, but as sources of real time data with the potential to inform the actions of consumers and providers alike. The practicalities of designing and providing these 'smart' devices, and of respecifying their role within systems of consumption and provision reveals deep ambivalence regarding relations between the state, the energy consuming public, the utilities and a host of intermediate service providers.

In both cases, debate focuses on the status of things which are situated at the interface between infrastructures (the grid) and appliances (including the electric vehicle and other 'plug-in' devices). In following these cases our aim is to detail debates about where the 'edges' of infrastructure and of device/appliance lie.

The chapter is organised as follows: the first section considers methods of conceptualising the relation between collective provision (and infrastructures) and individual consumption (and appliances) within science and technology studies and by those who write about the development of large technical systems. The two following sections describe the work involved in designing and positioning devices at the interface between provision and consumption and the wider consequences of such efforts first with respect to the plugging in of electric vehicles and then to the positioning of smart metering technologies. A fourth and final section reflects on the connections and disconnections at stake, and the wider implications of how interface controversies are provisionally resolved.

Independence and interdependence: conceptualising collective provision and individual consumption

With a few exceptions, the sociological literature on consumption rarely refers to infrastructures or to the networks of wires and pipes which constitute the typically invisible backcloth to daily life. In most Western societies, ordinary consumers are also routinely unaware of systems of collective provision unless and until they fail (Star, 1999; Nye, 2010, Amin, 2014; von Schnitzler, 2015). At the same time, it is obvious that infrastructures are *structures* that profoundly affect the way people move around (train, car, plane, bike), dwell (water system, waste collection, heating, electricity, etc.), and eat (transport infrastructures, water, cold chains of food provisioning, etc.). In short they define important aspects of how people live their lives (Strasser, 1999; van der Vleuten, 2004; van Vliet, Chappells and Shove, 2005). Consumers also interact with electricity infrastructures and with the world of public goods each time they plug an appliance in to the grid. In using and selecting appliances, they connect to, and in a sense sustain an infrastructure which exists beyond them, which they did not choose, but on which they depend. By the same token, infrastructures depend on consumer actions that are, in aggregate, crucial for matters of design, and for the economics and practicalities of operating and managing grids and networks.

This tension between the relative *independence* of provision and consumption and of providers and consumers – as usually represented, experienced and understood – and underlying aspects of *interdependence* comes to the fore when systems break down. This is so in that failures reveal the extent to which matters of infrastructural design – including issues of politics, financing and specialist expertise, along with questions of national security and of public versus market provision – are separated from the day-to-day practices of individual consumers. Breakdowns also demonstrate consumers' penetrating dependence on these systems. As outlined below, conceptual and empirical accounts of collective provision and individual consumption often hold these aspects of inter and in-dependence in tension.

This takes different forms. For example, in writing about how infrastructures of transportation, water, sewage and energy mutually shape contemporary urban environments there is a tendency to focus on the institutions and politics of city-scale provision (Graham and Marvin, 2001; Karvonen, 2011). Within this field there is considerable interest in the fate and future of what Graham and Marvin describe as the 'modern' infrastructural ideal, this being a vision in which public authorities are committed to the project of ensuring universal access to 'public' goods such as electricity, gas, telecommunications and water (2001). In such discussions the public goods of infrastructural provision are contrasted with the types of objects (and social relations) that are plugged into these systems. For example, electrically powered devices belonging to private citizens do not figure in descriptions of how 'networks' are organised and managed. Instead, such items are firmly positioned in the realm of the 'market', being sold, purchased and used in different ways, and being unevenly distributed across the population. Writing about urban infrastructures tends to reproduce these boundaries rather than specifying how they are organised.

Other literatures investigate the dynamics of the inter- and in-dependencies of collective provision and individual consumption. The literature on large technical systems (LTS) is close to the tradition referred to above but has a stronger interest in the connection between supply and demand. Studies of large technical systems emphasise the specialised technical expertise entailed in developing infrastructures and highlight the stability and obduracy of these systems, once established (Hughes, 1983; van der Vleuten, 2004; Hommels, 2005; Lagendijk, 2008). It also takes note of engineers' efforts to build demand for the infrastructures they construct (Platt, 1991; Rose, 1995). One well-known example is Hughes' account of Edison's role as a total system builder. As described, Edison took care to move between various 'registers' of activity (technical, social, economic), and to focus as much on the seemingly small details of demand-making as on the seemingly 'large' questions of generation and distribution (Hughes, 1979).

In zooming in on relations between technologies of provision and patterns of consumption, authors such as van Vliet and colleagues note that relations between utilities and their customers are generally more continuous and more multiply co-dependent than is the case when people buy discrete consumer goods. With networked systems of provision such as energy and water, relations between users and producers constitute forms of co-management, broadly defined (van Vliet, Chappells and Shove, 2005). For electricity, in particular, the timing of consumption and supply is closely monitored and managed in real time (see Silvast, Chapter 14). And in the longer run, decisions about investment in power generation clearly involve judgments about future consumption.

Contemporary engineers and others involved in the utility sector are consequently engaged in understanding and responding to the ways in which transformations in collective provision (e.g., new tariffs, demand-side management policies) play out in terms of the extent and timing of demand (Guy and Marvin, 1996; van Vliet, Chappells and Shove, 2005; Yakubovich, Granovetter and McGuire, 2005). Seen in this way, infrastructures represent quasi-living systems. Rather than viewing them as entities that are built, authors like Edwards et al. suggest that it makes sense to think of them as arrangements that grow, and that are always in motion (Edwards et al., 2009; Appel, Anand and Gupta, 2015; Barry, 2015; von Schnitzler, 2015).

The next sections of the chapter develop three insights drawn from this discussion. The first is to recognise the practical *interdependence* of infrastructural systems of provision and patterns of consumption, and to acknowledge that they are routinely represented as *independent* realms. Second, the details of this somewhat paradoxical relationship appear to form around critical points of ambivalence between collective provision and individual consumption. Methods of handling these uncertain interfaces define and reproduce boundaries between these realms, discursively forcing them apart in very particular ways. Third, and building on the point that infrastructural arrangements are always in flux, we suggest that the details of exactly how boundaries are provisionally drawn are important for the ways in which infrastructures and related complexes of practice develop over time. Rather than seeking to assess the extent to which consumers depend on infrastructures and collective systems of provision (or vice versa), this chapter focuses on *how* inter- and in-dependencies are organised.

Before examining our two empirical cases with these questions in mind we briefly comment on what have been described as 'intermediaries' within the field of utility management and provision. In essence, the literature on intermediaries shows that distinctions between 'supply' and 'demand' are difficult to locate in practice (Guy et al., 2011; Moss, 2009). Instead, these seemingly clear-cut categories are criss-crossed by an array of professions, objects and organisations. Developing this point, Stewart and Hyysalo consider what they call an 'ecology of intermediaries in and between supply and use' (Stewart and Hyysalo, 2008: 319). In this case, the focus is on intermediating people and organisations, not devices or non-human actors. However, within actor-network theory there is a long-standing interest in how things are implicated in the constitution of markets and consumers (Muniesa, Millo and Callon, 2007; Marres, 2011; Callon, Millo and Muniesa, 2007). Accounts of non-human intermediaries – including smart meters and low energy buildings (Marvin, Chappells and Guy, 1999, 2011; Grandclément, Karvonen and Guy, 2015) – therefore provide an interesting and methodologically useful point of entry, supporting our decision to interrogate objects at the interface.

The junctions on which we concentrate represent points at which the categories of infrastructure and appliance meet, and at which distinctions between collective provision and individual consumption collide. In keeping with the theoretical positions on which we draw, we do not suppose that things 'automatically' belong in one sphere or another: what counts as appliance or as infrastructure is consequently open to debate. The next two sections suggest that what happens at this interface serves to reproduce and regulate concepts and practices of provision and consumption.

Plugging-in the electric car

Our first example concerns the contested status of the boundary between an electric vehicle and the grid into which it is plugged.[1] Charging an electric vehicle (EV) depends on making and managing an effective connection to the electricity network. New devices (and institutional arrangements) positioned at this interface include a charging box, a charger, a lead, plugs, electricity billing systems and public charging stations. Exactly how these items are designed, operated, paid for and maintained depends on their status either as part of system of collective provision (in France, a public infrastructure), or as part of the car – which is, in effect, a private appliance. The different responses sketched below reflect the delicate partitioning of the world of cars, on the one hand, and the world of the electricity sector, on the other.

From the start, car manufacturers were reluctant to fully engage with the practicalities of the charging interface: the technologies involved were not normal car-parts and the expertise required to make them was outside the core competence of auto manufacturing. In addition, car manufacturers were keen to market electric vehicles as ordinary 'cars' and to position them in competition with petrol/diesel powered vehicles in terms of design, performance, etc. Promotional literature consequently emphasised themes of freedom and mobility and largely overlooked the practicalities of fuelling.

In essence, EVs are marketed as cars and not as electrical appliances. This makes sense. Any other strategy would potentially compromise the EV's cultural, economic and technological status as 'a car' and as something that affords and reproduces the same libertarian fantasies of independence and freedom to go (Steg, 2005). Not surprisingly, consumer evaluations of EVs are framed in similar terms. Whilst issues of range do figure in such evaluations (Rezvani, Jansson and Bodin, 2015), the challenges of charging do not. As a result, very little public attention is given to critical objects such as the specially designed charging point – called a wall box, or to the charging cable itself.[2] In effect this is situated not as part of the vehicle but as an extension of the invisible electricity infrastructure that exists beyond the scope of 'the car'.

However, this is not the whole story. Behind the scenes, car manufacturers are well aware of the fact that home charging points might prove to be a weak point – a missing link – in establishing a profitable and commercially attractive system of electrically powered mobility. They are reacting in different ways.

One strategy is to extend the scope of car-provision and to offer a total package including the supply and installation of a dedicated wall box. From the consumers' point of view, these proprietary 'turnkey' solutions, in addition to being expensive, extend the margins of the home infrastructure in ways that are unfamiliar and often unwelcome. In effect, the addition of specialised wiring represents a durable bond, tying the householder to a particular brand of car.

Another strategy is to leave the specification and provision of the charging interface to others – for example, to specialist electrical companies, or to third party providers. Car manufacturers adopting this approach are typically in favour of developing standardised and interchangeable rather than brand-specific interfaces. Sjoerd Bakker and colleagues have described the current proliferation of different standards surrounding the process of charging EVs and have pointed to the difficulty of harmonising these at an international scale. As Bakker and colleagues explain, failure to establish such standards has further consequences, potentially reproducing national or local 'lock in' to one regime or another and thereby limiting the geographical range of EVs (Bakker, Leguijt and van Lente, 2015).

In 2011 a consortium of organisations – some from car manufacturing, some from the electrical components sector, others representing energy suppliers, national governments and local authorities – came together in the CROME project to address issues of standardisation and interoperability.[3] As this ultimately successful effort revealed, managing the EV charging interface called for a combination of technical solutions and business models. In Eastern France and in neighbouring parts of Germany, the on-street charging infrastructure is now such that EV drivers are, in theory, able to travel from Alsace to Lorraine or to Bade Wüsour-rttemberg, confident that they can charge their car along the way. Because this project focused on cross-border mobility it concentrated on infrastructures for charging EVs in public places.[4] There were some subsidies for households but the question of whether home charging points *should* figure in such initiatives or not, and of whether public funding ought to be invested in making this 'new' infrastructure is at the same time a question about how relations between the state and the market ought to be organised.[5]

In practical terms these 'big' questions translated into a series of small-scale technical and bureaucratic troubles. Interviews with EV drivers involved in the CROME project, and potentially in receipt of public subsidy, revealed extensive confusion. Many new EV users only discovered that they had to pay extra to plug their car into the home electricity supply late in the purchasing process. It was only at this point that they learned that there were several different models of charging points – each available at a different cost, that they had to pay not only for the charging point but also for an electrician to install it, and sometimes for an additional cord to connect their car to the charging point if they planned to travel beyond the known zone of interoperability. While some resented these 'extras', others were happy to be involved in system building: learning about technical details and identifying cheaper and better solutions than those offered by the car+charger–provider. Either way, reactions underline the ambivalence of the home charging point: is it part of the infrastructure, part of the car, or a consumer device in its own right?

In reflecting on these questions, respondents explicitly commented on where and how boundaries should be drawn. For example, some EV drivers thought that the costs of the charging point should be incorporated in the cost of electric vehicle itself (the car+charger figures as a single unit of individual consumption). Others thought that the costs of installing charging points – whether at home, at work or in public spaces – should be covered by the state as part a wider mobility infrastructure, like the road or rail network (the charger+infrastructure figures as a single unit of collective provision). Finally, some viewed the charger as a separate consumer product: as with other such devices, chargers are available in a range of models offering different facilities, including fast charging (the charger, alone, is viewed as an item of individual consumption).

As these comments show, the EV home charging point represents a contested interface situated between the electrical infrastructure and the car. Competing interests and discourses gather around the cord, the plug and the communication system that manages the charging process and that links the electricity network to the car. On the one hand, there is the promise that EVs constitute cars like any other. On the other hand, they clearly come with what one user described as 'strings' attached. Whilst some can be charged without any intermediate technology, this basic method of fuelling fails to provide promised forms of flexibility, security and control. To become more car-like, further devices are needed. As EV owners navigate this field they encounter and are part of making a world in which multiple interfaces between the EV and the grid reflect deliberate but not necessarily coordinated interventions on the part of public bodies and market players. Current 'solutions' do not belong in one domain or the other: they are shaped by both. As Bakker puts it, the EV is 'a car as well as an electric device' (Bakker, Leguijt and van Lente, 2015). At the same time, the details of EV charging clarify and momentarily define boundaries between collective provisioning/state/infrastructure and individual consumption/market relations/appliances.

In writing about EV charging, we have been writing about forms of ambivalence and boundary making through which new relationships are built between consumers and providers and between electricity networks and cars. The next example illustrates a situation in which established roles are reconfigured from within.

Positioning smart meters and in-home displays

In this section we consider the status of smart metering devices and their position within a system of electricity provision or as separate consumer-facing 'appliances'.[6]

In France, as in other countries, smart metering is being rolled out on a massive scale.[7] One of the justifications is that smart meters will enable households to monitor and better control their energy consumption in real time.[8] In France, particularly, the rationale for deploying smart meters reflects what Graham and Marvin refer to as an 'infrastructural ideal' (Graham and Marvin, 2001). Accordingly, a standardised smart meter was to be installed in every home in order to enable better, more modern connections between the electricity market, the provider and the consumer as part of a commitment to infrastructural provision as a form of 'public good'.

However, field tests indicated that French smart meters were unlikely to fulfil this function particularly well (see Danieli, Chapter 13). The data display is rather basic, but the more limiting feature is that smart meters take the place of the traditional meters they replace which are generally located out of sight, in cupboards, under staircases or outside the home. As a consequence, and as the field trials demonstrated, the data they produce is likely to remain unread and unused.

The results of these tests led the French environment agency to conclude that smart metering, alone, would probably not deliver the promised energy savings and greenhouse gas reductions.[9] The consumer association *Que Choisir* was of the same view, also noticing that the cost of the new (but not very useful) meter would be passed on to the consumer through the electricity bill. The proposed solution was to introduce an additional device, an 'in-home display' capable of relaying information from the smart meter to the household in a more visible, 'user friendly' form. At this point the question was not about whether the real time display of energy consumption was itself of value. That debate was already side lined by the EU guidelines, and by an established commitment to the project of smart metering.

Instead the discussion was about who should provide and own this 'extra' bit of kit: should in-home displays be included and paid for as part of the smart meter roll out? Should they feature as 'optional' extras – and as new consumer appliances? Without in-home displays it would be difficult to claim that the smart meter programme was in the public interest, or that it would, of itself, help consumers reduce energy consumption and associated carbon emissions. The next few paragraphs summarise responses to the hotly contested issue of where in-home displays and data on domestic consumption should be situated within the spectrum of state, market and consumer concerns.

The environment agency, the energy ombudsman and consumer organisations were of the view that in-home displays should be provided to everyone along with the smart meter as part of France's response to the EU guidelines. Given that the meter was of limited value without the display and since the purpose was to provide all those who used electricity with data about their own consumption, it was essential to see the meter and the display as part of the same package.

Energy providers and the manufacturers of electrical components and home automation systems disagreed. Although these organisations had different and sometimes conflicting interests, all had a stake in trying to develop a market for in-home displays – constituted as consumer goods. From this point of view, including an in-home display as part of the metering infrastructure would reduce the scope for introducing new products in this field and undermine future business prospects.

The energy regulator, in charge of the proper operation of energy markets and of ensuring access to the public electricity and gas grids, was also against the universal provision of in-home displays, but for a different reason. In this case, the logic had to do with an essentially spatial demarcation of responsibility based on the physical and institutional positioning of the meter. Put simply, the view was that everything that happens upstream of the meter happens in the realm of the 'natural monopoly' of the grid, operated and managed by a regulated public company (in France). Since the realm of the market begins 'downstream' of the meter anything that is plugged in 'after' the meter is situated in the world of market competition. This spatial/political order would be disturbed if the grid operator or indeed any public service organisation were to provide a data display 'beyond the meter' and if it was to do so as a universal or basic service to all homes. In effect, any move of this kind would represent an inappropriate incursion into the realm of the market.

Finally, the grid operator – which might have been prepared to include the 'extra' display device along with the meter, and to see the provision of information and not only electricity as a public good – was reluctant to add to the already very large costs of the smart meter roll out or to introduce any further complexity.

How were these conflicting positions resolved?[10] In January 2012, those who argued for providing an in-home display along with the smart meter won a provisional victory. A ministerial order specified that a smart meter had to have an interface capable of displaying information to the consumer, and it had to have the capability of transmitting data so as to enable the remote control of appliances.[11] By November 2012, it became clear that the interface need not be a separate device like an in-home display. It could also take the form of a website were consumers could log in and retrieve information about their electricity consumption. While seeming to favour the universal provision of information as part of the new infrastructure, in practice this outcome created space for commercial actors to generate new market opportunities: if consumers want an in-home display they will have to buy one.

Connecting and disconnecting

In the two examples outlined above, distinctions and boundaries have been drawn in ways that enable certain market opportunities. Whilst the car manufacturers are standing back, public sector subsidies are helping to promote EVs and to build a private sector market for the charging technologies associated with them. The smart meter 'solution' has limited the cost of providing new infrastructure (in-home displays are not included) and in the same move opened up the possibility of a market in smart home devices. These arrangements are consistent with wider social, political and economic trends, but in each case, it is possible to imagine other scenarios.

For example, grid operators could have become much more involved in the provision of data, and of a plethora of associated energy-services, including opportunities to remotely monitor and control home electricity consumption. This would have extended the scope of collective provision. Similarly, car manufacturers could have taken a more active role in designing and managing charging systems: potentially colonising the 'terminals' of electrical supply as a first step in what might become a more extensive interpenetration of systems of mobility and of energy storage and supply. And in both cases, local authorities and governments could have become more actively involved: promoting EVs, and perhaps acting as intermediaries specialising in building energy management or home automation. For the time being, these are paths not taken. Instead, the two fields are settling down around different configurations – bit by bit standards are being agreed and organisational responsibilities are more sharply and also more consistently defined than they were just a few years ago.

However, debates at the interface are rarely settled for long. New challenges are already appearing on the horizon. For example, the 'vehicle to grid' (V2G) concept, in which private electric vehicles are used to store power hints at a further unsettling of relationships between individual consumption and collective provision. For the moment, EVs are bought and sold as discrete appliances – that is, as cars. In the future, it is possible that EVs will become more distinct and more distanced from petrol and diesel fueled vehicles and that new associations will be made. When in motion EVs represent momentarily detachable portions of an electricity infrastructure to which they are sometimes connected. Plans to use EVs as storage systems for the grid make these links even more transparent. Such scenarios imply further rejigging of the various and changing roles of car producers, interface designers/manufacturers, network operators and consumers.

As with the meter and the in-home display, the multiple systems we have described are always in flux. In this case, future possibilities revolve around the production and management not of electricity, but of data. Again the relations and politics involved are ambivalent and contested. The prospect of empowering consumers and enhancing choice through the provision of more and better information underpins the smart metering vision, but it is obvious that massive quantities of detailed data on consumption can and almost certainly will have other uses.

Our analysis of EV charging points and smart metering technologies points to a handful of generic conclusions. One is that interfaces like plugs and in-home displays have the dual quality of connecting and of disconnecting at the same time. They help specify the roles of consumers, providers, manufacturers and regulators, and in so doing constitute the terms of their interaction and the dimensions of interdependence. Second, the fact that interfaces are sites of controversy and contest is not an outcome of bad management, rather, it is an indication of how fault lines are drawn, and re-drawn at the points where collective provision meets individual consumption and vice versa. Third, the provisional outcomes of these boundary disputes have lasting effects, defining the scope of collective infrastructures, competitive markets and private homes, and specifying the contours of collective responsibility, public service and private profit. A fourth feature, not incompatible with the previous point, is that roles and responsibilities intersect in sometimes surprising ways. For example, our case studies show that public authorities may have an interest in configuring interfaces in ways that foster private sector interests. Hence home charging points are provided by private companies, benefiting from public subsidies which are, in the longer run, designed to promote the decarbonisation of private transport and help build a domestic market for national EV manufacturers. Likewise, smart meters represent a collectively funded platform which is a necessary precondition for new generations of privately developed in-home display and systems of home automation. Although we have concentrated on rifts and divisions, in both cases, the provisional solutions we have described represent an attempt to manage interface-relations not as sites of conflict but as points of potential convergence.

In this chapter we have explored some of the tensions that arise around the provision and consumption of electricity. The humble interfaces that we have considered – the in-home display and the EV wall box – shed light on a distinctive form of energy politics that has to do with the social and political organisation of state and market action. To put it more grandly, these interfaces provide a distinctly, perhaps uniquely revealing 'window' into social and political processes which exist beyond the electricity system, but which also make it what it is today. The definitions they embody organise and enable certain actions and prevent others: in this role they facilitate and foster specific innovations, simultaneously shaping forms of technological change and in the same move structuring the positioning and the contribution of 'consumers' and 'providers' and their respective roles in co-configuring the details of supply and demand. In the energy field as in others, devices at the interface have a potentially critical role in establishing, but also disrupting preconceived categories of the individual consumer on the one hand and the collective infrastructural provider, on the other. It is, for example, possible to imagine interfaces that redefine existing boundaries: shifting interpretations of what counts as a technical matter – calling for professional engineering/economic expertise, and what lies in the hands of the consumer. More ambitiously, there might be scope for deliberately blurring such distinctions and thus reformulating the politics of consumption and provision.

Notes

1 The data on electric vehicles is based on field studies conducted by Magali Pierre in 2012–2013 as part of a demonstration project designed to promote the diffusion of electric vehicles and especially the 'interoperability' of plug-in systems for EVs. The main goal of these field studies was to understand how consumers used electric vehicles and charging infrastructures. The fieldwork which was conducted in Eastern France, consisted of semi-structured interviews with stakeholders in the project (n=6) and with households which had acquired an electric vehicle in the previous year (n=27).

2 With a few notable exceptions, (Bühler et al., 2014; Ryghaug and Toftaker, 2014; Pierre and Fulda, 2015), this literature usually deals with topics like purchase intentions (Potoglou and Kanaroglou, 2007; Egbue and Long, 2012), adoption practices (Burgess et al., 2013) or barriers to diffusion – for an extensive review, see (Hui, 2017).

3 The CROME project consortium which started in January 2011 consisted of major car manufacturers (Daimler, Porsche, PSA, Renault), energy suppliers (EDF, EnBW), tier supplier (Schneider Electric, Siemens, Bosch) and research institutions (Karlsruhe Institute of Technology (KIT), EDF R&D and IFSTTAR) from France and Germany. Associated partners including Nissan and Toyota as well as Local Authorities (Communauté Urbaine de Strasbourg, Région Alsace, Conseil Général de la Moselle) in France and energy suppliers (E-Werk Mittelbaden, Stadtwerke Karlsruhe, Stadtwerke Baden-Baden, Star.Energiewerke Rastatt) on the German side of the border also took part. The project was funded by French and German Ministries.

4 The local authorities of the French regions where the project took place allocated a conditional subsidy for households which could show that they had installed a dedicated charging point for their EV. However, these individuals lacked formal advice on this topic, and many were unable to master the technical knowledge required to arrive at an optimal solution.

5 Note that Quebec and the UK among others have set up schemes to subsidise home charging points for EVs with public money. For Quebec see: Available at: http://vehiculeselectriques.gouv.qc.ca/particuliers/recharge-domicile.asp and for the UK, see www.gov.uk/government/publications/electric-vehicle-homecharge-scheme-guidance-for-customers-2015 (Accessed: 14.02.18).

6 The smart metering case draws on the research project 'Collener' (socio-technical collective and energy transition) funded by the French National Research Agency. Catherine Grandclément and Alain Nadaï conducted fieldwork on the emergence of French policy on smart grid technology in 2014. The fieldwork consisted of a review of 'grey literature', laws and regulatory texts, and news articles and a dozen interviews with relevant policy makers in France.

7 The Directive 2009/72/EC recommends that all member States roll-out a 'modern' electricity metering infrastructure by 2020. France launched its smart meter programme in 2008. This programme

has been severely criticised by numerous institutions and consumer groups for a range of different reasons. See Chapter 13, Danieli in this volume.

8 For a critical analysis of this vision, see Strengers (2013).

9 Press release of the Environment Agency, ADEME, December 2010. Available at: www2.ademe.fr/servlet/getDoc?cid=96&m=3&id=73790&ref=23980&p1=B, (Accessed 13.01.14).

10 The situation is more complicated in a deregulated market like the UK. Even so, the Department of Energy and Climate Change has decided that consumers should be provided with a stand-alone information display along with the smart meter, free of charge. However as the UK smart meter roll-out has been delayed, this obligation is not yet effective and energy providers still hope to reverse this decision.

11 Ministerial order of the 4 January 2012 pursuant to Article 4 of the decree n°2010–1022 of 31 August 2010 on metering devices on public electricity distribution networks.

References

Amin, A. (2014) 'Lively Infrastructure', *Theory, Culture and Society,* 31: 137–161.

Appel, H., Anand, N. and Gupta, A. (2015) 'Introduction: the infrastructure toolbox - cultural anthropology', *Cultural Anthropology Online.*

Bakker, S. ,Leguijt, P. and van Lente, H. (2015) 'Niche accumulation and standardization – the case of electric vehicle recharging plugs', *Journal of Cleaner Production,* 94: 155–164.

Barry, A. (2015) 'Discussion: infrastructural times—cultural anthropology', *Cultural Anthropology Online.*

Bühler, F., Cocron, P., Neumann, I., Franke, T. and Krems, J. F. (2014) 'Is EV experience related to EV acceptance? Results from a German field study', *Transportation Research Part F,* 25(A): 34–49.

Burgess, M., King, N., Harris, M. and Lewis, E. (2013) 'Electric vehicle drivers' reported interactions with the public: Driving stereotype change?' *Transportation Research Part F,* 17: 33–44.

Callon, M. and Latour, B. (1981) 'Unscrewing the big Leviathan: how actors macrostructure reality and how sociologists help them to do so', in Knorr Cetina, K. and Cicourel, A. (eds.) *Advances in Social Theory and Methodology toward an Integration of Micro and Macro Sociologies.* London: Routledge. pp. 277–303.

Callon, M., Millo, Y. and Muniesa, F. (eds.) (2007) *Market Devices.* Oxford: Blackwell Publishing.

Danieli, A. (2018) 'The French electricity smart meter: meters as interfaces', in Shove, E. and Trentmann, F. (eds.) *Infrastructures in Practice: the evolution of demand in networked societies.* London: Routledge.

Edwards, P. N., Bowker, G. C., Jackson, S. J., and Williams, R. (2009) 'Introduction: an agenda for infrastructure studies', *Journal of the Association for Information Systems,* 10: 6.

Egbue, O. and Long, S. (2012) 'Barriers to widespread adoption of electric vehicles: an analysis of consumer attitudes and perceptions', *Energy Policy, Special Section: Frontiers of Sustainability,* 48: 717–729.

Graham, S. and Marvin, S. (2001) *Splintering Urbanism: Networked Infrastructures, Technological Mobilities and the Urban Condition.* London: Routledge.

Graham, S. and Thrift, N. (2007) 'Out of order. Understanding repair and maintenance', *Theory, Culture and Society,* 24: 1–25.

Grandclément, C., Karvonen, A. and Guy, S. (2015) 'Negotiating comfort in low energy housing: the politics of intermediation', *Energy Policy,* 84: 213–222.

Guy, S. and Marvin, S. (1996) 'Transforming urban infrastructure provision—The emerging logic of demand side management', *Policy Studies,* 17: 137.

Guy, S., Marvin, S., Medd, W. and Moss, T. (eds.) (2011) *Shaping Urban Infrastructures: intermediaries and the governance of socio-technical networks.* London: Earthscan.

Hommels, A. (2005) *Unbuilding Cities: obduracy in urban socio-technical change, inside technology.* Cambridge, MA: MIT Press.

Hughes, T. P. (1983) *Networks of Power: electrification in Western Society, 1880–1930.* Baltimore and London: Johns Hopkins University Press.

Hughes, T. P. (1979) 'The electrification of America: the system builders', *Technology and Culture,* 20: 124–161.

Hui, A. (2017) 'Understanding the positioning of "the electric vehicle consumer": variations in interdisciplinary discourses and their implications for sustainable mobility systems', *Applied Mobilities* DOI: 10.1080/23800127.2017.1380977.

Karvonen, A. (2011) *Politics of Urban Runoff: nature, technology, and the sustainable city*. Cambridge, MA: MIT Press.

Lagendijk, V. (2008) *Electrifying Europe. The Power of Europe in the Construction of Electricity Networks*. Amsterdam: Aksant.

MacKenzie, D. A. (1990) *Inventing Accuracy: an historical sociology of nuclear missile guidance, inside technology*. Cambridge, MA: MIT Press.

Marres, N. (2011) 'The costs of public involvement: everyday devices of carbon accounting and the materialization of participation', *Economy and Society*, 40: 510–533.

Marvin, S., Chappells, H. and Guy, S. (2011) 'Smart meters as obligatory intermediaries: reconstructing environmental action', in Guy, S., Marvin, S. and Moss, T. (eds.) *Shaping Urban Infrastructures: intermediaries and the governance of socio-technical networks*. London: Earthscan. pp. 175–191.

Marvin, S., Chappells, H. and Guy, S. (1999) 'Pathways of smart metering development: shaping environmental innovation', *Computers, Environment and Urban Systems*, 23: 109–126.

Moss, T. (2009) 'Intermediaries and the governance of sociotechnical networks in transition', *Environment and Planning A*, 41: 1480–1495.

Muniesa, F., Millo, Y. and Callon, M. (2007) 'An introduction to market devices', in Callon, M., Millo, Y. and Muniesa, F. (eds.) (2007) *Market Devices*. Oxford: Blackwell Publishing.

Nye, D. E. (2010) *When the Lights Went Out: a history of blackouts in America*. Cambridge MA: MIT Press.

Pierre, M. and Fulda, A. S. (2015) 'Driving an EV: a new practice? How electric vehicle private users overcome limited battery range through their mobility practice', *Proceedings of the ECEEE Summer Study*: 907–1016.

Platt, H. L. (1991) *The Electric City: energy and the growth of the Chicago area, 1880–1930*. Chicago: University of Chicago Press.

Potoglou, D. and Kanaroglou, P. S. (2007) 'Household demand and willingness to pay for clean vehicles', *Transportation Research Part D*, 12: 264–274.

Rezvani, Z., Jansson, J. and Bodin, J. (2015) 'Advances in consumer electric vehicle adoption research: a review and research agenda', *Transportation Research Part D*, 34: 122–136.

Rose, M. H. (1995) *Cities of Light and Heat: domesticating gas and electricity in urban America*. University Park, PA: Pennsylvania State University Press.

Ryghaug, M. and Toftaker, M. (2014.) 'A transformative practice? Meaning, competence, and material aspects of driving electric cars in Norway', *Nature and Culture*, 9: 146–163.

Silvast, A. (2018) 'Co-constituting supply and demand: managing electricity in two neighbouring control rooms', in Shove, E. and Trentmann, F. (eds.) *Infrastructures in Practice: the evolution of demand in networked societies*. London: Routledge.

Star, S. L. (1999) 'The ethnography of infrastructure', *American Behavioral Scientist*, 43: 377–391.

Steg, L. (2005) 'Car use: lust and must. Instrumental, symbolic and affective motives for car use', *Transportation Research Part A*, 39: 147–162.

Stewart, J. K. and Hyysalo, S. (2008) 'Intermediaries, users and social learning in technological innovation', *International Journal of Innovation Management*, 12(3): 295–325.

Strasser, S. (1999) *Waste and Want: a social history of trash*. New York: Metropolitan Books.

Strengers, Y. (2013) *Smart Energy Technologies in Everyday Life. Smart Utopia?* Basingstoke: Palgrave Macmillan.

Van der Vleuten, E. (2004) 'Infrastructures and societal change. A view from the large technical systems field', *Technology Analysis & Strategic Management*, 16: 395–414.

van Vliet, B., Chappells, H. and Shove, E. (2005) *Infrastructures of Consumption: environmental innovation in the utility industries*. London: Earthscan.

von Schnitzler, A. (2015) 'Ends—cultural anthropology'. *Cultural Anthropology Online*. Available at: https://culanth.org/fieldsights/713-ends (Accessed 31.12.17).

Yakubovich, V., Granovetter, M. and McGuire, P. (2005) 'Electric charges: the social construction of rate systems', *Theory and Society*, 34: 579–612.

13

THE FRENCH ELECTRICITY SMART METER

Reconfiguring consumers and providers

Aude Danieli

Introduction

Electricity meters define and reveal the commercial relationship between customers and energy providers and have a critical role in enabling calculation and payment. To date, there is very little research on the meter's role in this relationship. Studies in the history of technology show that water and electricity meters, developed in the late nineteenth century, were designed to determine the rate of consumption as accurately as possible, and to combat fraudulent practices. This ambition reflected engineers' conception of the user as someone who might tamper with the supply in order to reduce their bill (Chatzis, 2006). When installed directly in a customer's home or business premises, the meter is a tool that helps energy providers and distributors manage the electricity grid,[1] control customers and determine how much each should pay (Coutard, 1999). To date, studies of metering tend to focus on the role of the engineers who designed these tools, on public policies and institutional debates (Klopfert and Wallenborn, 2011), or on public acceptance (Hess, 2014), rather than on what the metering of electricity involves in practice.

The growing social and political significance of the meter and of metering is the focus of this chapter. At different points in history, the standardisation of payment for domestic consumption as recorded by meters and smart meters has triggered social protest and raised questions about the ethics of monitoring homes and individuals. For example, the introduction of collective water meters in co-owned buildings caused tension, because it was associated with an allegedly unfair system of paying for water (Rabeharisoa, 1991). More recently, two European directives (2006; 2009) encourage member states to test and implement instruments and systems capable of producing regular bills based on actual consumption and not on six-monthly readings of consumption data. As a result, new technologies have been developed and many countries are now adopting 'smart meters'. In France, these new electric meters represent a significant advance in functionality, enabling automatic transmission of consumption data to computer servers, remote control (on/off, disconnection of service, change of voltage, etc.) and remote monitoring of electricity grids and their dysfunctions.

Up to the late 2000s, electricity meters were relatively straightforward devices that passively recorded consumption. The introduction of 'new' smart meters coincided with new ideas about the role of metering related to the ambition of liberalising energy markets and growing interest in the 'smart grid'. In this context, meters acquired a range of new, more active roles. One of these was to provide information to help domestic and industrial consumers manage and perhaps reduce their electricity or water consumption (Barraqué, 2013). In the electricity sector, additional measures were required to turn the traditional meter into an instrument that consumers could use for this purpose. In practice, this meant adding new digital functions, including a remote display, energy management options, a smart energy box and related digital applications. The design of these digital devices was in part influenced by the goal of providing customers with new possibilities for self-management, and of offering 'services' not possible with previous generations of electromechanical (Figures 13.1 and 13.2) or electronic meters (Figure 13.3).

In France, from 2005 to the present there has been significant debate and much negotiation about the precise definition and function of smart meters. These discussions were informed by industrial and commercial experiments leading up to the decision to roll smart meters out across France. Under the current plan, a total of 35 million traditional meters are due to be replaced by 'smart' meters over the next ten years (Danieli, 2014; 2015). Since 2015, debates about metering have intensified alongside this very significant programme of renewal and investment.

This chapter focuses on how meters are used in practice by professionals who are in direct contact with customers, engineers and consumers.[2] It is based on empirical data collected through observation and interviews conducted in 2014 and through four years of close

FIGURE 13.1 © AGIP/Bridgeman Images: The French electromechanical meter, introduced into homes in 1963.

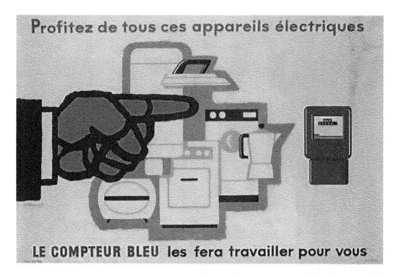

FIGURE 13.2 'Enjoy all the electrical appliances. The blue meter will make them work for you'. Commercial advertising from the French energy supplier EDF. Illustration by Bernard Villemot, circa 1964. © Bibliothèque Forney/Roger-Viollet.

interaction and research within the 'Research and Development Direction' of the French energy group EDF (*Electricité de France*). Ongoing experimentation with the smart meter – called Linky (2010–2015) – provided an opportunity to examine the development of the electricity meter in the digital age. As part of this work, I talked with just over 90 individuals, from design engineers to newly equipped customers, with whom I held long (one- to four-hour) semi-structured interviews. The Linky meter (see Figure 13.4) was created in 2008, first tested on a large scale in two regions of France (Rhône-Alpes and Centre-Val de Loire), mainly in 2010 and 2011 and subsequently installed by the national electricity distributor, ENEDIS.

By 2015, the tests had involved 250,000 customers, some of whom were located in secondary experimental smart grid areas (PACA, Ile-de-France, Midi-Pyrénées). In following this large-scale experiment, I spoke with project teams in both the strategic departments of the national energy provider and distributor in Ile-de-France (EDF LAB, legal department, marketing, metering) and in the operational departments (technical and commercial) that were in contact with customers in the areas in which the experiments took place. My research was not limited to an analysis of the internal functioning of the energy providers. I also investigated groups whose role has often been decisive, especially as regards battles over equality of treatment, fuel poverty and access to energy. These include organisations providing information on energy, urban authorities' energy services, energy syndicates and consumer unions. Other interviews took place in customers' homes. I observed the service relationship between customers and intermediate agents at call centres (such as tele-advisers) and went with meter readers[3] and technicians to customers' homes. Together, these materials provide valuable information on the actual experience of using a smart meter and on its embeddedness in professional and family environments.

Examining the evolution of meters in the digital age depends on paying particular attention to the figure of the customer that professionals in the energy industry construct and mobilise in defining the service relationship. How are the roles of domestic customers and of energy

FIGURE 13.3 Electronic meters, introduced into homes in 1990 (right, at the top). We can also see one Linky smart meter (left). From 'The saga of the meter', electric meters in the exhibition showroom of the French electric distributor Enedis in Paris. Personal photograph.

professionals imagined and understood and what features shape innovation processes regarding the smart meter? To what extent did the changing conception of the smart meter and its users correspond with the 'real' uses of this technology? The first part of this chapter provides some clues by examining the experiences of those who work in back-office departments, who are not in contact with customers and for whom the smart meter is an instrument which represents the results of customers' actions as revealed by the energy they consume. The second part focuses on professionals and experts who are in direct contact with customers. These experts construct and work with a very different figure of the customer: this being one who needs disciplining, who is potentially 'dishonest' or 'not interested' and who has to be made to pay their bill. In bringing these experiences together, I conclude with a discussion of the different routes through which definitions and uses of the smart meter have been stabilised.

FIGURE 13.4 User manual for the new generation of smart meter 'Linky' launched in 2010.
Personal Photograph

Creating an informed consumer

My interviews highlighted the fact that several groups in the energy field pictured customers
with smart meters as active controllers and managers of their own electricity consumption.
The representatives of consumer unions, the heads of the energy missions in the regions in
which the experiments were run and the design engineers who tested and developed customer services talked as if the smart meter was primarily designed as a tool *for* the customer.
What fostered this common perception?

These representations of the domestic electricity meter and these interpretations of its
'use' stem from developments over the past ten years and are closely associated with specific
ideas about the smart energy economy. In this context, smart meters are often presented as
one of the building blocks required for the full liberalisation of the energy market. Smart
meters are, it seems, a necessary precondition for fully informed consumer choice – a concept
associated with arguments that have been used to justify the opening up of public utilities to
competition (Poupeau, 2009). The smart meter is also associated with environmental issues –
apparently offering consumers the information they need to manage consumption and act
responsibly given concerns about the exhaustion of fossil fuel resources, climate change and
greenhouse gas emissions. In the words of the smart meter brochures given to customers
when the device is installed in their home or business:

> I will become a consum-actor, monitor my consumption, understand it better and take
> steps to control it.[4]

Many claims about the benefits of smart metering are based on a behaviourialist model, which assumes that if people really knew how much energy they were using they would change their consumption. Related to this, smart meters typically come with a number of offers: rates can be tailored to suit a user's consumption profile, detailed consumption statements are possible, there can be alerts and automated control of electrical appliances, including remote control of domestic heating. However, one practical difficulty is that the data that is constantly produced by a smart meter is not systematically accessible or easy to interpret.

Roughly 50% of meters are situated outside the main living or working space of a customer's home or business – they are to be found in the cellar, on an electricity pole, in a cupboard containing the building's incoming supply, or located outside the building altogether. In order to transform the smart meter into an interface that can be used for monitoring consumption, service providers have had to add new digital functions to allow ordinary users to learn about and better manage their energy consumption.

The idea here is that the meter, together with this information interface, will prompt customers to install less energy-hungry appliances and devices, to shift the use of some household appliances to the night and to install renewable energy systems such as solar panels. To reiterate, the social construction of a meter that promises to be useful to the customer is part of a proactive policy of developing energy markets and uses. By taking advantage of digital technology and the ability to make new rates and energy services available, energy providers (EDF, Direct Energie, etc.) have sought to offer different and competing services – a feature that has been a driver behind the construction of new market segments (Caron, 2015).

As outlined below, these ideas and ambitions acquire a material form. By focusing on how the various technical elements of the smart meter are negotiated we can see how the modern electricity meter materialises the role of energy companies (providers, distributors, and firms in the industry) and the relationship between these organisations and their customers. In studying these aspects of meter design, it is important to notice that the engineers responsible for developing smart metering systems are also responsible for devising technical solutions that facilitate the transmission of energy data to the household. These include the connection of an energy box; a USB port on the meter; 'smart sockets' in the home that can calculate the consumption of a specific device or appliance or control it remotely (e.g., remote programming of a heating system); radio transmitters to improve data transmission between the meter and the home and mobile applications.

These engineering solutions are intended to encourage users to develop competences and become, so to speak, technically-skilled managers. They are also intended to foster a sense of social distinction, and to situate juggling with watts, Euros and a personal library of energy data as something that can be fun. According to the technical experts I interviewed, providing customers with data on their own consumption makes sense, not only economically, but also ethically. It is true that meter readings are used for billing, but the engineers with whom I spoke insisted that ownership of the data remains with the customer. During our interviews, they referred to the 'customer tele-data' function, a sort of computerised calculator embedded in electronic meters and now in smart meters as well. The tele-data function means that consumers can easily find up-to-date information about their consumption. This is not new. Data on personal consumption was accessible online when electronic meters were introduced in the 1990s. However, as the engineers pointed out, customers rarely used this information, nor was it exploited commercially.

With the introduction of more efficient information systems and in the experimental age of smart grids, there are new incentives to manage consumption data and to make it available. Again, the idea is that providing households and businesses with detailed information about the energy consequences of daily practices will encourage them to 'optimise' their energy use in real time.

> The idea is to give you what's happening right now: we work on the consumption with watts … […] The idea is to show that you may be able to save and to change your subscription!
>
> *(Junior engineer, 18 March 2014)*

The idea that the meter might be useful from both a commercial and a customer point of view is not new within EDF's design department. It follows on from the already established tradition of providing different tariffs and energy services linked to peak and off-peak hours, along with options for an interruptible supply at times of peak-demand. Over the past three decades, the EDF LAB has used customer panels to test the impact of many home automation projects on domestic energy consumption (including tests with Minitel, computers, dedicated terminal, smart phones, etc.) and has used these insights to inform meter design.

Other organisations are also keen that consumers have access to useful, accessible and up-to-date information. For example, local collectives involved in energy issues (local consumer unions, energy agencies, municipalities) have played a leading role and national authorities (government administrations, national consumer associations) have insisted that a new consumption monitoring device (an in-home display) is included with every new smart meter. As these exchanges indicate, the meter remains the focus of ongoing tension between the discourses and ambitions of providers, on the one hand, and the 'interests' of consumers, on the other. For example, consumer bodies are concerned about the commercial purpose of smart metering and the details of meter design.

> Since ENEDIS puts forward the fact of saving energy [by means of Linky meters], can't we manage this a bit better, with a transmission of data on a device in the kitchen, that alerts one to excessive consumption?
>
> *(Representative of a local consumer union, 15 May 2014)*

Suggestions like these have been reinforced by elected councillors concerned about future votes and the persistent challenge of fuel poverty. From their perspective, the widespread introduction of smart metering is a project that is costly for society and is not something that customers feel is intended for them. On the other hand, some authorities are interested in the potential for using smart meter data to defend citizens' interests.

> I think that Linky can really be an energy-saving tool, provided that users are really given access to all their data, and that public authorities work together to ensure that people are able to decipher them.
>
> *(Head of the energy policy of a local authority, 2 July 2014)*

Although they differ on how to achieve this outcome, EDF LAB, consumer bodies and energy agencies share the objective of creating a new type of consumer, one that actively monitors his or her own consumption.

Despite this discourse, attempts by design engineers and consumer representatives to redefine the smart meter as a tool for the customer have been limited. This is in part because the definition of the meter's purpose (and its technical features) also depends on standards which reflect future commercial uses, as discussed in institutional and political arenas. To date, the capabilities of the smart meter have been strongly influenced by the energy regulator, the *Commission de Régulation de l'Energie*, which validated a functional specification designed to enable the new organisation of energy markets, before submitting the decree (for widespread smart metering) to the government. According to this specification the smart meter has three critical functions. As discussed above, one is to provide information on energy consumption to ensure that consumers' bills are accurate and to prevent fraud or financial exploitation. A second concerns 'upstream measurement' and relates to ENEDIS's management of the electricity grid. The third goal is to generate information relevant to the energy provider and the manufacturers of household appliances and devices, to enable 'downstream management'. These somewhat conflicting ambitions are materialised in the form of smart meter design. They also matter for the changing relation between consumer and provider.

Keeping the customer at a distance

Smart meters have an important but often overlooked role in reconfiguring the service relationship between consumers and energy providers. In particular, providers hope that smart meters will enable them to reduce direct interaction with their customers. Meters and circuit breakers (which cut off supply) are important when people move home or fail to pay their bills. In both cases, several actors are involved. For example, when someone moves into a new home, customer advisers (on the commercial side of the organisation) negotiate a contract and then leave it to technicians and meter readers to take care of the technical management of electricity provision, according to the contract.

In practice, meter design proves to be important for the day-to-day management of customer contracts. This becomes clear when observing the role of electromechanical and electronic meters, circuit breakers and power limiters at the time of the change-over to smart meters.

The job of the operations manager is to process electricity contracts and changes which are either requested by customers (different rates, connection to the network, repair services) or by suppliers (reading meters, cutting off the service due to unpaid bills). This is routine work, but in rare cases, more individualised treatment is required. For example, the provider might need to ensure that the conditions of the electricity contract are being complied with. Other problems might have to do with the level of power specified in the contract or with gaining access to read the meter. When the meters are electromechanical or electronic, such issues often lead to substantial delays in the payment of bills. The managers I interviewed all agreed that most such difficulties were encountered in private houses in rural or semi-urban areas and usually in properties equipped with electromechanical meters. In response, one solution is to introduce smart meters with circuit breakers that limit the level of power supplied. This helps combat fraud and allows the supplier to identify complex cases (active meters without a contract, so-called 'forgotten meters'[5] or 'abuse' of the *Accès Libre Service* option which enables someone who has just moved to consume electricity immediately, during the first weeks after moving in, before subscribing to a commercial contract).[6]

Putting these policies into practice and installing new meters increased the number of face-to-face encounters between technicians and customers, buildings and equipment. Managers mentioned that the search for 'forgotten meters' that were not recorded in customer files involved careful network mapping. They also spoke about the difficulties that technical agents encountered when customers were absent – sometimes interpreted as a deliberate attempt to avoid having their meter read or their electricity supply cut off when they failed to pay their bill: 'There were cases where they [the customer technicians] went there eight times but there was no one home' (Former technical agency manager, 2 April 2014).

Despite a huge effort to reduce 'abuse' of the *Accès Libre Service* and detect forgotten meters, deviant cases and net financial losses continue. From this perspective, the smart meter represents a means of normalising electricity contracts and customer relations. At present, technical service engineers (who go to people's homes) are not allowed to talk about bills and tariffs with customers, even though the metering equipment on site – used for measuring the voltage etc. – sometimes requires explanation and even though the meter and the circuit breaker on site all have to be calibrated with payment records. The liberalisation of the market and reforms in the sector over the past 20 years have had the consequence of prohibiting technicians and meter readers (of the energy distributor ENEDIS) from 'occupying the field' of the energy supplier – a role currently fulfilled by several competing firms. In this increasingly complex environment, the smart meter promises to reduce interaction with the customer and thus simplify and cut through these relations.

When positioned in these terms, the meter figures as an instrument of customer control. In this guise, it helps to reproduce a largely negative image of the customer who is suspected of misappropriating electricity and impeding its daily management. My interviewees talked about 'bad' customers who do not correspond to the firm's expectations and who have developed inappropriate expertise regarding the metering equipment (the meter itself, the circuit breaker, even connection to the grid) and their contract with the provider:

> Some of them play on the fact that we leave the electricity supply connected for a while. We can leave it for up to eight weeks. And some of them take advantage of this and push it even further.
>
> *(Head of the Linky project, 12 May 2014)*

Telephone advisers based at the national provider's call centre are responsible for taking incoming calls from new customers. Since this service relationship is established over the phone, it is difficult to detect problematic cases, especially when the meters are electromechanical or electronic. This difficulty is compounded by uncertainties about the state of the equipment that supplied the data on which the bill is based: Does the problem stem from wear-and-tear of the equipment or from fraudulent manipulation by the customer or by an electrician? In the absence of evidence from technical services, telephone advisers have no option but to give customers the benefit of the doubt: 'It's tricky to say to the customer 'Sir, you've cheated'. No, one just can't say that' (Call centre tele-adviser, Linky expert, 16 May 2014).

The smart meter offers new possibilities for telephone interaction, for the organisation of front-office work and for discussions between sales agents, technical advisers and customers. For example, Linky meters can be remotely controlled by EDF sales agents who can involve customers in setting them up and activating them and who can offer informed advice over the phone. This contrasts with the need to plan a technician's visit to the customer's home as is the case for people who have electromechanical or electronic meters. In one of the experiments I studied, the creation of a new telephone-based technical agency involved reorganising technicians' and the meter readers' rounds and a gradual change from face-to-face interaction to remote intervention, presented as being at the customers' request:

> When you have customers who want changes to the contract, [earlier meters] demanded from those who work [that they take] a half-day's leave [to be at home to receive the agent] … [By contrast, smart meters avoid this appointment] … [these] are really new services that are being offered to customers.
>
> *(Head of the Linky project, 12 May 2014)*

Another challenge for operations managers has been to motivate technical agents, especially when having to cut off supply because of unpaid bills. Such encounters are often a source of anxiety for the technicians themselves. Even in ordinary situations, it is necessary to limit the risk of assault and avoid arguments with customers, for example, if they refuse to grant access to the meter or obstruct efforts to disconnect. In some rural areas and in sensitive urban areas, meters are sometimes located in basements or in areas where illicit activities go on. In such circumstances, technicians and meter readers have to negotiate carefully with customers and intermediaries (caretakers and neighbours) to 'open doors' and sometimes have to install a tele-reading device or rely on 'confidential readings' transmitted directly by the customer, called a *Relevé Confiance*.[7] In many such cases, it is difficult to really speak of a 'customer relationship':

> We have customers, they've got more than nine absences for readings. That means that in five years we haven't read their meter once. And we write to them, we demand appointments, we send them registered letters.
>
> *(Technical customer manager for meter readings, 9 July 2014)*

Often, there is little possibility of checking problems in situ, at the customer's address. The diffusion of the smart meter facilitates remote verification of customers' reported meter readings as well as the technicians' activity. Where there is a smart meter and where supply has to be cut off, the technicians are obliged to inform the customer on site, but can then proceed to request the back office to disconnect without having to perform the act themselves. This is an important development in that disconnection is a contested topic that gives rise to competing interpretations and reactions. Some technicians defend the principle of disconnection to prevent customers from going even deeper into debt, whereas others argue that more should be done to maintain access to what they see as an essential service. Smart metering does not change these debates, but it does change the way they are positioned within the organisation.

Smart meters also matter for how complaints are handled. Customers with electromechanical and electronic meters often contact the call centre to express dissatisfaction – for example, about waiting for a technician to arrive, or to contest estimated bills. These calls are a source of stress for tele-advisers who resort to a string of arguments to justify technical and commercial actions. As I observed first hand, the installation of smart meters also generated many conflicts, but once installed, they appear to have reduced complaints or made them easier to resolve, perhaps because technical managers and EDF tele-advisers have all the relevant data to hand.

In addition, smart meters change the scope for 'fiddling' and fraud. Electromechanical meters are fitted with security seals designed to stop customers tampering with them. A broken seal or window (which protects the numbers representing the energy consumed) or holes in the case are evidence of attempts to open it, but are not necessarily proof of fraud by the customer. In my interviews, design engineers explained that electronic meters had made fraud more difficult. Smart meters take this a stage further in that they record data in the event of an unauthorised attempt to open the case.

Finally, the smart meter is capable of limiting the electricity supply – a feature that can be activated remotely by the provider's tele-advisers as soon as a contract has been cancelled, or when someone moves house. For example, within 24 hours, the available power can be reduced to one kilowatt hour (rather than remaining at the level for which the previous occupant had a contract). This restricts consumption to a minimum number of devices when the new occupants move in, thus encouraging them to sign up for a new contract and pay for their electricity right away. In practice and in response to complaints, telephone advisers tend to be more relaxed about implementing this feature. As described, some are willing to let customers move in and subscribe to an electricity contract without having 'suffered' a limited power supply for the first few days of occupancy.

As all these examples show, the meter is pivotal in mediating between consumers and providers and in co-configuring the respective roles of each.

Conclusion

In this chapter, I have discussed the rise of two imagined types of smart meter enabled consumers: on the one hand, there is the informed, rational consumer who adapts his or her behaviour when provided with more and better data. On the other hand, there is the cheating, troublesome consumer who is capable of taking advantage of the new technology by circumventing the law and obstructing the service provider.

From the provider's point of view, smart meters figure as increasingly useful instruments with which to reduce oral and written complaints and to ensure that bills are paid. Proper management of the meter and of the circuit breaker are important in achieving these objectives. However, these goals have little or nothing to do with the parallel aspiration of creating a rational and responsive consumer. My analysis of recent experiments with the smart meter (2010–2015) generates two major findings, both of which reflect this tension.

First, attempts by design engineers and consumer representatives (unions, energy syndicates, etc.) to redefine the function of the meter have had limited success. The closer we get to actors who are in contact with the customer, the more the meter is perceived and used as a tool for regularising customers' files and for optimising procedures and processes for distributors and service suppliers – and the less the meter figures as an instrument of energy transition or as a tool that helps consumers monitor and adapt their consumption.

Second, this suggests that despite the official rhetoric, the smart meter is primarily important as an instrument with which to control and manage contracts, including disconnection, detecting fraud, identifying worn-out equipment and limiting encounters with difficult customers. From this point of view, the smart meter increases the distance between customers and suppliers – the site of the meter is no longer of defining importance, nor is it the key physical interface: not only are smart meters harder to tamper with, they can also be 'read' remotely and they enable new functions, including limiting supply. As a result, the smart meter calls for new models of contract management and 'back office' organisation, meaning that the roles of technicians and meter readers are redefined.

Apart from what it reveals about the customers' limited role in the detailed technical design of the smart meter, this case study shows how the meter materialises and relates to broader organisational changes in French energy provision. As described here, the smart meter is an active agent in defining and differentiating between the roles of professionals (suppliers, distributors, technicians) and customers. Its capabilities are defined and framed by the rules of the *Commission de Régulation de l'énergie*, which clearly distinguish between commercial, public and private roles in the energy market. As such, smart meters are designed to fit, and fit in with, a regime in which a commercial enterprise provides energy (in a now deregulated sector), in which various firms are involved in distribution (a regulated sector) and, in which customers are expected to manage and monitor their energy demand.

Notes

1 For example, in the case of failure in the electricity grid, detected by way of active or inactive electricity meters.

2 The survey draws on Ph.D. research conducted under a research convention between EDF and Université Paris Est on innovation processes and controversies concerning smart meters in France and on the social worlds that they mobilise, from design engineers to customers in newly equipped domestic environments. New research was also organised in 2016 to study the evolution of these debates. I wish to thank the reviewers Magali Pierre and Isabelle Moussaoui, the translator Liz Libbrecht and especially Olivier Coutard. I thank Elizabeth Shove and Frank Trentmann for editing this chapter. I am particularly grateful to Cécile Caron (GRETS, EDF LAB) who provided enormous intellectual support during my PhD studies and with my publications. An earlier version will be published in French in Moussaoui, I. and Pierre, M. (2016) *Pratiques sociales et usages de l'énergie*. Paris: Lavoisier.

3 The meter reader is responsible for two annual cycles of compulsory meter readings at the customer's home and for transmitting consumption data as recorded by each electricity meter, whether it be electromechanical (Compteur Bleu) or electronic. In the latter case, the reading can be automated by means of a remote reader often placed on the pavement outside. These data are then transmitted to the distributors and suppliers of electricity, to be used in drawing up bills. Note that most meter reading have been outsourced to private companies since the 2000s.

4 'Le compteur Linky et moi' ('The Linky meter and me'), ENEDIS brochure, July 2013.

5 These are meters that exist without any contract. The customer is able to receive electricity but is unknown to EDF and ENEDIS.

6 This is a facility granted by ENEDIS when a customer moves to a new home or new business premises. The new occupant can thus use energy provided through a contract with the previous homeowner, even when that contract has been cancelled. The electricity meter remains active and the new occupant has six to eight weeks to subscribe to a new contract with an electricity provider of their choice. Should they fail to do so within the prescribed time, an ENEDIS technical agent goes to the address and cuts off the supply without warning. There are cases in which the new occupants fail to subscribe to a new contract even after the eight-week period, without the supply being cut off and thus continue to consume energy without being billed for it, and sometimes without ever having to pay for it.

7 EDF's *Relevé Confiance* entails customers taking their own meter reading on the dates indicated on their bill if they are absent when the meter reading is to be taken. They then transmit this data directly to their provider, so that their bill reflects their actual consumption as closely as possible. Alternatively, they may tape a note to their front door, giving the meter reading.

References

Barraqué, B. (2013) 'Le compteur d'eau : enjeux passés et actuels', *Revue SET*, 10: 98–109.

Caron, C. (2016) 'Ambivalences Experimental Devices on the Appropriation and Diffusion of Eco-Innovations in the Field of Energy', 3rd ISA Forum of Sociology, 10 July 2016, Vienne.

Chatzis, K. (2006) 'Brève histoire des compteurs d'eau à Paris, 1880-1930', *Terrains & Travaux*, 11: 59–178.

Coutard, O. (1999) 'L'accès des ménages à faible revenu aux services d'eau et d'énergie en France et en Grande-Bretagne', *Flux*, 36: 7–15.

Danieli, A. (2014) 'Les controverses autour des compteurs communicants d'électricité «Linky» dans les médias locaux (2009-2013): de la dénonciation publique à l'affaiblissement médiatique local'. Intern research report, GRETS, EDF LAB.

Danieli, A. (2015) 'Enquêter sur un compteur d'électricité: un objet technique à la conquête de mondes sociaux (premières observations empiriques).' Intern research report, GRETS, EDF LAB.

Directive 2006/32 /EC of the European Parliament and of the Council of 5 April 2006 on energy end-use efficiency and energy services and repealing Council Directive 93/76 /EEC. Available from: http://eur-lex.europa.eu/legal-content/EN/TXT/?uri=celex:32006L0032 (Accessed 23/02/18).

Directive 2009/72 /EC of the European Parliament and of the Council of 13 July 2009 on common rules for the internal market in electricity and repealing Directive 2003/54 /EC. Available from: http://eur-lex.europa.eu/legal-content/EN/ALL/?uri=celex%3A32009L0072 (Accessed: 23/02/18).

Hess, D. J. (2014) 'Smart meters and public acceptance: comparative analysis and governance implications', *Health, Risk & Society*, 16(3): 243–258.

Klopfert, F., and Wallenborn, G. (2011) 'Les « compteurs intelligents » sont-ils conçus pour économiser de l'énergie?' *Terminal*, 106–107: 87–99.

Poupeau, F.M. (2009) 'Domestic customers and reform of the gas sector. An organisational sociology perspective', *Energy Policy*, 37, 5385–5392.

Rabeharisoa, V. (1991) 'Mesures «techniques», mesures «morales». De l'institution d'un habitant raisonnable face aux économies d'énergie', *Techniques & Culture*, 16: 63–82.

PART V

Steering, managing and disrupting demand

As the previous sections have shown, demand for energy is not just 'out there' as something to which infrastructures and utilities then respond. Rather, it arises from home, leisure and work practices, multiple material arrangements, and various forms of planning, standard setting and deliberate intervention. The dynamics of demand operate not in a vacuum but within a field that is structured and regulated by state, markets and experts.

The chapters in this section examine how managers and consumers steer and manage demand in different settings and circumstances. In focusing on what goes on in an electricity control room, how customers respond to variable electricity pricing and how people have managed in times of drought and energy shortage, they reveal multiple forms of 'demand management'. These include instant actions, such as raising or switching off the air conditioning, through to long-term changes in routines associated with shifting interpretations of what constitutes a 'normal' way of life.

In their emphasis on the linkage between actions and expectations, all three chapters alert us to the interdependence between practices and politics in framing demand. The managers in the electricity control room in Finland, for example, monitor and manage the electricity network within a market setting. Their orientation is towards commercial signals and imperatives rather than towards municipal service, as was the case before privatisation. Similarly, in seeking to reduce peak demand with the help of dynamic pricing in Australia and California, utilities work within a market model that treats price as the primary mechanism for modifying consumption. Political framing is also critical for how people respond to droughts and energy shortages and how responsibilities are assigned for overcoming them. Is a disruption blamed on the state, profit-oriented companies or the freak of nature? Who should help get things back to 'normal' – consumers by adapting their lifestyles, networks or the state?

This attention to the interweaving of practices and politics leads to two innovative steps regarding methods and scales of analysis. The first relates to the intersection of micro and macro processes. The fine-grained observation of energy managers in their day job or the detail of domestic routines is situated within, and not outside what look like 'wider' matters of politics, economics and public discourse. Similarly, monitoring a control room and cooking the family dinner occur in specific locations, but it is a defining characteristic of networked infrastructures that they connect these practices to distant places.

The second insight has to do with the histories of these arrangements. Practices that use energy happen at a particular point in time, but they carry within them habits, skills and expectations that have evolved over time. People respond differently to an ice-storm or a drought if they have lived through a similar disruption and acquired relevant socio-technical knowledge and skills, or if they have not. Policy makers and energy providers, similarly, work with past experiences and assumptions at the back of their minds. Practices can be learnt and unlearnt, but they are rarely instantaneous. Capturing these processes calls for an imaginative approach to empirical research and sources. The chapters in this section make use of ethnography and surveys along with details of political discourse, surveillance and legislation through to media representations and supranational regulatory frameworks.

This section highlights the flexibility of practices and the potential for creative intervention in managing demand. Today, and in the shadow of neoliberalism, many experts think of price signals as the natural mechanism for 'steering' demand. The chapters included here remind us that practices (past and present) change for many other reasons, from a sense of civic duty and social learning to the availability of different fuels and technologies. By implication, there are many more opportunities for steering demand today than is usually appreciated.

14

CO-CONSTITUTING SUPPLY AND DEMAND

Managing electricity in two neighbouring control rooms

Antti Silvast

Introduction

This chapter discusses the practical management of electricity infrastructure and concentrates on two electricity control rooms in a Finnish city's electricity supply company. One is an *electricity network room*, the other is an *energy market centre*. The electricity network room, which is adjacent to the energy market centre, manages the city's electricity network by monitoring a number of 'inputs' and 'outputs': electric voltages along the network, the standard frequency of the distributed electricity and the stability and temperature of electric network components. This work happened in shifts covering 24 hours a day and seven days a week and mainly involved working with a great number of computer screens. This arrangement is replicated in the market centre control room, in which the task is that of overseeing the city-owned electric energy production, monitoring many variables (from market prices to customers' energy demands and the weather) and bidding for and offering electricity on an energy stock exchange organised around the Nordic countries, called the Nord Pool.

The research described in this chapter explores the two control rooms and their political and professional contexts. By combining observations and interviews with workers from both rooms with higher-level political and organisational documents (EU directives, Finnish legislation and annual reports of the electricity company) I was able to discover how and why the control rooms had been 'unbundled' as part of the organisation of the city's electricity supply company. The method of moving between multiple research sites let me explore the forms of situated conduct and of sense-making and skill enacted in the two control rooms, viewed as specialised centres of coordination. This approach draws on other workplace (Heath and Luff, 2000; Gobo, 2008) and organisational studies (De Bruijne, 2006; Roe and Schulman, 2008) and on research in science and technology studies that also investigate the situated character of organisational procedures and arrangements (Collier and Ong, 2005; Pollock and Williams, 2010; Vertesi, 2012).

By utilising these diverse concepts and data, the chapter develops two main points that complement each other. First, the ethnographic research provides new insight into the practicalities of making and operating infrastructures on a daily basis. Second, and by taking a step back, I show how important political visions about electricity supply and demand are in shaping the organisational contexts, spatial arrangements and legal mandates through which infrastructures function. Together these observations allow me to show how the electricity infrastructure works within and as part of the wider politics of provision, and to better understand how infrastructures and everyday consumption constitute each other.

Introducing the two control rooms

The two control rooms that I investigated were both part of a company supplying electricity. Staff working in each room had clearly defined roles and functions. The pattern and rhythm of their work had differences, but also similarities. In describing these – and following the terminology employed in the company – I refer to the control room responsible for the electricity grid as the 'electricity network room' and describe the room in which people operated in various energy markets as the 'energy market centre'.

To put this study in context, my research concerns an electricity company in a Finnish city. Before the 1990s, a single electricity utility was responsible for the entire supply chain of electricity to the city, ranging from energy generation in power plants to electricity distribution, customer sales and billing, and maintenance of the network. Following energy market liberalisation, a process that started in the 1990s in many Western countries (Graham and Marvin, 2001) and now includes all EU Member States (European Parliament and Council, 2009), the electricity system is no longer organised in this way. Although the whole company was in principle owned by the city and dedicated to serving the energy demands of that city, its organisation had been subdivided to handle different aspects of the infrastructure, including various energy carriers (from electricity to gas and district heating), along with more or less commercial functions (such as marketing). The separation of the two control rooms followed this reorganisation.

In terms of physical appearance, the two rooms differed from most other offices in that they had a large number of centrally located computer screens. A control room operator, one in each room, sat in front of a half circle of screens that he or she could observe at all times. The screens in the electricity network control room (Figure 14.1) generally showed a map (both geographical regions and more schematic industrial control systems). However, they sometimes showed information systems into which supply faults or video camera feeds recording different locations across the grid were entered. A large video wall, behind the computers, could repeat any of the smaller screens or a number of them.

FIGURE 14.1 Inside the electricity network room.

FIGURE 14.2 Inside the energy market centre.

In the energy market centre (Figure 14.2), the computer screens displayed information on electricity production, the electricity network, district heating, email and spreadsheets, and had windows that enabled operators to interact with several different markets (gas, day-ahead electricity, real time electricity). Both rooms had a normal television which the operators were also allowed to watch (this was sometimes on during my interviews). In addition to monitors, other communication devices (landlines, radio, phones) were critical, especially in the electricity network control room (Figure 14.1).

All but one of the control room workers were men in their late 50s or early 60s, professionally trained in electric power generation technology – a vocational degree in Finland. The one exception was a new female worker in her 20s who was studying electrical engineering. As most of the male workers explained, they had learned how to do their daily duties on the spot by training in the control rooms alongside more experienced staff. Formally, the electricity network control room 'uses' the electricity network and maintains, plans and helps build it. This essentially technical job description includes various practices of patching/repair to ensure the consistent operation of the electricity infrastructure. More labour intensive operations of building and maintenance were assigned to another part of the company.

The energy market centre's duties involved:

> continuously analysing a whole formed by many variables, … making prognoses and … optimisation. The most significant variables on the whole are the weather situation, the prices of fuels, the electricity and heating need of the end customers, as well as the market prices of electricity and emission permits.
>
> *(Annual Report, 2005)*

This extract gives a sense of the sheer number of anticipatory practices – covering market prices, energy demands and even the local weather – that are involved in keeping the electricity infrastructure going and keeping it afloat from day-to-day in the open energy market. At the time of my study, the technicians working in the market centre had mostly been retrained as energy brokers through a short course organised by the Nordic stock exchange Nord Pool in the 1990s.

In order to provide more insight into what this arrangement means for understanding how the electricity network and the electricity market work, I will begin by describing what happens in the electricity network control room before moving to the energy market centre.

What happens in the electricity network room?

Those working in the electricity network control room ensured that electricity generated by the company, or bought from the Nordic energy markets, was distributed to energy consumers in the city. This depended on: (a) maintaining a functioning electricity distribution system and in so doing, (b) maintaining a reliable power supply – thus enabling 'physical well-being of the energy customers' (as one worker put it) – whilst, (c) managing the electricity distribution grid in a way that avoids large-scale material losses including the management of peak demands.

Another operator explains what this means in practice:

> we monitor the electricity grid and also use remote operated stations and switches and other accessories. And the normal use is that when a load change causes a situation or because of building operations, the switching of the energy grid has to be occasionally changed.
>
> *(Electricity network room operator)*

According to this operator the most typical routine on a working day is the remote testing of newly installed components (e.g., lines, transformers, power stations) in cooperation with teams of mechanics who are outside 'in the field'. The task of continuous monitoring also involves oversight of the so-called 'waste power' that electricity cables contain. This routine pattern is punctuated by alarms. Components of the grid trigger alarms when their voltage, current or temperature exceeds a certain level. Although the operators do not necessarily keep count, an event list on computer screens showed 36 pages of events on one particular day. Not all of these events set off an alarm; some are solved by automatic fail-safe devices. When an alarm occurs, the task is to first report the details of the fault to a computer system, then determine whether a maintenance team is needed and if it is, to send the team into the field and coordinate the field work in relation to the information showing on the control room computer screens.

Thus far, what is at stake is relatively straightforward. As well as managing risks to the electricity supply, actions were often designed to reduce such risks and increase security. This was indicated by the existence of highly standardised methods of solving a fault. The steps taken are discussed in the following extract:

Interviewer: Are there many rules that are followed even though situations change?

Operator: Well, of course there are security and other sets of rules about what should be done. You have to go according to them. And every operator has to have the same point of view about those things. That doesn't change according to who sits here.

> *(Interview, 2008)*

On the one hand, the working practices of those in the room depend on following strict rules and standards when 'security' is involved. On the other hand, the way 'security' is guaranteed is to some extent dependent on circumstances. As the technician continued, 'each fault is a little different and you have to consider separately each time how to act'. Another operator reflected on a similar tension between security and on-the-spot actions:

> In principle, electricity work is usually highly standardised. If everyone follows the standard, then it is highly structured. There is a problem, however, that when you go

to a work site, the situation might vary greatly. And then comes your own adaptation about how you want to do things.

(Electricity network room operator)

In this account, one aspect of unpredictability stems from the actual worksite. Another stems from the need to maintain the welfare of customers. As a rule, maintenance work requires that part of the electricity grid is shut down to avoid dangerous electric shocks. Yet, this safe working practice requires a trade-off, some customers will lose their electricity supply when maintenance work is going on. One operator highlighted this when he pointed out that each maintenance task needs to be carried out in a manner that does not pose 'unreasonable harm to other customers'.

I was able to observe one occasion when an operator fixed a fault for a customer. This job started with a phone call from a domestic customer (customers can call technicians directly). In this case, the technician first talked with the customer who reported lights blinking in the home. The technician then determined whether this fault was the responsibility of the electricity company. Eventually, he decided to send a maintenance team into the field. At first it seems as if there was a problem within the customer's home and not on the company's electricity grid. However, blinking lights can indicate a 'ground fault', which carries with it the risk of an electric shock to the customer. The technician found the location of the house on a computer map, phoned an outsourced maintenance team and told them about the technical details of the fault. He determined how many other houses might have to be cut off whilst the fault was fixed, 'in the worst case' and then waited for the maintenance team to reach the customer's house. He then interacted with a computer screen and started writing a fault report. He talked with the maintenance team on the phone again once they arrived. After several attempts at finding the cause of the fault, he determined together with the maintenance team, that this was not a ground fault after all, but a loose electricity line, typical of 'these old battlefront soldier houses' as he noted to me. He then concluded the job by sending the maintenance team off and checked the details about their working hours, for purposes of billing. The bill was then sent to the relevant part of the electricity network company.

This detailed description reveals different aspects of the management of maintenance work. The routine management of risk and security, in which statistics from previous incidents are turned into risk assessments which guide risk mitigation activities in a highly standardised way (O'Malley, 2004) was only part of the story. The above example also illustrates improvisations, independent decisions, teamwork, skills, help from computer systems, practical rules of thumb and experiential knowledge of the region. Furthermore, it is clear that the anticipated threat to the system shifts as the situation unfolds. First, what occurs is blinking lights, perhaps suggesting an impending blackout for the customer. However, the operator also foresees a dangerous ground fault, potentially indicated by the blinking. A maintenance team is sent and there is some consideration of how many other customers might have a blackout if a repair is needed. In this case, the prevention of one risk potentially causes another, in the form of a power failure for customers not affected by the initial fault. After a long period of work, the operator concludes that the fault was not a ground fault. Instead, it was sagging lines, which are to be expected with this kind of housing. In summary, the nature of the risks involved can change and be reinterpreted almost minute-by-minute, as habits and experience combine with observations, as problems emerge and as information is added.

From an organisational point of view, the problem – signalled by blinking lights – becomes the responsibility of the electricity network control room. The allocation of problems and responsibilities and their reintegration to ensure the system continues to function, reflects and depends on the wider management of the electricity sector as a whole. The work that goes on in the two control rooms is part of this overall system, but as described below, the tasks in each have been formalised in very different ways.

The energy market centre

Staff working in the electricity network room only dealt with electricity once it flowed into the distribution grid and was on its way to the end customer.

In a liberalised infrastructure, this electrical energy comes from another subsystem, formed by the energy generators, themselves operating on open international energy markets in Finland. It is at this system level that the reliable provision of electricity entails other costs – including prices on energy wholesale and customers' retail markets: costs which those working in the network room do not strictly speaking see (the electricity network makes a charge for distribution which is included in customers' electricity bill). The activities that go in on the network room and in the energy market centre are therefore interdependent.

The tasks undertaken in the two control rooms were so specialised that only one worker could or was allowed to work shifts in both of the rooms. This one operator made the following comparison:

> The energy market centre is like keeping watch of over a campfire. You have to constantly keep a small flame burning, that is, you shouldn't fall behind the energy stock exchanges. Working in the electricity network control room, on the other hand, is like being a tin soldier. Things don't happen all the time, but when someone calls you have to be ready on the spot.
>
> *(Electricity network and energy market centre operator)*

What he saw was a market place that has to be constantly 'made' by economic actors. By comparison, the electricity grid was managed primarily through reactive monitoring and maintenance. In his interpretation, the electricity network is relatively static most of the time, while the market is continuously changing, a dynamic entity in relation to which one needs to stay alert.

In many ways, the energy market centre had experienced constant change for more than ten years at the time of my study. All those who worked in the centre during the 1990s had been retrained as 'stockbrokers' though all were originally educated as electricity power technicians. During this period, changes in international energy markets have been reproduced in the Nordic countries and Europe at large (e.g., Kaijser, 1995; Summerton, 2004; Lagendijk, 2008). For example, Finland (and the other Nordic countries) already had forms of electricity trading prior to the market opening in the 1990s. Before the 1990s, the Finnish electric utilities were mostly engaged in long-term contracts with the state-owned power company, but in some cases, small individual trades were made if surplus energy existed. Power plants also produced a small number of differently priced 'forms' of electricity. The trades in all these cases happened on the phone and were between two known parties. There are examples of similar forms of trading still taking place today, especially in the regulation power market where the Finnish high-voltage company contracts with large industrial organisations to help restrict consumption in case of national energy balance problems.

In contrast to this case-by-case energy trading, with the opening of the energy market, energy is supposed to become like any other commodity 'like, for instance, grain and oil' (Nord Pool Spot, 2009: 2). This depends on an organisational separation between a wholesale market and a retail market for electricity and the existence of a range of actors who mediate between the wholesale energy, retail energy and end consumers, including energy producers, retailers, traders and brokers, all of whom transfer electricity from generators to the customers for a charge. In my case, the Nord Pool wholesale market involves energy companies in Denmark, Finland, Sweden, Norway, Estonia, Latvia, Lithuania and parts of Germany. There are two main temporally related energy markets that these companies engage in: the day-ahead auction market (called Elspot) that concerns purchase orders for the day ahead and the intraday market (called Elbas). The Elspot orders are prepared in local energy market centres, like that of my study, once per day and then used by Nord Pool to calculate the international energy system price for each hour of the day. The more or less real time Elbas market is used by companies during the day to make corrections to their order due to power plant shutdowns, weather fluctuations, changing demand or other real time factors. If the companies involved do not achieve a balance between supply and demand, the gap is filled by the national transmission company, which sets its own price, on its own 'balancing market', which risks being high (or at least difficult to anticipate on the local level) (Silvast, 2011; 2017). In addition to these arrangements, there is a financial market in which futures can be traded further than one day ahead.

Some academics have highlighted the particularities of electricity as a product even after it goes on the free market, and even after it is constituted as a 'commodity'. For example, two sociologists conclude that electricity markets cannot separate 'actual prices' from 'material variables', which include 'the role played by material parameters such as yields, traffic and network loads in the calculation of rates' (Çalışkan and Callon, 2010: 18). This suggests that the materialities of the electricity infrastructure and the economics of the infrastructure – calculation of rates, actual prices – are always intertwined. Yet, it is difficult to maintain a sense of this interdependence when studying how the infrastructure works in practice and from the viewpoint of the control room.

In terms of daily operation, working practices in the control room seem to resemble trading in many other financial commodities. That said there are some relatively distinctive features. For example, historical records of previous energy demand patterns (prepared by the electricity network room) and of the weather played a large part in making a spot bid for the day ahead (Silvast, 2011). In theory, the price of a stock is only predicted by its current price, not its past prices. Having said that, actors in many kinds of financial markets also examine evidence from the past, like price records, before making trading decisions. Another seemingly specific aspect is that traders pay great attention to the weather – mainly because electricity and heat are produced in the same power plant and the demand for heat is closely related to the outside temperature. As one of the traders said, 'you can never tell what the temperature is and [trading] depends on that completely'.

What one finds through interviews is that the workers routinely talk about what they do in financial terms: such as 'balancing', 'offers', 'good prices', 'cost prices', 'price protections', 'burning money' (in the case of a severe imagined breakdown at a power plant) and 'serious financial risks' (in the case of being coerced into buying national balancing energy). Their everyday working practice tended to follow largely predetermined trading routines on the computer screen – for instance, they had to prepare and make a spot order before one o'clock, communicate that order to the power plant so that its managers know what to generate, then trade in the real time energy markets every hour of the day and during the night.

The electricity company was still owned by the city, but given the market discourses and practices described above, it is perhaps not surprising that many of the traders felt they were no longer really providing a municipal service. They were acting within a market context and for a municipality which sought to maintain a cheap and reliable electricity supply and which owned the infrastructure and had to justify its costs. As one informant said 'the city wants to have cheap electricity … The city has its targets for the invested capital'. Operating under this logic of return on investments, workers in the energy market centre viewed themselves as economic actors – but did not see this as being problematic. As one of the traders explained: 'We have these units and we are a profit-responsible unit. We have a certain hourly rate that we bill others for our services'. Seen in comments like this, the logic of the market permeated daily work in a way that seemed almost automatic. Market-related discourse, metaphors and practical tools were simply adopted and used – being taken for granted by what were in effect public sector market traders.

Links between the two control rooms

Although the working methods and practices enacted in each of the two control rooms differed markedly, both were tied to linked and related events. In terms of temporal sequence, activities in the two rooms followed in succession: the spot orders in the energy market centre preceded the distribution work in the neighbouring network control room, which patched the distribution infrastructure in real time, especially if something went wrong or when routine maintenance was needed. For unforeseen events that had financial repercussions – concerning the foreseen energy market price, such as a power plant shutting down or other major energy resource fluctuations – the market centre drew on the real time market to maintain supply at the best possible price. For events like electrical power failures or other reliability problems, the markets did not 'see' them at all (unless they figured as a minor price fluctuation) and neither did the energy market centre. In this respect, at least, energy markets and the electricity networks really were separate worlds just as recent energy policies have predicted.

Previous works in science and technology studies have argued that social organisation has to be enacted as local order to become effective (Vertesi, 2012). One key outcome is that activities in markets and other local orders are also always part of wider processes and social organisations, a view which my study supports.

However, this observation generates a further question: which forms of social organisation were the two electricity control rooms meant to be performing and did they act as anticipated? From the perspective of those working in each of the control rooms, activities in the market, the markets themselves, as well as overarching security standards and the more or less reliable operation of large technological systems were in many ways simply 'out there', figuring as external entities that shape the work to be done and the rules that need to be followed almost all the time (Silvast and Virtanen, 2014: 100). However, these markets and systems are not inevitably arranged in the way that they were at the time of my study. In the next section, I consider the political and institutional origins of this separation between 'electricity networks' and 'electricity markets'.

Unbundling electricity markets from networks: political visions

The last empirical part of the chapter looks back at how and why the two control rooms were separated such that one was concerned with the networks and the other with the market. As will be shown, this configuration partly reflected the requirement to 'unbundle' – in practice, to separate on a legal, operative or accounting sense – that aspect of electricity supply that involves maintaining physical networks (often monopolistic) from its 'market-based' aspects which include sales to customers and trade on international energy markets. Such unbundling is closely related to the idea that large-scale modern organisations have to be split into special-ised units that can 'network' globally (DiMaggio, 2001).

Mandates for this separation were, and continue to be, part of international and national policy to liberalise, deregulate and partly privatise monopolistic infrastructure industries (Graham and Marvin, 2001). While such unbundling dates back to the original Finnish elec-tricity liberalisation from the Electricity Market Act (1995) and the European Parliament and Council's (1996) first energy market package, stronger mandates were enacted in Finland in 2004 following the European Parliament and Council's (2003) second package. Furthermore, around 2008 and the years that preceded it, decision makers in my case study city had their own aspirations for organisational reform in the electricity utility. The ambitions also shaped the separation of the two control room's professional duties and practicalities. I will briefly comment on these different institutional 'levels' and on what policies regarding electricity distribution were about.

The European common electricity market stems from the aspiration of a single market in Europe and has been ongoing in EU legislation since 1996 through a series of legal packages in 2003 and 2009 (with new energy market design currently being drafted, see European Commission, 2016). The aim was to promote the competitive generation of electricity and separate it from the networked distribution of electricity, handled by so-called natural monopolies. The hope was that this would lead to the creation of a large market area all over the EU where member states' energy generation companies could compete for energy con-sumers and where consumers could choose between different suppliers. The EU legislation, as its name implies, sets these rationales in motion by creating common rules for the internal market of electricity, which member states implement in their national electricity market laws.

One of these rules concerns electricity unbundling. In the first 1996 electricity mar-ket directive (European Parliament and Council, 1996), unbundling simply meant separate accounting for electricity generation, transmission and distribution activities if they were managed by the same integrated company. While this was meant to increase public transpar-ency, it did not prevent mergers of electricity utilities, especially between European borders, which may have ended up reducing rather than increasing competition in the electricity sector (Karlstrøm, 2011: 128–129). The next EU electricity market legislation (European Parliament and Council, 2003) redefined the meaning of unbundling: for electricity distribu-tion system operators, such as the one in my study, independence was required in legal form, and in terms of organisation and decision making (but not ownership) – and in this sense separation from other company activities that were not about distributing electricity (such as generation or energy market operations).

These stricter EU requirements were anticipated by Finnish policy makers, energy market regulators and the industries. The earliest suggestions by the Ministry of Trade and Industry (KTM, 2001) and the Finnish Government (HE, 2004) aligned with those of the EU, but were opened to a public hearing (KTM, 2001: 246–249). While many welcomed unbundling as a means of increasing competition and lowering prices, some energy companies anticipated increasing administration and rising electricity prices and other commentators noted that unbundling could disrupt municipal utilities in particular and interfere with how cities organise their activities. The parliamentary discussion before the Finnish 2004 Electricity Market Act highlighted this same worry: a political question was whether 'the government proposal would include a responsibility to incorporate after unbundling, namely to establish (utilities as) stock companies'. Hence, unbundling was supported or opposed for seemingly ambivalent reasons: while it brought new players into the markets and hence increased competition, it also paved the way for privatising city utilities.

The Finnish Electricity Market Act was amended in 2004 to separate 'electricity system operations from other electricity trade operations and the electricity trade operations from its other trade operations'. In this, it enacted a new distinction between legal and operative unbundling. This meant that the largest operators, measured by how many gigawatt hours of electricity they transmit, would be *legally unbundled* and that sub-units within them would have independent legal form, organisation and decision making power, as per the EU's terms. Other large operators, this time defined in terms of how many customers they served, would also have *operative unbundling*, meaning there would be restrictions on who could sit on the boards and be the managing directors of the different unbundled units.

In the company I studied, organisational specialisation predated the Finnish electricity law of 2004. Two years prior to the Finnish Government proposal that established the different 'objectives', 'business basics' and 'profit responsibilities' in electricity networks, generation, sales, maintenance, fixing and building (HE, 2004: 16), the company had already been split, if not yet unbundled, into seven business 'operation units' – a move that was designed to create 'a customer-oriented process organisation' (this and all of the following quotes from the company's Annual Reports). These units included an energy centre (explained above), energy sales (both for electricity and district heating), energy production, district heating and gas provision, business support, business development and electricity distribution.

The legal requirement for unbundling came in 2005 and led to a redefinition of the remit of these business units. The owners divided the electricity distribution function into two corporations, albeit still owned by the city: 'a network company regulated by the Energy Market Authority and an electricity network building and maintenance company that operates on the competitive markets'.

This was a method of delineating the system in market-based terms that had significant repercussions in the electricity network room. The electricity utility continued to be operated by the city and contain five business units dealing with electricity generation, district heating and gas, marketing and sales, energy markets and business support. At the same time, forms of communication had to be redesigned as the units of the company became much less integrated than before. In practice, the new corporations were to become 'expert organisations' as well as 'subscribers' of each other's 'services', communicating through a formalised 'service contract system'.

The nuances of these arrangements and terminology are not always easy to follow, but the outcome is crucial: through new concepts as well as tools – such as contract systems – they create specific conditions, redefining how staff in each of the control rooms viewed their professional role. As opposed to the older terminology of the municipal utility (*sähkölaitos* in Finnish) and its dispatchers, one sees the reimagining of control room work as an 'expert' role involving working for an 'organisation' (with the loan word *organisaatio* frequently used in these discussions), which provides 'services' that others 'subscribe' to by making 'contracts'.

Critically, the emphasis on fair competition and common market rules is not just a matter of EU and national policy; it also has repercussions for the day-to-day work of where, when, how and by whom the electricity infrastructure is managed. Expanding the role of the energy markets has implications for technical maintenance and monitoring, which tends to become a secondary function that supports and patches distribution systems when they do not function properly. It also emphasises the temporality of the markets, which are not so much concerned with long-term maintenance, but are instead focused on prognoses for a single day ahead and the real time management of events once they occur. I now consider what these features mean for an understanding of the electricity infrastructure and the practices of its management more generally.

How the unbundled electricity infrastructure works in practice

This chapter has shown how the electricity infrastructure is managed in practice. Detailed accounts of two control rooms, one relating to the network itself, the other to the electricity market, show how EU and Finnish national law on unbundling electricity networks and markets is enacted. These accounts also show how the city (which owned the company) partly utilised and embraced external legal requirements to serve its own ambitions for streamlining and managing electricity provision. As well as reflecting formal institutional distinctions and ambitions, work within the two centres revolved around a range of often unrecognised systems of supervision encompassing spatial arrangements, trading routines, contracts, professional identities and the artefacts (Silvast and Virtanen, 2014). I conclude by thinking about how these two very different forms of control might create new understandings about what is involved in balancing infrastructure supply and demand, flagging the latter aspect in particular.

Although I have emphasised the different forms of network management and the types of expertise involved in each control room, it is important to explain that the operators in both rooms monitor electricity consumption, but do so in very different terms. The energy market control room deals in abstract and aggregate measures of demand – representing consumers whose needs and ability to pay are anticipated in an attempt to generate the best possible energy market price. In contrast, those responsible for the network focus on households and end users facing specific and localised problems with the reliability of their electricity supply. In comparing these coexisting and to some extent related forms of control, this chapter has provided new insight into the daily operation of the electricity infrastructure and of the market arrangements involved – especially by showing how supply and demand are co-managed in practice through electricity distribution systems and electricity markets.

The two control rooms, their work and the demands that they deal differ in terms of the temporalities, rhythms, metrics and responses involved. From the consumers' point of view, centralised infrastructures of electricity and heat often appear to be static (Jalas, Rinkinen and Silvast, 2015). However, this impression does not match the experiences of those who manage the system on a daily basis. As this chapter has shown, electricity infrastructures and markets reflect and constitute a wide variety of temporalities. The energy market does not exist 'out there' in the global stock exchange or in some sense apart from the more situated electricity infrastructure. Conversely, the regional electricity network needs the market (or information about the market) to guide almost all of its inputs and production processes. Both working arrangements ensure the consistency of the infrastructure – as experienced by consumers – but achieve this through different but closely related forms of adjustment: those working in the market control room respond to fluctuating prices and weather conditions, whilst those in the network room adapt and react to actual and potential faults.

As we have seen, organisational separations between markets and networks of electricity supply stem from specific political histories: in the city, in Finland and in the EU. This much is clear. In following these arrangements through to the practical work of keeping both systems going, this chapter provides further insight into how energy politics configure the challenges of managing electricity supply and demand at the local level.

Acknowledgments

I acknowledge the helpful comments received from Elizabeth Shove, Dominic Berry, Tanja Winther, Vincent Ialenti and Rosemary Taylor. The preparation of this chapter was financially supported by the Scottish ClimateXChange, UK and Princeton University, Princeton Institute for International and Regional Studies, US. I am thankful for comments and help from the Global Systemic Risk Research Community, Princeton University, where I began to draft this chapter as a postdoctoral research associate.

References

Annual Reports (2003, 2004, 2005, 2006, 2007, 2008) of an anonymised Finnish city electricity utility.

Çalışkan, K. and Callon, M. (2010) 'Economization, part 2: a research programme for the study of markets', *Economy and Society*, 39: 1–32.

Collier, S. and Ong, A. (2005) 'Global assemblages: anthropological problems', in Ong, A. and Collier, S. (eds.) *Global Assemblages: Technology, Politics, and Ethics as Anthropological Problems*, Malden: Blackwell. pp. 3–21.

DiMaggio, P. (2001) 'Introduction: making sense of the contemporary firm and prefiguring its future', in DiMaggio, P. (ed.) *The Twenty-First-Century Firm: changing economic organization in international perspective*. Princeton: Princeton University Press. pp. 3–30.

De Bruijne, M. (2006) *Networked Reliability: institutional fragmentation and the reliability of service provision in critical infrastructures*, Doctoral thesis, Technical University of Delft, Faculty of Technology, Policy and Management, Delft: TUD Technische Universiteit Delft.

European Commission (2016) 'Proposal for a directive of the European Parliament and of the council on common rules for the internal market in electricity (recast)'. COM/2016/0864 final/2 - 2016/0380 (COD).

European Parliament & Council (1996) 'Concerning common rules for the internal market in electricity'. Directive 96/92/EC.

European Parliament & Council (2003) 'Concerning common rules for the internal market in electricity and repealing Directive 96/92/EC'. Directive 2003/54/EC.

European Parliament & Council (2009) 'Concerning common rules for the internal market in electricity and repealing Directive 2003/54/EC'. Directive 2009/72/EC.

Finnish Electricity Market Act (2004) 386/1995, amendments up to 1772/2004 included. Unofficial translation by the Finnish Ministry of Trade and Industry.

Gobo, G. (2008) *Doing Ethnography*. London: Sage Publications.

Graham, S. and Marvin, S. (2001) *Splintering Urbanism: networked infrastructures, technological mobilities and the urban condition*, London: Routledge.

HE (Hallituksen esitys, Finnish Government Proposal) (2004) 'Hallituksen esitys Eduskunnalle laeiksi sähkömarkkinalain ja markkinaoikeuslain muuttamisesta'. HE 127/2004. ['Government proposal for changing the electricity market act and market court act'. HE 127/2004].

Heath, C. & Luff, P. (2000) *Technology in Action*. Cambridge, UK: Cambridge University Press.

Jalas, M., Rinkinen, J. and Silvast, A. (2015) 'Infrastruktuurit järjestävät aikaa' ['Infrastructures organize time'], in Pääkkönen, H. (ed.) *Ajassa kiinni ja irrallaan - Yhteisölliset rytmit 2000-luvun Suomessa* ['Attached and detached to time - social rhythms in the 21st century Finland'], Helsinki: Statistics Finland. pp. 135–145.

Kaijser, A. (1995) 'Controlling the grid: the development of high-tension power lines in the Nordic countries', in Kaijser, A. and Hedin, M. (eds.) *Nordic Energy Systems: Historical Perspectives and Current Issues*, Canton: Science History Publications. pp 31–54.

Karlstrøm, H. (2011) *Empowering Markets? The Construction and Maintenance of a Deregulated Market for Electricity in Norway*. Doctoral thesis: Faculty of Humanities, Norwegian University of Science and Technology.

KTM (Kauppa- ja teollisuusministeriö, Finnish Ministry of Trade and Industry) (2001) Sähkömarkki-noiden kehitystarpeet: Sähkömarkkinalain 5-vuotishuoltotyöryhmän loppuraportti. ['The development needs of electricity markets: the end report of the five year maintenance working group of the Electricity Market Act.'] Kauppa- ja teollisuusministeriön työryhmä- ja toimikuntaraportteja 18/2001.

Lagendijk, V. (2008) *Electrifying Europe: the power of Europe in the construction of electricity networks*. Doctoral thesis, Eindhoven University of Technology. Amsterdam: Aksant Academic Publishers.

Nord Pool Spot (2009) *The Nordic Electricity Exchange and the Nordic Model for a Liberalised Electricity Market*. Lysaker: Nord Pool Spot.

O'Malley, P. (2004) *Risk, Uncertainty and Government*, London: Polity Books.

Pollock, N. and Williams, R. (2010) 'E-infrastructures: how do we know and understand them? Strategic ethnography and the biography of artefacts', *Computer Supported Cooperative Work*, 19: 521–556.

Roe, E. and Schulman, P. (2008) *High Reliability Management: operating on the edge*, Stanford: Stanford Business Books.

Silvast, A. (2011) 'Monitor screens of market risks: managing electricity in a Finnish control room', *STS Encounters*, 4: 145–174.

Silvast, A. (2017) *Making Electricity Resilient: risk and security in a liberalized electricity infrastructure*. London: Routledge.

Silvast, A. and Virtanen, M. (2014) 'Keeping systems at work: electricity infrastructure from control rooms to household practices', *Science & Technology Studies*, 27: 93–114.

Summerton, J. (2004) 'Do electrons have politics? Constructing user identities in Swedish electricity', *Science, Technology and Human Values*, 29: 486–511.

Vertesi, J. (2012) 'Seeing like a Rover: visualization, embodiment, and interaction on the Mars exploration rover mission', *Social Studies of Science*, 42: 393–414.

15

PRICES AS INSTRUMENTS OF DEMAND MANAGEMENT

Interpreting the signals

Yolande Strengers

Introduction

Variable, cost-reflective or dynamic pricing is a key demand management strategy in many governments' energy policies. The concept refers to tariffs in which the cost of electricity varies throughout the day, week or year, in line with peaks and troughs in electricity's supply and demand. The goal is to 'correct' the signals of flat rate pricing, which have become 'something of a curse' for utility providers (Sioshansi, 2012: xl). As Sioshansi (2012: xxxvii) explains, the aim is to alert customers 'that a kWh consumed at 2 p.m. on a hot summer afternoon is *not* the same as a kWh consumed at 2 a.m.'. This is because 'the former costs a lot more to generate and deliver' (Sioshansi, 2012: xxxvii).

Variable tariffs have been around for a long time. Telecommunication, airline, hotel, rail-road, car hire and entertainment industries routinely employ dynamic tariffs to reflect changes in supply and demand and the peaks to which their products or services are subject. Dynamic pricing has been more cautiously approached in the energy sector, partly because the industry's historical 'build and supply' legacy has given rise to an overarching ethos that demand should be met, rather than shifted or shaved (Healy and MacGill, 2012) and partly because of equity concerns about protecting consumers from price volatility associated with this essential service (Faruqui, 2012). Nonetheless, peak demand pressures and investment in 'enabling technologies' such as smart grids and meters mean that variable and dynamic tariffs are receiving heightened attention as a way to 'smooth' peaks and troughs in electricity demand and supply (Sioshansi, 2012).

A somewhat obvious but important assumption is that the key variable in variable pricing is price. In other words, it is the changing *rate* or *cost* of electricity which makes variable pricing variable. The magnitude of demand response is thought to depend primarily on the degree of price difference, with higher prices resulting in more substantial demand shifting (Faruqui and Sergici, 2010). Other factors also noted to result in greater demand variation include the presence of an air conditioner (or heater) and the availability of enabling technologies, such as, a programmable or smart thermostats (Faruqui and Sergici, 2010). However, the focus is on 'getting the price right'. That is, establishing a tariff structure which generates the most elasticity in demand, without unnecessarily burdening or penalising consumers.

This is neither the only nor necessarily the best way of understanding variable pricing. Indeed, there are a number of perplexing anomalies in this dominant narrative that warrant a different investigation. For example, contrary to cost-benefit predictions, residential air conditioned cooling becomes *increasingly* negotiable with hotter temperatures and when *more* households own or use these devices, *regardless of price* (Faruqui and George, 2005; eMeter, 2010; Strengers, 2013). Similarly, some 'information-only' trials, which notify householders of an impending peak event but do not change the price of electricity during this time still achieve significant demand response (Strengers, 2013; IEA, 2005; Pasquier, 2011).

The usual method of understanding these seeming contradictions is to recruit economics-related disciplines or sub-disciplines, such as behavioural economics, to explain the predictable *ir*rationality of some consumers' responses, without fundamentally challenging the assumed importance of price. For example, Stern's (1986: 203) seminal paper from the 1980s sought to rectify the 'blind spots' in economic analyses of price. In doing so, he remained committed to price as the dominant variable, asking 'how does the information embodied in price enter a consumer's awareness?' and 'how does awareness of price affect action?' (Stern, 1986: 203). More recently, in Thaler and Sunstein's (2008) popular behavioural economics book *Nudge*, the authors argue for a better 'choice architecture' in which there are favourable default settings and purposefully aligned economic incentives to steer people away from undesirable behaviours. Price features here as one of the tools to reorient human action through individual choices. Common 'confounding factors' that help explain why price may not operate as expected include low household energy use knowledge (CSIRO, 2013) and the problematic value-action gap (Blake, 1999), where motivations (to save energy, for example) do not match what people do. These psychological and behavioural explanations seek to rectify or 'correct' deviation from the expected demand response, thereby allowing price instruments and economic theories to retain their dominant status in planning and policy.

I consider an alternative perspective in this chapter: one which puts price second, or more radically, moves it completely to one side. Instead of assuming the primary importance of the tariff itself, I am interested in what we can learn from assuming that what matters is a tariff's variability or dynamism. What if we focused on the *duration, frequency* and *regularity* of pricing as a means to explore its effectiveness as an instrument of demand management? This approach leads away from economic questions of price points, utility maximisation and cost-benefit analyses, instead inviting us to explore how the temporalities of electricity pricing intersect with the routines and rhythms of everyday life. This involves a reconceptualisation of tariffs: from economic or market signals to modes of sustaining and potentially disrupting the everyday temporalities which constitute energy demand (Walker, 2014).

This chapter explores the relevance of such an approach with reference to exemplary studies of pricing trials conducted with Australian and other households. The discussion focuses on two distinctive variable pricing arrangements: time-of-use (TOU) tariffs and dynamic or critical peak pricing (CPP). The first of these tariffs – TOU – involves charging households different rates during fixed time points on the weekdays and weekends. The second, CPP, charges a very high rate for electricity on a small number of short peak 'events', which are called up to 24 hours in advance in response to anticipated changes in supply or demand. In comparing these tariffs, my aim is to draw attention to the temporal dynamics of each and how they aim to temporarily disrupt or permanently shift everyday routines. Additionally, I consider a third demand management instrument – peak alerts – which embody the temporal dynamics of CPP, but without changing the price of electricity. This example illustrates the more radical proposition that price is not needed to achieve significant demand response. I conclude by considering what this means for the orchestration of demand and for those who are tasked with the job of attempting to intervene in temporary and temporally-dependent peaks.

Pricing the peaks: reinterpreting the signals

Most consumers, including many in developed nations, are still billed for their electricity using a flat multiplier – the cents/kWh – multiplied by the volumetric consumption for the period (Sioshansi, 2012). However, these 'flat tariffs' have proved problematic in countries where short bursts of electricity supply are needed to cope with increasing air conditioning, heating and other demand, particularly on very hot and cold days. In North America, these peaks typically occur during just 1% of hours, during which 9–17% of the annual peak demand is concentrated (Faruqui and Sergici, 2010). In Australia, which has experienced rapid growth in air conditioning demand over the last 50 years (DEWHA, 2008), around 15% of Australia's National Electricity Market capacity is only needed for four days of the year (Lohman, 2011). Aside from these critical peaks, hourly, daily, weekly and seasonal demand fluctuations are a regular feature of electricity systems, creating 'hot' and 'cold' spots of demand (Guy and Marvin, 1996).

From the electricity industry's perspective, peak demand creates both network and economic inefficiencies in the electricity system, whereby expensive infrastructure is built, but only used for a few days of the year to meet peaks in demand (Faruqui and Palmer, 2011). In Australia, around AU$11 billion investment in network equipment is needed to meet just 100 hours of electricity provision (Lohman, 2011). This means that billions of dollars of electricity assets sit idle for the majority of the year, a cost which is passed onto all electricity consumers through their bill. The goal, then, is to 'smooth' demand across as much of the network as possible and avoid situations where supply cannot meet these peaks. Alternatively, where demand cannot be smoothed, the aim is to ensure that consumers who use electricity during peak periods pay disproportionately more during these times, in order to cover the extra infrastructure and generation costs involved. Variable pricing is one of the key instruments by which this smoothing of demand, or more equitable distribution of costs, can be achieved (Faruqui, 2012).

Evidence from over 30 years of economic research demonstrates that substantial reductions in household electricity demand during peak times can be achieved through variable pricing (Faruqui and Sergici, 2010). However, there is significant and often unexplained variation in the demand response achieved through different tariffs. There have been several recent attempts in the social sciences to reconceptualise the relationship between variable pricing and household energy demand in order to explain these differences. In previous work, I argued that is the 'meanings' that prices convey and the way these intersect with everyday practices, which account for variation in tariff demand responses (Strengers, 2013). I suggested that prices can convey meanings of scarcity and abundance, which in turn reposition some practices as wasteful or normal during different pricing scenarios. In another study, I suggested that the notification of CPP events partly explained their success, associating a sense of urgency, importance or 'crisis' with these occasions (Strengers, 2010).

Another approach, pursued by scholars interested in the flexibility and temporality of routines through demand response has focused on how variable tariffs, particularly TOU pricing, disrupt or change everyday routines (Higginson, Thomson and Bhamra, 2013; Powells et al., 2014; Nicholls and Strengers, 2015b; Torriti et al., 2015; Anderson, 2016; McKenna et al., 2017; Curtis, Torriti and Smith, 2018). Here, the emphasis is on what makes some practices more flexible than others in response to TOU pricing (Powells et al., 2014; Higginson, Thomson and Bhamra, 2013) and how practices performed during the weekday peak 'hang together' at this particular time of the day (Nicholls and Strengers, 2015b). These studies have drawn on social practice theories to focus on the temporal rhythms of practices and how they constitute energy demand (Shove, Trentmann and Wilk, 2009; Southerton, 2009; Walker, 2014).

Viewed as an outcome of social practice, these studies frame peak demand as a product of the compression of multiple practices into a specific time period, such as during the afternoon and evening (Powells et al., 2014; Nicholls and Strengers, 2015b) or as the intensity of energy associated with a specific practice, like air conditioned cooling (Strengers, 2010). During a compressed period of time, practices consume electricity which *make* peak demand. What makes specific practices hang together at such moments to compress and/or intensify the consumption of electricity is rarely an outcome or expression of solely economic 'factors' as envisaged in mainstream market perspectives. For example, the daily morning or afternoon peak can be understood as the compression of practices into specific periods of the day, which are 'squeezed' by intuitionally timed events, such as school and work hours and the sequence of household dinner, bathing and other routines (Southerton, 2009; Higginson, Thomson and Bhamra, 2013; Nicholls and Strengers, 2015a).

While these and other studies reveal the temporal dynamics of different practices and the peaks they create, they have tended to downplay the temporalities of pricing schemes themselves. Taking forward these studies' conceptualisation of peak demand as the temporal compression or intensity of practices, variable pricing simultaneously mimics and deliberately attempts to disrupt these practice 'bundles' or 'complexes' (Shove, Pantzar and Watson, 2012) through more expensive tariffs. Variable tariffs are sequenced *with* the practices that create peak time and designed to dislodge those same practices, by moving them to 'off-peak' or 'shoulder' tariff times. I now explore these temporal dynamics through a discussion of two variable tariffs: time-of-use (TOU) and critical peak pricing (CPP).

Time-of-use tariffs: routine (dis)lodgement

A TOU tariff differentiates between off-peak, shoulder and peak periods. It is a routinised form of pricing, in which the daily breakdown of rates is known, predictable and rarely changes. These different breakdowns are synchronised with predictable peaks and troughs in daily demand, such as the early pre-work and pre-school rush and/or the afternoon/early evening post-school, post-work routines (Powells et al., 2014; Nicholls and Strengers, 2015b). Prices are lowest during the off-peak period and highest during the peak, reflecting the extra costs of supplying electricity during these times. In Australia, the daily peak typically occurs between 2–9 p.m. on weekdays (Nicholls and Strengers, 2015b) for a duration of approximately six hours. However, in other countries, like Italy (Torriti, 2012) and the UK (Powells et al., 2014), the peak tariff can also apply in the morning. Regardless of the precise timing, TOU tariffs are universally characterised by temporal regularity. They are designed to achieve ongoing and reliable load smoothing across the network, thereby ensuring the more efficient use of electricity assets. In this way, describing TOU as a 'dynamic' tariff is misleading. Indeed, it is this tariff's consistency and stability which defines it.

Internationally, TOU tariffs have been found to promote a drop in peak demand of 3–6% (Faruqui and Sergici, 2010). This is one of lowest rates of demand shifting achieved by variable tariffs, but is considered significant by many utility providers because it is dependable and reliable. Nonetheless, there is considerable lament within the industry about why TOU tariffs do not achieve more significant shifts in demand. Many claim it is the low price volatility which keeps the demand shifting modest. NERA Economic Consulting exemplify this view when they explain that demand response 'depend[s] on the proportion of electricity demand that is capable of being shifted between peak and off-peak periods *and the change in the price of peak and off-peak tariffs compared against original flat tariff* (NERA, 2008: 13; emphasis added). 'Capability' is the key term here, referring to consumer decisions and choices to shift energy demand to other times of the day, which is assumed to be a direct outcome of the change in price.

Evaluations of TOU commonly uphold these assumptions, featuring survey questions asking which 'discretionary' appliances are 'capable' of being shifted in response to the price signal, such as switching the timing of pool pumps or using the dishwashing in the evening rather than straight after a meal. In contrast, analyses of TOU pricing informed by theories of social practice explain how the effectiveness of TOU tariffs are dependent on the temporal rhythms of everyday practices such as 'doing the laundry' (Higginson, Thomson and Bhamra, 2013; Anderson, 2016), along with the dependence of some practices (such as cooking and eating dinner) on the availability of multiple household members (Powells et al., 2014) and the compression of multiple practices during peak periods (Nicholls and Strengers, 2015b). In other words, it is the routinised temporalities of practices, rather than individual choices and price, which determine opportunities for TOU demand shifting.

These dynamics are illustrated in a study of family household routines conducted with my colleague Larissa Nicholls (Nicholls and Strengers, 2015a). Here we found that family routines are compressed during the 'family peak period', which coincides with the usual timing of the Australian TOU peak tariff (e.g., 2–8 p.m. or 3–9 p.m. on weekdays). There was a clear sequence to the afternoon/evening peak in many of these households, which culminated around a period described as 'crazy time', 'feral o'clock', 'arsenic hour' or 'hectic, stressful, chaotic, exhausting, frantic, tiring and rushed' (Nicholls and Strengers, 2015a: 20). Crazy time was commonly linked to children's dinnertime, before, during and after which meal preparation, bathing, homework, clean-up and bed time were coordinated. The family peak period is thus a 'time squeeze' (Southerton, 2003) or a 'compression of practices' (Shove, 2009) into a tight sequence coordinated around institutionally-timed events, such as school and work times. In family households, this 'squeeze' refers to the synchronisation of parents' activities with 'kid rhythms', such as children's tiredness and hunger common around dinnertime. The family peak is further squeezed by many parents' desire to reach a period of 'downtime' after children go to bed (Nicholls and Strengers, 2015a).

The implications of the family peak period for demand shifting are that many routines are unable to be regularly or permanently moved, as is the intention of TOU pricing. While some family households in our study had shifted some activities, like running the dishwasher, to other times of the day due to a TOU tariff, others indicated why this would be difficult, noting that additional household members (e.g., children) needed to be awake to pack/ unpack it at certain times or noting that dishwashing noise would disrupt children's sleeping if run later at night. Regularly or permanently changing these routines was not dependent on price, but on the availability of household members, children's needs (for food and sleep) and desires to create shared familial experiences during dinnertime and generate downtime at the end of the day (Nicholls and Strengers, 2015a). These dynamics serve to limit the potential demand response of TOU pricing, in contrast to the considerable demand response achieved through CPP.

Critical peak pricing: occasional disruption

While TOU tariffs are tied to average peaks and troughs in daily demand, they do not reflect the high price associated with providing electricity during the critical or network peaks (top 1% of hours), when many electricity systems struggle to provide enough supply to meet demand. CPP, also known as dynamic peak pricing or interruptible electricity rates, aims to reflect the additional costs of providing electricity during these network peaks. Contrary to the regularity of TOU, the high CPP rate is only applied on a limited number of irregular peak demand days which normally coincide with very hot or cold weather. In most versions of this tariff, somewhere between 12–20 CPP 'events' are called throughout the year with a duration of two to five hours, during which time the price of electricity rises significantly (10–40 times the off-peak rate (Herter, 2007; Strengers, 2010)). These exceptionally high rates are generally offset by lower rates at other times. Consumers are usually notified of these critical peaks via a range multiple communication channels (SMS, email, automated phone message, in-home display) approximately one day in advance. A variation of CPP is the critical peak rebate (CPR), also known as the peak time rebate or a dynamic peak rebate, which financially *rewards* customers for reducing electricity during these critical peaks with a rebate or incentive on their bill (Faruqui, Hledik and Tsoukalis, 2009). CPR schemes are becoming a particularly popular demand management technique in Australia due to affordability concerns associated with rising energy prices.

The duration (two to five hours) and notification (usually 24 hours advance warning) of critical peak events is mostly predictable, as is the frequency of events in any given year (e.g., maximum of 20). While the exact timing of these events is unpredictable, more occur during the height of summer or winter, depending on climate and the region's peak demand profile. CPP therefore balances the predictable with the unpredictable. Unlike the completely unplanned nature of a blackout, CPP aims to generate a form of 'normal disruption' (Trentmann, 2009) which allows for some degree of planning and foresight alongside unplanned infrastructural and climatic variations which contribute to network peaks. Compared with the relatively modest demand reductions associated with TOU tariffs, CPP trials demonstrate substantial and sustained reductions in household electricity demand during events – between 13–20% or much more (27–44%) when combined with energy feedback and enabling technologies such as smart thermostats (Faruqui and Sergici, 2010). In keeping with economic theory, the higher demand response compared to TOU is generally thought to be a product of the higher peak price generating greater demand 'elasticity'. However, information-only trials of CPP, which are characterised by the *absence* of a higher or changed tariff, suggest this is not the whole story. These trials mimic the temporal dynamics of CPP by calling peak events and notifying households when these will occur, but they do not raise the price of electricity. In one Australian trial of CPP, the information-only group reduced their peak consumption by an average of 13% in the summer and 11% overall (Strengers, 2010). This was much higher than the demand response achieved through TOU pricing in the same trial, but still substantially lower than the CPP response.

Focusing on the temporalities of CPP helps explain these differences. If we conceptualise CPP as a temporary disruption of 'normal' electricity service (Strengers, 2013), we can draw comparisons to the temporary blackouts, breakdowns or restrictions that have long been part of the electricity system (Trentmann, 2009). Importantly, blackouts and breakdowns are not always considered disasters. As historians Nye (2010) and Trentmann (2009) have argued, blackouts can engender outpourings of connectedness and 'mirth-making', as well as disorder, chaos and degeneration. Likewise, considerable research demonstrates that CPP is not normally negatively experienced. Despite Faruqui and Palmer (2011: 17) warning that 'a negative mythology has taken root' which has 'prevented dynamic pricing from germinating', they find that most residential customers (over 90%) who have experienced some form of CPP would participate in dynamic pricing trials again and are generally satisfied on this tariff.

There are several key distinctions between blackouts and CPP that help explain this high satisfaction. First, while irregular, CPP is characterised by a degree of predictability, while blackouts are often not. Most households on CPP trials are aware that extremely hot or cold days are likely to result in a CPP event and they are also normally given up to 24 hours notice if one is to occur (Strengers, 2010). Notification of an impending CPP event is thus another central feature of CPP, giving households time to plan and prepare for the disruption. A third feature is the temporary nature of a CPP event, which, unlike a blackout, is not always conceptualised as a 'failure'. Like other temporary measures of 'saving electricity in a hurry' (IEA, 2005), CPP does not fundamentally challenge the dominant ethos of meeting, growing and expanding consumer 'needs', but it does place those needs in a negotiable and contestable space for a short period of time. In this sense, CPP does not seek to overturn the dominant 'build and supply' ethos underpinning the electricity sector, nor does it signal a 'failure' of those services. CPP's temporary and planned nature ensures that the system can 'bounce back' to this status quo. Viewed this way, CPP creates 'ordered disorder', or an exceptional circumstance during which time electricity infrastructures are repositioned as scarce, restricted or *temporarily* unavailable (Strengers, 2013).

Reflecting these observations, some evaluations of CPP trials demonstrate that householders treat a CPP event as a self-imposed blackout. For example, the PowerCentsDC™ Program in the District of Columbia, US, found that 28% of households turned off nearly all of their electricity-consuming appliances during a CPP event (eMeter, 2010: 67). This is consistent with other trials, which find that householders report turning off a large number and range of appliances during CPP events, such as hot water systems, lights, air conditioners, heating, fridge/freezers, TVs, DVD players, stereos, the oven/hob, washing machines, clothes dryers and dishwasher (Strengers, 2013). One way of understanding this blackout-like response is to think of CPP as transforming a 'hot spot' of consumption into a 'cold spot', where the normal harriedness of everyday life calms down and practices are temporally suspended in favour of 'family time' or 'quality time' (Southerton, 2003). In support of this idea, some households report using a CPP event as an opportunity to take the family out for dinner, light some candles, 'have a bit of fun' or play games (Strengers, 2013). Resonating with the social intimacy experienced during New York's 1965 blackouts (Nye, 2010), disruptions like CPP can create an opportunity to slow down and reconnect.

However, unlike TOU peak periods, which most commonly occur at the busiest time of the day, the normal intensity of energy demand during a critical peak does not necessarily reflect or map on to the normal rhythms of regularly occurring practices. While critical peaks represent hot spots of electricity demand, extreme heat (and cold) often restricts activity and slows the body down. In this way, CPP heightens the climate-related disruption to household routines which are normally experienced on a very hot day. For example, self-imposed household-level blackouts reported in some CPP trials can be understood as householders leaving the home to visit friends, swim at the pool or watch a movie at an air conditioned cinema – activities which many Australian households routinely participate in to manage the heat on extremely hot days (Strengers, 2010; Nicholls and Strengers, 2015a).

This interpretation helps explain another cost-benefit contradiction common in CPP trials: namely that demand response commonly *increases* when the temperature becomes more extreme. In neoclassical economics, this response is viewed as irrational, the assumption being that the benefit of air conditioning on a hot day will increasingly outweigh the cost of providing it as the temperature rises (Strengers, 2010). However, in many instances, the opposite occurs. Trials indicate that the demand response (cutting down on electricity consumption) increases with higher temperatures and air conditioning penetration, because householders simply turn this appliance off (Faruqui, Hledik and Tsoukalis, 2009; Strengers, 2010). Contrary to popular industry opinion, CPP has been shown to sustain these reductions in peak usage over time and during prolonged peaky periods (such as a heatwave) (Faruqui and Palmer, 2011). Furthermore, research by the Brattle Group in the US cites trials where customers not only maintain their response to CPP, but increase it over several years, leading to further reductions in peak usage (Faruqui and Palmer, 2011: 20).

Put another way, on the hottest days of the year, which are arguably when people are most likely to want to use air conditioning, householders are more likely to turn their thermostat up, adopt alternative cooling strategies or turn their air conditioner off (if there is a meaningful reason to do so). This is similar to the response recorded during the 2001 Californian electricity crisis, when the air conditioner was already firmly entrenched in US households' practices of cooling. An evaluation of the crisis revealed that 40% of surveyed households either turned their air conditioner off or used it more sparingly during this time (Lutzenhiser, Gossard and Bender, 2002: 8.158). In contrast, raising the thermostat was only reported by about 4% of households, despite this action being promoted through pro-conservation advertising. Instead, Lutzenhiser, Gossard and Bender (2002: 8.164) found that households opted for 'alternative cooling' or 'rethought' cooling in response to a range of conservation programmes initiated to alleviate the crisis. They point out that these changes constitute 'actions that conventional energy policy wisdom would expect consumers to be quite unwilling to even consider on the grounds of comfort and convenience' (Lutzenhiser, Gossard and Bender, 2002: 8.164).

These findings demonstrate the close coupling of disruptions in infrastructure arrangements and seasonal weather events and the routines and strategies householders *already* have for dealing with these (Strengers and Maller, 2017). But it still does not explain *why* householders respond to CPP and how important price is in this equation. To answer these questions, we conducted an experiment to consider what might happen if we removed price and focused on generating a temporary disruption to peak electricity demand.

Variable pricing without price: critical peak alerts

In our family energy study (discussed earlier), we set out to investigate the significance of nonfinancial 'peak alerts' by presenting householders with a hypothetical scenario where they were asked whether they would consider cutting back their electricity use for a few hours during a critical peak period (the example given was in relation to a hot summer day) without any financial incentive or disincentive (Strengers and Nicholls, 2013; Nicholls and Strengers; 2013, 2015a). We tested the peak alert idea in a national survey responded to by 547 family households (Nicholls and Strengers, 2015a). The peak alert scenario was posed as follows:

> The weather is forecast to be very hot (over 35°C) tomorrow and there may be a shortage of electricity. Everyone is asked to reduce their electricity use where possible between 2 p.m. and 9 p.m. on this hot day. This might happen a few times each year ... Would you try to reduce home electricity use between 2 p.m. and 9 p.m. on those occasions?

In response, 85% of all respondents answered 'yes' to this survey question. The response was high regardless of gender, household type, income status, work status or climate (Nicholls and Strengers, 2015a).

Importantly, the survey asked why householders were interested in responding to a peak alert scenario. Few householders indicated they would respond because 'it would be easy' (12%), contradicting common energy-saving rhetoric which cites 'easy actions' as the most promising way to change behaviour (Loux, 2008) and also contradicting TOU evaluations which commonly find that only 'discretionary' appliances that can be easily shifted will constitute the demand response (NERA, 2007).

The most popular reasons selected for wanting to respond to a peak alert were 'to help prevent electricity outage (blackout)' (64%), 'to be part of a community effort' (59%) and 'to reduce stress on the electricity grid' (52%). Additionally, 37% of respondents selected 'to help other people or places that need the electricity more than us'. These responses indicate social or community interest in (and shared responsibility for) the electricity system, which runs counter to current market-based propositions that position householders as 'consumers' or 'customers' of energy as a market commodity. In other words, these findings challenge the dominant assumption that householders' primary (and only) relationship to energy is an economic transaction, in which the cost of electricity is the key variable. Instead, electricity is viewed here as a social asset (providing important health benefits) and a *temporarily* limited infrastructure.

Resonating with CPP findings discussed above, the possibility of *occasional* weather-related disruptions to the electricity system was not always viewed negatively by households. Fifteen per cent stated that they would respond to a peak alert because 'it would be fun or educational for my child(ren)'. Thus, peak alerts were an opportunity to generate 'slow time' for some. Over a third of households (35%) said they would respond to a peak alert simply because they were asked.

Survey findings about what these householders said they would do or change in response to a peak alert are also revealing of the dynamics at play. Interestingly, activities that most households considered unsuitable to change on a regular basis for the financial incentive offered by a TOU tariff were much more flexible on an occasional basis under a peak alert scenario. For example, 48% of respondents with air conditioners thought they could change their use of the air conditioner to reduce energy use for a peak alert compared with 13% on a TOU tariff. Again reflecting the peak alert's (and CPP's) synchronisation with normal, weather-dependent disruptions, 40% of respondents considered leaving the home for a few hours in the peak alert scenario (Nicholls and Strengers, 2015a). Normally, this heightened interest in demand response would be explained by the variation in price, but here, that variable is removed. Instead, what is varying under a peak alert scenario is the timing of occasional 'events' and their synchronisation with the changing weather. This in turn repositions the meaning of the signals themselves: they are no longer framed as economic transactions and trade-offs (cost versus comfort). Instead, peak alerts appear to convey or engender a sense of social responsibility towards the electricity system and a shared obligation to ensure everyone has adequate access to electricity in exceptional circumstances (such as extreme heat).

While these results are hypothetical, unrepresentative and unlikely to fully reflect actual demand shifting, they do highlight a currently under-explored demand management opportunity. If nothing else, it is clear that the variable pricing demand response involves much more than setting the right price. In focusing on the *variability* of pricing schemes themselves, and their synchronisation with the compression or intensity of practices which constitute peaks, this analysis provides a reinterpretation of pricing signals which points to opportunities for alternative demand management strategies.

Reinterpreting the signals

This chapter has sought to uncover the different temporalities of several variable tariffs which underpin many residential demand management programmes and which are advocated as part of national energy policies. TOU tariffs, characterised by their predictability and stability, aim to permanently move routines normally conducted during the peak tariff period into off-peak and shoulder tariff times. Conversely, CPP aims to occasionally and irregularly disrupt household routines, mimicking and often coinciding with normal everyday disruptions, such as extreme weather events.

While price is clearly not irrelevant, this chapter demonstrates that adopting a traditional economic perspective on variable pricing may be counterproductive to demand management objectives. In focusing on financially motivating consumers to regularly shift their energy demand, TOU achieves modest demand shifting. In contrast, peak alerts and information-only CPP trials unintentionally reposition the problem of peak demand as a community, health and/or national issue, similar to the ways in which blackouts, droughts and natural disasters are often approached: that is, with a focus on community concern and 'common good', rather than an individualistic assessment of 'what's in it for me'. Viewed from this perspective, price is repositioned as *enhancing* the urgency and importance of the temporary disruption generated by CPP and by extension, the demand response, by further reinforcing electricity's scarcity during short periods of high demand or limited supply.

In reinterpreting price signals with reference to patterns of temporal stability or disruption, there is scope to consider a range of other demand management instruments. One possibility involves designing strategies which are deliberately designed to generate an exceptional circumstance, such as the peak alert scenario described above. Similarly, demand managers could consider a range of other techniques for generating occasional periods of exception, during which routines are likely to be dislodged and shifted. There are many international examples the electricity sector could turn to for inspiration in this regard, such as water restrictions, health campaigns, bushfire warning systems and temporary energy crises, which have all generated and/or sought to respond to exceptional situations.

A second complementary approach is to incentivise or enable those practices *already* performed during seasonal disruptions which help to reduce residential peak demand. For example, in Australia, very hot days are already experienced as an exceptional circumstance involving various practices designed to 'beat the heat'. Demand management strategies in this situation might involve providing better and free access to cool spaces during critical peak demand days, such as extending library and pool opening hours, providing ways for people to spend time in shopping centres without needing to spend money, or providing free or discounted movie tickets during peak times (Nicholls and Strengers, 2015a).

Importantly, these strategies are not all nonfinancial or uneconomic – providing households with free movie tickets still involves an economic transaction. The distinction is one of scale. Whereas prices appeal to individual consumers and their electricity consumption, free movie tickets appeal to different ways of spending time. The cost-benefit equation is no longer about how to save money – it is about how to make, shift and take time for different activities in ways that support peak demand reduction.

At first sight, the idea that demand managers might deliberately attempt to orchestrate periods of disruption in a system commonly perceived as being unlimited and capable of producing power indefinitely is challenging. But in many instances, this is what demand managers *already* do, through CPP, planned rolling blackouts or brownouts, and other temporary disruptions. What is novel here is the suggestion that these strategies can be understood and potentially pursued as means of 'generating' exceptional circumstances, by incentivising different ways of spending time that already make sense to householders. Such opportunities are ripe for investigation and experimentation in demand management research led by the social sciences.

References

Anderson, B. (2016) 'Laundry, energy and time: insights from 20 years of time-use diary data in the United Kingdom', *Energy Research & Social Science*, 22: 125–136.

Blake, J. (1999) 'Overcoming the "value-action gap" in environmental policy: tensions between national policy and local experience', *Local Environment*, 43: 257–278.

CSIRO. (2013) 'Change and choice: the future grid forum's analysis of Australia's potential electricity pathways to 2050'. Newcastle: CSIRO.

Curtis, M., Torriti, J. and Smith, S. T. (2018) 'Demand side flexibility and responsiveness: moving demand in time through technology', in Hui, A., Day, R. and Walker, G. (eds.) *Demanding Energy: space, time and change*. Cham: Springer International Publishing, pp. 283–312.

DEWHA. (2008) 'Energy use in the Australian residential sector 1986–2020'. Canberra, Australia: Australian Government: Department of the Environment, Water, Heritage and the Arts (DEWHA).

eMeter. (2010) 'PowerCentsDC™' program final report'. Foster City, California: eMeter Strategic Consulting for the Smart Meter Pilot Program, Inc.

Faruqui, A. (2012) 'The ethics of dynamic pricing', in Sioshansi, F. P. (ed.) *Smart Grid*. Boston: Academic Press, pp. 61–83.

Faruqui, A. and George, S. (2005) 'Quantifying customer response to dynamic pricing', *The Electricity Journal*, 18: 53–63.

Faruqui, A., Hledik, R. and Tsoukalis, J. (2009) 'The power of dynamic pricing', *The Electricity Journal*, 22: 42–56.

Faruqui. A. and Palmer, J. (2011) 'Dynamic pricing and its discontents', *Regulation*, 16.

Faruqui, A. and Sergici, S. (2010) 'Household response to dynamic pricing of electricity: a survey of 15 experiments', *Journal of Regulatory Economics*, 38: 193–225.

Guy, S. and Marvin, S. (1996) 'Transforming urban infrastructure provision – the emerging logic of demand side management', *Policy Studies*, 17: 137–147.

Healy, S. and MacGill, I. (2012) 'From smart grid to smart energy use', in Sioshansi, F. P. (ed.) *Smart Grid*. Boston: Academic Press. pp. 29–59.

Herter, K. (2007) 'Residential implementation of critical-peak pricing of electricity', *Energy Policy*, 35: 2121–2130.

Higginson, S,. Thomson, M. and Bhamra, T. (2013) '"For the times they are a-changin": the impact of shifting energy-use practices in time and space', *Local Environment*, 19: 520–538.

IEA. (2005) 'Saving electricity in a hurry: Dealing with temporary shortfalls in electricity supplies'. Paris: Organisation for Economic Cooperation and Development (OECD) and International Energy Agency (IEA).

Lohman, T. (2011) 'Ausgrid spruiks smart grid consumer tools'. *Computerworld*. https://www.computer-world.com.au/article/410340/ausgrid_spruiks_smart_grid_consumer_tools/ (accessed 15 December).

Loux, R. (2008) *Easy Green Living: the ultimate guide to simple, eco-friendly choices for you and your home.* New York: Rodale Inc.

Lutzenhiser, L., Gossard, M. and Bender, S. (2002) 'Crisis in paradise: understanding the household conservation response to California's 2001 energy crisis'. *Proceedings of the 2002 ACEEE Summer Study*. Washington: American Council for an Energy-Efficient Economy.

McKenna, E., Higginson, S., Grunewald, P. and Darby, S. (2017) 'Simulating residential demand response: improving socio-technical assumptions in activity-based models of energy demand', *Energy Efficiency*. https://doi.org/10.1007/s12053-017-9525-4

NERA. (2007) 'Cost benefit analysis of smart metering and direct load control. Work stream 4: consumer impacts. Phase 1 report' Sydney, Australia: NERA Economic Consulting for the Ministerial Council on Energy Smart Meter Working Group.

NERA. (2008) 'Cost benefit analysis of smart metering and direct load control. Work stream 4: consumer impacts. Phase 2 consultation report'. Sydney: NERA Economic Consulting, prepared for the Ministerial Council on Energy Smart Meter Working Group.

Nicholls, L. and Strengers, Y. (2013) 'Co-managing home energy demand. Stage 4: endeavour energy peaksaver and coolsaver program research'. Melbourne: RMIT University for TransGrid.

Nicholls, L., and Strengers, Y. (2015a) 'Changing demand: flexibility of energy practices in households with children. Final report'. Melbourne: Centre for Urban Research, RMIT University for Consumer Advocacy Panel.

Nicholls, L., and Strengers, Y. (2015b) 'Peak demand and the 'family peak' period in Australia: understanding practice (in)flexibility in households with children', *Energy Research & Social Science*, 9: 116–124.

Nye, D. E. (2010) *When the Lights Went Out: a history of blackouts in America*, Cambridge, MA: The MIT Press.

Pasquier, S. (2011) *Saving Electricity in a Hurry: update 2011*. Paris: International Energy Agency.

Powells, G., Bulkeley, H., Bell, S. and Judson, E. (2014) 'Peak electricity demand and the flexibility of everyday life', *Geoforum*, 55: 43–52.

Shove, E. (2009) 'Everyday practice and the production and consumption of time', in Shove, E., Trentmann, F. and Wilk, R. (eds.) *Time, Consumption and Everyday Life: practice, materiality and culture.* Oxford: Berg. pp. 17–33.

Shove, E., Pantzar, M. and Watson, M. (2012) *The Dynamics of Social Practice: everyday life and how it changes.* London: SAGE.

Shove, E., Trentmann, F. and Wilk, R. (2009) 'Introduction', in, Shove, E., Trentmann, F. and Wilk, R. (eds.) *Time, Consumption and Everyday Life: practice, materiality and culture.* Oxford: Berg. pp. 1–16.

Sioshansi, F. P. (2012) 'Introduction', in Sioshansi, F. P. (ed.) *Smart Grid.* Boston: Academic Press. pp. xxix–lvi.

Southerton, D. (2003) '"Squeezing time": allocating practices, coordinating networks and scheduling society', *Time & Society*, 12: 5–25.

Southerton, D. (2009) 'Re-ordering temporal rhythms: coordinating daily practices in the UK in 1937 and 2000', in Shove, E., Trentmann, F. and Wilk, R. R. (eds.) *Time, Consumption and Everyday Life: practice, materiality and culture.* Oxford: Berg. pp. 49–63.

Stern, P. (1986) 'Blind spots in policy analysis: what economics doesn't say about energy use', *Journal of Policy Analysis and Management*, 5: 200–227.

Strengers, Y. (2010) 'Air-conditioning Australian households: a trial of dynamic peak pricing'. *Energy Policy*, 38: 7312–7322.

Strengers, Y. (2013) *Smart Energy Technologies in Everyday Life: Smart Utopia?* London: Palgrave MacMillan.

Strengers, Y. and Maller, C. (2017) 'Adapting to "extreme" weather: mobile practice memories of keeping warm and cool as a climate change adaptation strategy', *Environment and Planning A*, 49: 1432–1450.

Strengers, Y. and Nicholls, L. (2013) *Co-managing Home Energy Demand. Final report.* Melbourne: RMIT University for TransGrid.

Thaler, R. H., and Sunstein, C. T. (2008) *Nudge: improving decisions about health, wealth, and happiness.* New Haven: Yale University Press.

Torriti, J. (2012) 'Price-based demand side management: assessing the impacts of time-of-use tariffs on residential electricity demand and peak shifting in Northern Italy', *Energy*, 44: 576–583.

Torriti, J., Hanna, R., Anderson, B., Yeboah, G. and Druckman, A. (2015) 'Peak residential electricity demand and social practices: deriving flexibility and greenhouse gas intensities from time use and locational data', *Indoor and Built Environment*, 24: 891–912.

Trentmann, F. (2009) 'Disruption is normal: blackouts, breakdowns and the elasticity of everyday life', in Shove, E., Trentmann, F. and Wilk, R. (eds.) *Time, Consumption and Everyday Life: practice, materiality and culture.* Oxford: Berg. pp. 67–84.

Walker, G. (2014) 'The dynamics of energy demand: change, rhythm and synchronicity', *Energy Research & Social Science*, 1: 49–55.

16

DISRUPTION IN AND ACROSS TIME

Heather Chappells and Frank Trentmann

Introduction

Disruptions reveal the hidden dynamics of everyday life, but what and how much they reveal depends on conceptual focus and analytical scale (Bennett, 2005). From one perspective, disruption can appear as a discrete and extreme event, a sudden break in time, normality and equilibrium. Power outages that last for several days, weeks or even months fit this 'punctuated' profile. From another point of view, however, disorder and order may seem to fuse into one another. Cyclical and seasonal water scarcities that modulate everyday life in California, for example, fit this second perspective. Although droughts may have intensified, people have become acclimatised to severe conditions: dryness has become 'normal' (Pincetl and Hogue, 2015). As the sociologist Hendrik Vollmer notes, it may be more appropriate to think in terms of a 'continuum of disruptiveness', ranging from ordinary troubles to full-scale breakdowns (Vollmer, 2013).

How disruption is perceived has profound socio-political and material consequences, for it shapes how resilience is understood and how responsibilities are assigned between providers and users. Disruption can be viewed as a temporary intrusion into normal life to be mitigated and overcome as quickly as possible. Alternatively, it can be treated, even welcomed, as part of a continuous reordering of daily life. The former approach is exemplified by policy responses that look to flexible consumers to cope with 'crises', such as the International Energy Agency (IEA) report *Saving Electricity in a Hurry*, (IEA, 2005). Yet an emphasis on collapse and crisis obscures the more prosaic efforts of repair and maintenance that keep networks operating as normal (Graham and Thrift, 2007).

Viewing disruption as part of a continuing story rather than an exceptional occurrence requires a more historical approach. During the twentieth century people in the developed North came to rely increasingly on externally provided resources and centralised modern infrastructures. In Canada, for example, a mere 765,000 residential and farm customers were connected to electricity networks in 1920. By 1975, that number that had risen to seven million, and by 2007 to 13.7 million (Statistics Canada, 2007). However, it would be misleading to deduce from such aggregate connection figures that disruption has disappeared in the rich North. The very interconnectivity of current networks has arguably made urban industrialised societies more vulnerable (Lovins and Lovins, 2001; Taylor and Trentmann, 2011). While interconnected grids may be more efficient when working, when they go wrong, they go completely wrong. The United States saw a tenfold increase in major power outages (those affecting more than 50,000 customer homes or businesses) between the mid-1980s and 2012. The cascading power failure in North America in 2003 affected an estimated 50 million people (NERC, 2004; Kenward and Raja, 2014). And grids vary significantly between and within countries. The average American electricity consumer has to cope with 30 times as many service interruptions each year as their Japanese counterpart (CRO Forum, 2011). In British Columbia, rural residents living in the most remote regions go without power for an average of 20–30 hours a year, whereas those living in cities such as Vancouver lose only one (Skelton, 2015).

This chapter explores contrasting understandings of disruption over time in energy and water systems. Disruptions give us short, momentary glimpses of the fabric of 'normality' as it is fraying and reveal the patterns in which practices and infrastructures are woven together. Rather than being isolated instances, disruptions over time shape expectations of a 'normal life'.

Our historical analysis follows disruption in four directions: (1) what people actually did in times of disruption, (2) how what they do is shaped by particular socio-technical regimes, (3) how disruption and normality intersect *across time* and what legacy this leaves for future reactions and (4) the impact of networks on resilience and responsiveness.

Disruption in time

We begin with a specific case *in* time – the 2006 drought in southeast England – drawing on interviews with households that lived through it (Medd and Chappells, 2008). This drought was a consequence of two successive winters of below average rainfall. The eight water companies serving the region introduced water use restrictions for their customers. Domestic water users were the primary targets – 15.6 million people were restricted in their use of hosepipes, roughly one quarter of the British population (Environment Agency, 2006). Water companies viewed many outdoor water uses as 'non-essential' and thus beyond their statutory duties of supply. What people actually did in the drought, however, and how they experienced and coped with disruption reflected many different interpretations of 'normal' use. Many of those interviewed claimed already to be sensible about their water usage and to see little scope for cutting back. As one middle-aged, householder put it: 'we do everything we need to do but we don't do it with excess, and I think that's reasonable' (Interview Mr A, 24.08.2006).

People assessed the 2006 drought against background knowledge of previous shortages, especially the record-breaking drought of 1976. A middle-aged father recalled this excruciatingly hot summer of his childhood and believed that citizens had been asked to do more to reduce consumption back then. Several householders remembered having put a brick in the toilet cistern. As no such measures were discussed in 2006, many concluded that the current water problems were less severe. Collective memories of 1976 framed the 2006 drought, but so did personal memories of other disruptions. One middle-aged businessman, for example, recalled an overseas trip where he had been three days without running water, having to rely on seawater and bottled water to wash. The real hardship he found was facing the 'ghastly' reality of not having water to flush the toilet. It was a sharp reminder of the essential importance of water, so easily taken for granted at home.

In 2006, water use restrictions did prompt changes in daily practices, but to become permanent, a favourable mix of practical knowledge and technologies within a household was required. For some gardeners, watering cans were a purely temporary arrangement needed to see them through until the rains predictably returned. Several other households had kept rainwater tanks in the garden for years, but developed additional routines as the drought intensified. A retired older couple, for example, added containers to collect more water. The couple had a sense of an impending regional water shortage due to a perceived rise in the local population, a long-standing ethic of conservation and caring for plants, a particular configuration of plumbing that made it easy to collect water directly from the drain outlet and the right combination of practical skills and outdoor space, meaning that containers could be located in a convenient spot for garden watering. These favourable preconditions were reinforced by social networks and learning. The couple was impressed by a younger neighbour's recycling efforts and they had also followed a friend's advice concerning chemical-free dishwashing and laundry detergents that would not harm plants. Though this is only one household, we get a clear sense of the social, cultural, spatial and infrastructural factors that came together in shaping water use. These considerations included inherited values (past), current challenges (present) and an anticipation of water and population stress (future).

For gardeners who had previously learnt to live with dry, sandy soils or other natural challenges, the drought did not entail a sharp break in normal practices, but instead formed part of a continuation of trial and error with limited watering. Such acquired knowledge also reinforced people's preparedness to consider long-term changes such as abandoning watering plants altogether. A less dramatic response was to rearrange seasonal activities, for instance, by switching patio pressure washing from summer to winter or spring.

How people respond to disruption depends on the circumstances before, as well as after, a disruptive event hits. In their specific adaptations, people drew on established skills and knowledge, including their experience of what is 'normal' and what works. Such individual and collective pre-framings of normality constitute an important backstory to any disruption.

Macro structuring of disruption at different points in time

That people's responses are context specific does not mean that they are driven entirely by the social and cultural dynamics of the household itself. Beyond the household, the experience of disruption is shaped by politics that affect the substitutability of a scarce resource, infrastructural development and the collective dynamics of supply and demand. These structural conditions vary from one location to the next and under different politico-economic regimes. In some situations, water scarcities, energy crises and climate change have been used to promote certain scientific and political agendas (Bakker, 2000; Mehta, 2010). The 1995 drought in Britain was the product of meteorological modelling, demand forecasting, corporate restructuring and deregulation under a neoliberal regime (Bakker, 2000).

As well as shaping the extent and type of shortage, the political context also affects users' sense of responsibility and blame. In England in 2006, leakage was often treated as symptomatic of negligent profit-focused privatised companies and contrasted with a public ethos of conservation in 1976, when water was still nationalised (Taylor et al., 2008).

Droughts across the twentieth century provide an opportunity to follow the impact of different politico-economic regimes on institutional ideas about the rights of water users and the relative roles of consumers and providers in overcoming shortage. In England

and Wales, water provision evolved first from locally fragmented to mixed public-private arrangements in the mid twentieth century, then to national centralisation coordinated through regional water authorities in the 1970s, and finally, since the late 1980s, to privatisation overseen by a national regulator (Taylor et al., 2008). These regimes placed radically different expectations on consumers and providers. In the early twentieth century, water companies had a statutory duty to provide constant domestic supply, but this did not apply in times of unusual drought when private users were called upon to reduce consumption. In the 1990s, by contrast, the need for restrictions was publicly questioned since supply had become the responsibility of private water companies and was regarded as a customer service that should maintained.

The drought in West Yorkshire in 1995 was consequently as much a crisis of governance as of physical scarcity. While hosepipe bans, rota cuts and standpipes all played a part in drought alleviation, the unresponsiveness of many consumers was taken by some water companies as evidence that restrictions no longer had much effect in what had become a customer service based business geared towards giving consumers what they wanted (Bakker, 2003). Many people were unprepared to see their water supply cut to help what were, after all, profit-making companies. Some metered customers argued that, since they paid for it, they would continue to use as much water as they liked. Ultimately, water companies were compelled to deliver water by tankers to villages at huge expense.

By the time of the 2006 drought, there was greater concern for 'the environment' and for the preservation of rivers and habitats. Abstracting more water for public supply was no longer considered a legitimate response, as it had been in 1976 when dramatic engineering interventions saw every last drop squeezed out of reservoirs (Andrew, 1976). Emphasis shifted instead to strategic long-term thinking and a shared responsibility for water stress. The government adopted a more proactive, precautionary approach and water companies focused on the need for careful water use, trying to instil in their customers a sense that drought was a 'normal' expectation when living in a relatively dry climate (DEFRA, 2006).

Connections between disruptions across time

If we see disruptions not as stand-alone moments but structured by regimes and experiences before and after moments of crisis, we can ask next what is carried over from one disruption to another and what is lost. How are infrastructures or persistent cultural scripts implicated in responses to recurrent disruptions? What role do political regimes play in sustaining or changing expectations and practices? In exploring these questions, we turn from water to coal and examine features of disruption and normality that recurred over several generations in the first half of the twentieth century.

Coal shortages were a frequent occurrence in Canada during the early twentieth century, but were largely localised. It was the two World Wars that propelled coal to the centre of national political debate. Coal was the dominant fuel in Canada in 1917. It was used to power railways and factories and heat homes. By mid-1917, national coal shortages had escalated to a point where the Federal Government was forced to appoint a fuel controller, who ordered an increase in coal mining to ensure that the people of Canada got all the coal they needed (House of Commons, 1917a). Reality proved tougher: coal shortages continued into the harsh winter of 1917–1918 causing significant disruption to everyday life that culminated with the introduction of heatless Mondays (Blake, 2011).

Disruption to daily life during the winter of 1917–1918 did not come without prior warning. In June 1917, the fuel controller had already beseeched patriotic citizens to keep house temperatures down to prevent coal shortages in the coming winter (Keshen, 1996). Householders were advised to build bigger storehouses to stockpile coal. While a few large industries responded to calls to conserve fuel, relatively few local coal dealers or their customers did. Domestic and commercial users were reluctant to tie up money stockpiling when there was not yet any actual shortage of supply. Coalfields in the United States, upon which some provinces heavily relied, had reportedly increased their output (House of Commons, 1917b).

The main problem in 1917 was one of distribution: insufficient transportation capacity to deliver coal to where it was needed the most. The situation was exacerbated by competing demands from railroad operators, firms and households as well as from war-related industries in the United States. Why did Canada not manage to overcome the fuel shortage by tapping into its own considerable coal reserves? The answer partly lay in the spatial nature of the challenge. Canada's coal shortage was an outcome of multiple local and regional problems that were exacerbated by a priority system for meeting demands from different groups of consumers. Quebec, for example, usually relied on the delivery of two million tons of bituminous coal from Nova Scotia to see it through the winter, but in 1917–1918 the bulk of the prospective mine output was targeted instead for local needs and railways. Mines in Pennsylvania were expected to fill some of this gap, but the cumulative pressures of coal demands from Ontario and increased wartime needs within the United States meant that this could not be guaranteed. In the Western Prairie provinces, meanwhile, supply was precarious because of labour strikes in Alberta.

The wartime coal shortages had all the ingredients of a perfect storm. In addition to natural factors, such as heavy snow and ice blocking roads and railroads, there were political, social and infrastructural pressures. One member of parliament openly blamed the government's laissez-faire policy: if the mines in the Maritime provinces and prairies had been kept running during the summer, then there would have been more coal for the winter. But clearly, the problem was one of demand as well as supply. Households and coal merchants had failed to plan ahead and store sufficient coal when it had been available. What proved decisive in turning a fuel shortage into a full-blown disruption to everyday life, however, was householders' almost complete reliance on coal in certain areas, such as the prairies. The ability to cope was weakest where the lack of alternative fuels was greatest.

By December 1917, coal production and internal demand in the United States had worsened to the point that Canada faced a genuine supply shortage. The authorities now took more drastic steps. In Toronto, schools were closed. In the city of Guelph, people doubled up in homes. In Brantford, Ontario, women fought over scarce supplies outside the civic distribution centre. Here, some consumers were also charged with illegal hoarding (The Globe, 1918a). Such strategies reveal how some people had learnt to cope with shortages by storing and planning for worse to come. What had changed was the nature and severity of disruption. Ordering coal ahead for future consumption was lauded as a civic act in the summer of 1917 when there was still coal to go around. Six months later, when stock had run out and the price of coal was going through the roof, it was a criminal act of hoarding.

Serious coal shortages returned in the Second World War, in the winter of 1942–1943. The situation was marked by several of the same factors – Canada was dependent for two-thirds of its coal from south of the border as well as from the United Kingdom. The war, again, resulted in labour shortages in mines. Meanwhile, overall levels of coal consumption had risen to 43 million tons per year in 1943. On top of this, Canada suffered the most severe winter for half a century. As in the previous war, the government in the summer of 1942 urged consumers to plan ahead and take delivery of their winter coal in the summer, this time with help to pay for advance bulk purchases (House of Commons, 1943a).

Vulnerability was again highly regionalised. So was the potential for resilience. The situation was especially bad in Alberta, where the lack of labour had simultaneously meant a sharp fall in wood fuel. Shipping coal from Alberta to markets in Ontario was prohibited. In British Columbia, labour shortages similarly closed down the option of switching to alternative fuels for many households. The inhabitants of Vancouver instead took the axe to any piece of wood in and around their homes (House of Commons, 1943b).

These two coal shortages were separated by more than three decades but connected by a recurring debate about Canada's over-reliance on US coal and the threat this posed to national and provincial energy security as well as to national development. In Ontario, newspapers asked how in one generation thousands of potentially valuable acres of timber had been cleared, depriving the province of a vital substitute fuel (The Globe, 1918b). But it was especially hydropower from Canada's own waterways that caught the attention of politicians and the media in the 1920s–1930s (The Globe, 1921; 1933). Companies involved in producing hydropower had good reasons for wanting to increase the number of electrified households and thereby increase demand and revenue. The promise of greater energy autonomy and freedom from shortages of foreign coal certainly aided hydro's position in national politics and infrastructure development. As a Canadian newspaper already stressed in 1923: 'Every house wired for cooking saves Canada from importing two tons of coal – residential heating by electricity to make Canadians independent of American coal strikes and profiteers' (The Globe, 1923). 'White coal' was the political beneficiary of the shortages of 'black coal'.

Coal shortages reveal the dialectic between disruption and normality. By boosting new energy systems and infrastructures (hydropower), disruption helped bring about a new 'normality' that was premised on rising electrical dependency. Similar indirect effects can be observed in other national contexts. Coal shortages in Britain and the disruption of electrical and town gas supply in Germany during the Second World War made many households turn to new portable electrical heaters and other electrical appliances, as well as rediscovering wood fuel. In Britain, electricity consumption per person soared by 40% between 1939 and 1944. Such increased demand favoured an expansion of electric power generation and infrastructures after the war (Hannah, 1979; Trentmann, 2017). At the level of daily life, these transitions were rarely smooth or straightforward. In Canada in the 1920s, the initial hope was that hydro would enable households to cook and heat with electricity, thus reducing the coal burden (The Globe, 1933). In reality, Ontario still imported 98% of its coal from the United States in 1957 and efforts to reduce dependence through a substitution with hydro or oil were only partly successful (Snider, 1957). Coal was cheap and versatile, and many industries and households continued to rely on it as a supplementary fuel, especially when hydroelectric networks faced their own disruptions due to drought or infrastructure failure (The Globe, 1920).

Connecting the present to the past

The shift from coal to hydro-powered electricity did not only concern a substitution of one fuel for another. It was part of a larger transition from decentralised to centralised networks and from multiple fuel sources to single-fuel grids. What has been the effect of this shift for resilience, for the ability of people to cope with disruption and for the distribution of responsibility between infrastructures, collective bodies and individual consumers? Has centralisation increased or decreased the vulnerability to disruption?

Ice storms in twentieth century Canada, load shedding in Britain in the years after the Second World War and coal shortages in communist East Germany between the 1950s and 1980s provide a set of contrasting cases that let us observe recurring disruptions across time in association with network expansion. Severe ice storms are common in Canada and the 1959 ice storm was not the first to hit Toronto. But it was one of the first major storms after dependence on electricity had become the norm, prompting demands to move power wires underground to improve the city's resilience (The Globe and Mail, 1959; 1968). The expansion of the grid, moreover, meant that an ice storm would increasingly result in blackouts for rural as well as urban households. In 1969, for example, the ice storm that downed hydro lines caused a blackout for 10,000 families for up to five days in the rural municipality of Norfolk County, Ontario (Gilles, 1969). The recent conversions of these rural homes and farms to all-electric provision had introduced new levels of vulnerability: no power here also meant no water, since pumps were electric too. Some households had hung onto older technologies such as coal stoves or oil lamps, but found it hard to get the necessary fuel, as their supply and distribution networks had all but disappeared with the advance of electricity.

The record-breaking 1998 ice storm cut power for 1.4 million customers in Quebec and a further 230,000 customers in Ontario for up to 25 days. It illustrates how vulnerability continues to vary, depending on a region's particular trajectory of electrification (Bonikowsky, 2012). In Quebec, insurers found that the heavy historical investments in hydroelectric power in the province had created an over-dependency on electricity (Van Zyl, 2001). In 1996, electricity supplied 41% of all energy consumption needs in Quebec compared to a national average of 24%. The share of electricity for household consumption was even more pronounced at about 70%; the other 30% came from biomass, petroleum products and gas (Lecomte, Pang and Russell, 1998; Gouvernement du Québec, 2016). In eastern Ontario, just across the border, the ice storm also hit hard, but here disconnection times ended up being shorter and, significantly, it was reported that many people had back-up options when electric power failed. The 1998 ice storm not only toppled power lines, it also called into question the legacy of the socio-technical regime that had established the conditions for the monopolisation, nationalisation and over-centralisation of Quebec's power system. Power outages triggered a discussion about the decentralisation of grids and power structures as a means of ensuring future resilience.

Longer-term responses to the 1998 breakdown took a number of forms. One was at the level of infrastructures: Hydro-Québec made significant improvements to their electrical power grid in the hope of decreasing the likelihood of future lengthy power outages. Equally revealing, though, were changes in the fuel systems and practices of households and firms. Many Quebec homeowners and businesses, for example, purchased generators and non-electrical stoves and heaters (RMS, 2008). For them, resilience was no longer something to entrust to distant network managers, but a task to be taken into their own hands and homes. Disruption also intensified social cooperation and bonding (Trentmann, 2009). In the eastern Ontario town of Vankleek Hill, where residents at the outskirts were without power for three weeks, the local restaurant was fortunate enough to cook with gas and staff were able to feed local residents and the hydro crews working to restore power. The local hardware store was another vital hub where people could get hold of candles, kerosene and lamp oil. Others faced the ice storm of 1998 with a fair bit of learning and skill acquired during earlier disruptions. A householder in rural Ontario recalled how her family's move from the city to the countryside had necessitated learning all about 130-volt light bulbs, power surges and outages (Government of Canada, 2015). As a consequence, they had collectively learnt not to rely on a single source of energy. Timely household acquisitions prior to the ice storm included a woodstove and natural gas supply. What was a catastrophic nightmare for others, this family experienced as a mere inconvenience. The experience of disruptive events – both extreme and recurrent – involved social learning that shaped future expectations of service and capacities to respond.

Comparing the British with the Canadian experience is useful in revealing several differences, as well as parallels, in how people coped with recurrent energy shortages as networks and dependencies on them evolved. Although coal in Britain was not rationed and electric power stations received preferential treatment, by the winter of 1946–1947, it was necessary to restrict electricity consumption. In February 1947, industrial consumers in large parts of the country were prohibited from using electricity altogether and households were banned from using it between 9 a.m. and 12 p.m and 2–4 p.m. Britons coped fairly well with the disruption, mostly treating it as a manageable nuisance. Significantly, and in stark contrast with the later situation in Quebec, very few households were locked into all electric homes at this time. Most were therefore able to substitute their energy from a mix of gas, coal and electricity. In rural areas, some had wood-burning stoves and were able to get their fuel straight from the forest. Some shops dimmed or reduced their lighting. People also adapted by changing their temporal rhythms, getting up earlier to cook breakfast before the restrictions came into force or rearranging hoovering, washing and other household tasks that required energy (Shin and Trentmann, forthcoming).

A widespread criticism was the extension of existing restrictions on food and clothing (which were rationed) to sport, leisure and entertainment. In February, cinemas were no longer allowed to run their afternoon shows. Dog racing and mid-week sports events were prohibited entirely, with the partial exception of international cricket, which was considered too crucial for relations with the Commonwealth. The BBC had to reduce its programming from 23 hours to six and a half. In addition, households in restricted areas were urged to switch off their radios during specified hours. In general, housewives suffered most, since they were stuck at home and had to reschedule household tasks, in the cold and without entertainment. As one of many complained to a newspaper in March 1947, she was 'tied all day to the house, with a young child, no coal, not enough food'. At least she wanted to have 'music while she works' (Farmer, 2013: 31).

While the Labour government was acutely aware of the unpopularity of these measures, there was neither popular rebellion, nor a sense of crisis. Tellingly, the government relied on an 'honours' system without recourse to wholesale disconnection or heavy-handed controls. True, some people continued to turn on their cookers and radios regardless, but most households appeared to have respected the system. Many felt worn down and frustrated that wartime constraints and disruptions never seemed to end. At the same time, such wartime experience provided valuable lessons in how to absorb these temporary interferences and keep on living. There had already been twelve incidents of load shedding between 1944 and 1946 and they reached a formidable 267 in 1950–1951. By this time, the war and blackouts had prepared Britons to shift activities from one hour to another. The collective spirit of the Blitz was an important ingredient in this preparedness, but it was also helped by the consultative and democratic process through which energy shortages were mediated for households. Load shedding after the war continued the local organisation of fuel control established during the war. When coal, gas and electricity were nationalised in 1947–1948, consumers were represented on consultative councils. These favourable contexts protected domestic consumers from more serious and costly forms of intervention, such as peak pricing.

Resilience was distributed radically differently in socialist East Germany. Comparing this case with the British and Canadian experiences highlights the importance of politics in shaping the very nature and effects of disruption for people and practices. Energy shortages were a systemic challenge for East Germany, from its foundation in 1949 all the way into the 1970s. Partly they were the product of geography and history. East Germany was almost exclusively dependent on its own lignite or *Braunkohle*. Lignite, unfortunately, has a high water content, which created difficulties for mining and transport in freezing winters. But a lot of the shortages were also human-made political consequences produced on the demand side. In its first few years, East Germany had repeatedly targeted private households and rolled out power cuts during peak hours. The uprising of 17 June 1953, which almost toppled the regime, led to a radical change in approach. Households continued to receive patriotic calls to do their bit and save electricity, but the regime now thought it better to abstain from direct interference in the home. Instead, industry had to bear the brunt of shortages. Large industrial consumers were set electricity quotas for peak hours and pressed to introduce night shifts.

The reactions of industrial and private consumers during energy shortages reveal how the political context makes changes in practice more or less attractive. The response of industries was mixed. Some firms adapted their operating schedules or tried to save energy by switching off 'unnecessary' lights and whitewashing rooms to reflect light better. Many others ignored the quotas and preferred a fine to slowing down production. Reaching production quotas mattered more than exceeding an energy quota. This observation reminds us that each disruption is relative – not only in relation to normality, but in relation to other disruptions. For a socialist firm, the constant disruption in the arrival of raw or semi-manufactured materials necessary for their own production was a much bigger headache than repeated energy shortages – after all, calls to reduce consumption during peak hours could be ignored (at the risk of a fine), and the problem passed onto other users. The regime tried hard to lower the evening demand by shifting activities into night-time, but with limited success. In 1963, a spot check revealed that only a third of enterprises had been prepared to move working hours (Landesarchiv Berlin, 1963).

There was also little incentive for private consumers to change their lifestyle – although additional nightshifts had a big knock-on effect on women and children, not least for the hours of childcare. Household coal and electricity were cheap and, like housing itself, heavily subsidised by the regime, which treated them as a basic need. Activists put up posters in stairwells urging households to abstain from using irons, hoovers and heaters in the morning and evening hours, but few took any notice. Energy saving campaigns were themselves hampered by product shortages – low wattage 15 or 25 W light bulbs were much praised but almost impossible to obtain. The housing shortage exacerbated problems. One reason why portable electric cookers and heaters were so popular was that they enabled lodgers who were given a room in an apartment to cook in the privacy of their own room instead of running into conflict with the main tenants in what the latter considered 'their' kitchen. It was only in the early 1980s that the regime forced users to hand over electrical heaters and night-storage heaters unless they obtained a special license. That three quarters of the tens of thousands of applications for such licenses were granted gives a sense of how few East Germans were able to switch to substitute fuels.

Finally, there was lack of political understanding and collective will. In 1971, for example, there were plenty of East Germans who blamed that year's energy shortage on the regime itself and its lack of investment in coal mining and power stations. Lack of power was treated as symptomatic of the wider failure of socialism. Such sentiment did not bode well for energy savings campaigns. Young pioneers did set up warm chambers for freezing pensioners and the National Front did manage to entice a few households to cook for vulnerable neighbours, but overall such instances of activism had little long-lasting effect. The minute such campaigns were over, electricity consumption rose again. Unlike Britons, most East Germans did not see any reason for changing the normal rhythm of their day (Bundesarchiv Berlin, 1971).

Conclusion

Disruption and normality are inextricably connected in time. By feeding into each other, they help shape the relative resilience of infrastructures and practices. At first glance, disruptions may appear as departures from normal life, but once placed in their historical context, they emerge as part of it. Our examination of specific cases of disruption is meant as an invitation to others to deepen our understanding of the social interweaving of order and disorder over time.

The sociologist Vollmer (2013) has stressed that disruption is not something that can be externally defined. It demands an understanding of the social situation in which it takes place and micro-sociological attention to what precisely is disrupted and repaired. Our analysis of the 2006 drought shows how disruption was experienced in highly differentiated ways. For some it was an acute crisis, for others a minor irritation. Such micro-sociological observations of the here and now need to be complemented by temporal analyses of learning and memory across time. People's personal life histories interact with collective experiences to frame how a particular disruption is received, what counts as 'normal' and how people respond.

Sociological studies of disruption have tended to focus on interpersonal relations, social skills and social networks. These matter but not at the expense or to the exclusion of politics. Our analysis highlights the importance of politics in structuring how disruptions proceed and in defining what normality and disruption mean in the first place. People's responses to disruption have been framed by the politics of provision that govern services and material supply and distribution at a particular moment. These arrangements have changed over time, and the distribution of responsibility between providers and consumers and between infrastructures and practices has shifted with them. Nationalised systems are different from privatised ones. At the same time, recurrent disruptions can generate a political momentum across time that contributes to future expectations of what should be 'normal' and what kind of infrastructures and policies should be deployed in service of such visions. Disruption, in this sense, is often not a temporary blip but a political spur to action that mobilises arguments and interests for national policies and development. The generation of these new 'normal' arrangements, in turn, feed into the dynamics and experience of future disruption. A disruption emerges from social situations as a nexus of occasions in which activities and expectations are coordinated, but the force of the nexus and the type of coordination is a function of both history and politics.

Finally, what differences have networked infrastructures made to people's resilience and the responsiveness of daily practices at moments of disruption? Responsiveness to disruption varies in relation to past decisions about network development and the relative ease with which people can switch to substitute fuels and materials. Just as important, however, is social and technical learning over time. Disruption is usually defined in terms of a deficit of material resources. But human capacity matters, too. Coping with ice storms, fuel crises or food shortages involves skill, competence and ingenuity. These human resources can be rallied by calls for collective action, but they cannot be called into existence by them. They are partly built up (or depleted) by long-term processes of social learning (and forgetting). A high degree of dependence on centrally coordinated infrastructures can minimise but never entirely replace repair, maintenance and adaptation as ongoing processes in daily life. Modern networked societies have not been able to eliminate disruptions. What has changed is the delegation of repair and the distribution of responsibility and cost. As the future of centralised infrastructures is called into question by climate change and the need to bring basic services to poor and developing societies by less costly and less centralised means, there is a lot that can be learned from viewing disruption and normality as members of the same family rather than as enemies or opposites. Instead of treating disruption as a deficit to be overcome, it might be time to reclaim it as a moment that cultivates valuable knowledge and forms of adaptation that pave the way for the normalities of the future.

Acknowledgements

In addition to DEMAND, funded by EPSRC-ESRC (EP/K011723/1), the authors wish to acknowledge support from the AHRC for 'Material cultures of energy' (AH/K006088/1), and the ESRC for funding 'Drought and demand in 2006' (RES-0177-25-0001).

References

Andrew, C. D. (1976) *We Didn't Wait for the Rain.* London: National Water Council.
Bakker, K. (2000) 'Privatizing water, producing scarcity: the Yorkshire drought of 1995', *Economic Geography,* 76(1): 4–27.
Bakker, K. (2003) *An Uncooperative Commodity: privatizing water in England and Wales.* Oxford: Oxford University Press.
Bennett, J. (2005) 'The agency of assemblages and the North American blackout', *Public Culture,* 17(3) Fall: 445–466.
Blake, R. (2011) *Narrating a Nation: Canadian history post-confederation.* Toronto: McGraw-Hill Ryerson.
Bonikowsky, L. N. (2012) 'Ice Storm of 1998', *The Canadian Encyclopedia;* 11 August, Available at: www. thecanadianencyclopedia.ca/en/article/ice-storm-1998/ (Accessed 12.06.16).
Bundesarchiv Berlin (1971) DY 6/4990: Nationale Front, Informationsberichte Bezirk Suhl.
CRO Forum (2011) *Power Blackout Risks.* Amsterdam: CRO.
DEFRA (2006) 'Water supply in the long term', DEFRA News Release, 20 June.
Environment Agency (2006) *Early Drought Prospects for 2007.* Bristol: Environment Agency.
Farmer, R. (2013) 'All work and no play: British leisure culture and the 1947 fuel crisis', *Contemporary British History,* 27(1): 22–43.
Gilles, J. (1969) 'Norfolk blackout gives taste of life on the farm 50 years ago', *The Globe and Mail,* 4 January: 2.
Government of Canada (2015) 'Ice storm – ready in the country, get prepared'. Available at: www. getprepared.gc.ca/cnt/str/str001-en.aspx (Accessed 12.06.16).

Graham, S. and Thrift, N. (2007) 'Out of order', *Theory, Culture and Society*, 24(3): 1–25.

Gouvernement du Québec (2016) 'Energy in Québec: the 2030 energy policy'. Available at https://politiqueenergetique.gouv.qc.ca/wp-content/uploads/Energy-Policy-2030.pdf (Accessed 29.06.16).

Hannah, L. (1979) *Electricity Before Nationalisation*. Basingstoke: Macmillan.

House of Commons (1917a) 'Appointment of a fuel controller', 12th Parliament, 7th Session, Vol.3, Dominion of Canada, 12 June: p.2235–2236.

House of Commons (1917b) 'Address by Sir George Foster, Minister of Trade and Commerce', 12th Parliament, 7th Session, Vol.5, Dominion of Canada 22 August: p.4789.

House of Commons (1943a) 'Mr. Ilsley address', Dominion of Canada, 19th Parliament, 4th Session, Vol.1, 5 February: p.175.

House of Commons (1943b) 'Mr. Reid address', Dominion of Canada, 19th Parliament, 4th Session, Vol. 1, 4 February 1943: p.134.

(IEA) International Energy Agency (2005) *Saving Electricity in a Hurry*. Paris: OECD/IEA.

Kenward, A. and Raja, U. (2014) *Blackout*. Princeton, NJ: Climate Central.

Keshen, J. (1996) *Propaganda and Censorship During Canada's Great War*. Edmonton: University of Alberta.

Landesarchiv Berlin (1963) C Rep., 135-01, nr 253, Aktenvermerk, 14 Oct 1963.

Lecomte, E. L., Pang, A. W. and Russell, J. W. (1998) *Ice Storm '98*. ICLR Research Paper Series – No. 1. Toronto: ICLR.

Lovins, A. B and Lovins, L. H. (2001) *Brittle Power: Energy Strategy for National Security*. Andover, MA: Brick House (Second Edition).

Medd, W. and Chappells, H. (2008) 'Drought and demand in 2006. Final report'. Lancaster: Lancaster University.

Mehta, L. (ed.) (2010) *The Limits to Scarcity*. London: Routledge.

(NERC) North American Electric Reliability Council (2004) *Technical Analysis of the August 14, 2003, Blackout*. Princeton, NJ: NERC.

Pincetl, S. and Hogue, T. S. (2015) 'California's new normal? Recurring drought', *Local Environment*, 20(7): 850–854.

RMS (2008) 'The 1998 Ice Storm'. Online report. Available at: www.rms.com/resources/publications/natural-catastrophes (Accessed 30.06.15).

Shin, H. and Trentmann, F. (forthcoming) 'Living with energy shortages', in Albritton Jonsson, F. Brewer, J., Fromer, N. and Trentmann, F. (eds.) *Scales of Scarcity in the Modern World, 1800–2075*. London: Bloomsbury Press.

Skelton, C. (2015) 'Power failures far more common in remote parts of B.C.' *Vancouver Sun*, 22 August.

Snider, M. (1957) 'Fueling the future', *The Globe and Mail*, 16 March.

Statistics Canada (2007) *Canada Electricity Consumers, 1920–1975*. Ottawa: Statistics Canada.

Taylor, V. T., Chappells, H., Medd, W. and Trentmann, F. (2008) '"Drought is normal", the socio-technical evolution of drought and water demand in the UK, 1893–2006', *Historical Geography*, 35(3): 568–591.

Taylor, V. and Trentmann, F. (2011) 'Liquid politics: water and the politics of everyday life in the modern city', *Past and Present*, 211(1): 199–241.

The Globe and Mail (1918a) 'Had 1 1-2 tons ordered, quarter-ton delivered', 9 January: p.10.

The Globe and Mail (1918b) 'Standing timber at $60 to $200 dollars per acre', 2 January: p.25.

The Globe and Mail (1920) 'Manufacturers score hydro for storage', 20 April: p.9.

The Globe and Mail (1921) 'Cook by hydro, solve problem', 11 May: p.3.

The Globe and Mail (1923) 'Happy day coming when hydro will replace coal', 3 April: p.13.

The Globe and Mail (1933) 'Hydro heating', 9 January: p.4.

The Globe and Mail (1959) 'Our vulnerable cities', 30 December: p.6.

The Globe and Mail (1968) 'Hundreds of power lines down', 15 January: p.1.

Trentmann, F. (2009) 'Disruption is normal', in Shove, E., Trentmann, F. and Wilk, R. (eds.) *Time, Consumption, and Everyday Life*. Oxford: Berg. pp.67–84.

Trentmann, F. (2017) 'The lessons of war', in Berghoff, H., Logemann, J. and Römer, F. (eds.) *The Consumer on the Home Front*. Oxford: Oxford University Press. pp.331–356.

Van Zyl, S. (2001) 'The big chill: holding state monopolies accountable', *Canadian Underwriter*, 1 February. Available at: www.canadianunderwriter.ca/features/the-big-chill/ (Accessed 12.6.16).

Vollmer, H. (2013) *The Sociology of Disruption, Disaster and Social Change*. Cambridge: Cambridge University Press.

17

INFRASTRUCTURES IN PRACTICE

Implications for the future

Elizabeth Shove, Matt Watson and Frank Trentmann

The chapters in this book demonstrate that infrastructure-practice relations are more than material: they are shaped by the ambitions and actions of states, companies, citizens and consumers. Nor do they flow in one direction only, from supply to demand. Supply also depends on demand just as businesses depend on consumers and infrastructures depend on the practices of which they are a part.

Since resource consumption and carbon emissions are outcomes of these arrangements, it is important to establish whether infrastructure-practice relations might be steered in more sustainable directions, and if so, how. Although many existing infrastructures will be with us in the years ahead, Western countries have long term plans to decarbonise their energy supply and to promote technologies such as electric vehicles, heat pumps and district heating systems in order to meet carbon reduction targets.

We now review some of these strategies and the assumptions they make in the light of lessons and findings from our analyses of how infrastructures and practices co-evolve. We begin by commenting on climate change policies in Britain. These are guided by a dominant 'vision' in which future habits and practices are expected to be very much like those of today, but in which these 'needs' are met more sustainably thanks to the adoption of decarbonised technologies and systems of provision. In the United Kingdom's infrastructure development plan (H.M. Government Infrastructure and Projects Authority, 2016), the fifth carbon budget (Committee on Climate Change, 2015), a recent report on future-proofing the energy system (Strbac et al., 2016) or the Clean Growth Strategy (BEIS, 2017), the priority is typically to decarbonise the energy system and to do so without changing existing 'standards' of living.

Framed like this, the aim of meeting carbon reduction targets resolves into a largely technical problem of substituting carbon-rich fuel with lower-carbon or renewable alternatives. Attempts to shape future energy systems consequently depend on scenarios in which smart grids and meters, demand-side response, on- and off-shore wind, storage technologies, hydrogen, electric vehicles, solar power, district heating, heat pumps, carbon capture and storage, and so forth, figure prominently. Demand for energy is taken for granted and treated as if it had an existence of its own, independent of the means by which it is met. As a result the strong normative commitments involved in reproducing present standards of living are not visible, and there is no space for a discussion of alternative ways of life (Hui and Shove, 2013).

This is important because dominant discourses and related patterns of planning and investment influence the kinds of decarbonising strategies that are proposed and adopted. For example, the unwavering ambition of 'keeping the lights on' (all lights? at all times?) justifies a brute level of investment and the construction of networks and systemic interdependencies that hold certain practices and patterns of demand in place.

The goal of decarbonising society and enabling economic growth *without* substantially changing everyday practices significantly limits the list of potential options and interventions and slows down the speed at which carbon targets might be met. As Strbac and colleagues observe, '[i]f we are flexible towards our electricity consumption, much less infrastructure will be required allowing us to meet decarbonisation targets at a severely reduced cost' (2016: 16). For the time being, at least, there is no such flexibility.

The strategy of taking present forms of consumption for granted provides governments with a guide for future action. This, however, conveniently bypasses uncertainties about how society might evolve, and it side-steps contentious debates about the moral value of different ways of life. In effect, contemporary programmes of decarbonisation and efficiency presume that 'the pool of practices remain unchanged', even though this is rarely the case (Urry, 2016: 90). Such programmes also suppose that lower carbon technologies substitute for those they replace. Again this is often precisely not what happens. For example, while heat pumps are good for providing background heat they do not offer full-on, instant control of the kind associated with gas: at a minimum, their use implies a different thermal-temporal rhythm (Jalas, Rinkinen and Silvast, 2016). Likewise, electric vehicles do not match 'conventional' cars in absolutely all respects. At present the tendency is to play down these discrepancies, but this is not the only option. New infrastructures, technologies and systems of provision also enable new forms of everyday life.

In highlighting both the malleability and also the diversity of infrastructure practice-relations this book sets the scene for a more ambitious approach to carbon reduction. Given that the future will not be the same as the present, and given that practices and relations between them are inherently dynamic, there are opportunities for intervening not to reproduce existing conventions but to imagine and develop new ways of living and related infrastructures that are less resource intensive than those of today.

Rather than designing future systems to meet a contemporary 'template' of normality, there is scope to exploit the rich variety of processes and possibilities for change. These include the emergence of 'non-traditional' business models, the hollowing out of the grid and an array of coexisting systems of provision that range from the bundling of packages of energy to DIY forms of 'self' or community provisioning. As this book shows, different visions and versions of 'normal' always coexist: there is no single template to follow and no one model of consumption.

In examining disputed or at least unsettled junctions and interfaces: the meter, the plug, the roadside verge, the relation between the market control room and network management, and so forth, various chapters have examined processes through which such systems are shaped. Exactly how the plugging in of electric vehicles is resolved is at the same time a matter of resolving boundaries of rights and responsibilities between car makers and electricity providers. Such interfaces are indicative of perhaps momentary but nonetheless significant opportunities for reconfiguring entire systems of provision. Whilst some developments have to do with the insertion of 'new' devices (smart meters, new tariff structures), others arise from the conjunction of institutional and infrastructural legacies; Johnson's account of district heating in Belgrade is a telling example (see Chapter 9). The outcomes are uncertain but the general message is clear: the future is being made in innumerable moments and places, but perhaps most intensely at such junctions.

Of course, the future is not entirely open: it is not possible to re-imagine either infrastructures or conventions of daily life from scratch. Instead, efforts to configure and steer the future are in large part efforts to manage the rolling frontiers of adaptation and concern the repair and modification of existing infrastructures and practices. Many of the next century's infrastructures and related institutions, forms of social organisation, ideals, habits and routines are already in place. It is only through and from these existing arrangements that 'new' configurations will be made. That said, it is important to articulate the different visions and versions of 'normality' around which policies revolve and which they help construct. This is a critical task and one that should be as vital for those developing mega-cities in China, extending electrical power to villages in Laos, or justifying investment in new generation nuclear power plants such as Hinkley Point C in the United Kingdom.

In recognising that aspects of past, present and future coexist this book provides important insights into the manner in which successive versions of 'normal' are constituted through sequences of disruption and readjustment and across multiple sites and scales (see Chapter 16, Chappells and Trentmann). For instance, chapters have documented how different 'generations' of heating regimes and related habits persist in parallel, never truly supplanting each other but jointly constituting ranges of experience and expectation. Together they offer a subtle and graduated picture of change. Instead of recording linear progress towards 'modernity', we observe a patchwork of surprise and flux: visions of suburban life shifted with the arrival of the car; the internet has transformed shopping; the politics of heating change; wood makes a come-back as a fuel, and so forth.

On a global scale, the parameters of infrastructural provision have not settled down. There has been a growing need for networks of power and data that are 'always on' and the taken-for-granted goals of economic growth are woven in to policies and investment strategies at every scale. This is not in the least surprising: as we have noted, such arrangements have come to be defining features of 'modern' industrial societies. However, big infrastructure is not the only paradigm. There is evidence that some developing nations are moving directly towards smaller infrastructures and mini-grids and correspondingly to more varied patterns of consumption and demand. In 2014, the United Nations launched its 'decade of sustainable energy for all' (2014–2024). Its goal is to provide cheap and affordable access to energy for the poor. The consensus is that electricity cannot possibly reach the 1.3 billion of people who are currently without it via big electrical grids. It is equally clear that imperatives of public health and climate change make it impossible to follow the Western route of adopting coal-fired power stations. Instead, the focus has shifted to cleaner 'mini-grids'. Sustainable Energy For All cites an example from Bangladesh:

> where the Rahimafrooz Renewable Energy Ltd will install a hybrid mini-grid that includes a 80 kWp PV plant and a 40 kW diesel generator set on the Island of Muradpur: this mini-grid will benefit 310 households and 40 small producers.
>
> *(Sustainable Energy for All, 2015: 16)*

The developing world highlights many opportunities for such alternative types of infrastructures.

The conditions and challenges of the developed North are very different from those in the global South. However, debates about mini-grids and changing practices in poorer regions of the world are a reminder that it is possible to approach innovations in infrastructure and practice in conjunction. This book offers a conceptual toolkit with examples and lessons from the industrial West that remind us that here, too, arrangements have been flexible and have taken a variety of different forms.

Importantly, international programmes for sustainable energy recognise that future provision requires changes in consumption, as well as production. One of the UN's ambitions is that initiatives should

> create more incentives for a change in behaviour to manage and allocate resources in a more sustainable manner: activities … should promote sustainable energy production and consumption so that energy resources are used in a more equitable manner.
>
> *(United Nations, 2013: 21)*

In so far as infrastructures are deliberately constructed and to the extent that they make certain practices, forms of consumption and courses of action more likely than others, it is possible and in fact necessary to consider the scope for crafting combinations of infrastructures and practices that are much less resource-intensive than those with which we are familiar today (see Chapter 2, Coutard and Shove). Lopez' chapter (Chapter 6) reviews such efforts in the field of architecture. Other contributions, including those by Smits (Chapter 4) and by Rinkinen (Chapter 5) provide evidence of functioning social worlds organised around diverse forms of provisioning, consumption and practice. As these examples indicate, there is no shared or stable agreement about the meaning of progress, comfort or the good life. Indeed, utopian and dystopian visions are themselves outcomes and expressions of culturally and historically specific moments and practices (Urry, 2016). The fact that interpretations of well-being vary and change suggests that industrialised countries are not necessarily locked in to a one-way trajectory of escalating consumption.

Future lives will depend on certain combinations of devices/appliances, infrastructures and resources. It is not clear what these will be but it is entirely possible that some will include methods adopted in the past or in other parts of the world. Relevant examples might be wearing more insulation and wearing it close to the body (clothing), managing and living with more decentralised systems of provision (Vannini and Taggart, 2014) or shifting the timing of activity to match the supply of renewable power (wind, solar). Since strategies for coping with intermittent supply have been such an important feature of energy histories, it is entirely possible that they might figure again, in some new form, in the future.

The fact that infrastructural systems interconnect is a further source both of uncertainty and of opportunity for carbon reduction. For example, when levels of online shopping reach 80%, as they already do in some cities in China, the meaning of 'shop' and related patterns of urban land use shift, with a myriad of other consequences for transport, logistics, servicing and more. Something similar may be happening to the concept and the reality of office work. In this case, wireless connections, battery powered laptops and online data storage enable new forms of mobility, decoupling previously necessary physical links between the formal office infrastructure and the enactment of office work.

These examples illustrate the highly provisional character of seemingly 'fixed' infrastructures and the potential for radical reconfiguration in how they are organised and managed.

As mentioned by Coutard and Shove (Chapter 2), commercial interests might also lead to significantly new ways of conceptualising and selling 'energy' – in the form of light, heat or communication. And these might be bundled together in ways that set the scene for as yet unimagined forms of personal and collective de-synchronisation with on- and off-peak rhythms. Since future-oriented ideas and plans have real, if unpredictable, effects, it is important to consider which imaginaries shape 'future' thinking and to ask where future infrastructures are being envisaged, in what terms, and by whom.

Attempts to conceptualise the future are inevitably partial. They reflect and reproduce specific and often present-oriented preoccupations. For example, the conservative approach that characterises UK energy policy is in large to measure an outcome of the purposes and limits of the state. In the policy context, scenarios have to meet certain conditions: they need to be credible in the short term and they need to align with dominant ideologies and values, hence maintaining and not challenging processes that contribute to current market-oriented models of economic growth and social order. However, policy is not the only sphere in which scenarios are formulated or in which futures are constructed and represented. Different filters colour the more speculative worlds envisaged by product developers and science fiction writers. In between political pragmatism and utopian fiction, there is scope for generating multiple scenarios of future ways of living that are consistent with the limits, possibilities and affordances of the present and yet involve a radical reduction in carbon emissions. This is not an impossible task. As this book shows there are ways of making sense of the complex relations and politics at stake and ways of learning from past conjunctions of infrastructures and practices, and from those that exist elsewhere.

References

Chappells, H. and Trentmann, F. (2018) 'Disruption in and across time', in Shove, E. and Trentmann, F. (eds.) *Infrastructures in Practices: the dynamics of demand in networked societies.* London: Routledge.

Committee on Climate Change. (2015) 'The fifth carbon budget.' Available at: https://documents. theccc.org.uk/wp-content/uploads/2015/11/Committee-on-Climate-Change-Fifth-Carbon-Budget-Report.pdf (Accessed 14.02.18).

Coutard, O. and Shove, E. (2018) 'Infrastructures, practices and the dynamics of demand', in Shove, E. and Trentmann, F. (eds.) *Infrastructures in Practices: the dynamics of demand in networked societies.* London: Routledge.

Department of Business, Energy & Industrial Strategy. (2017) 'The clean growth strategy: leading the way to a low carbon future'. UK: BEIS. Available at: www.gov.uk/government/publications/clean-growth-strategy (Accessed 14.02.18).

H.M. Government Infrastructure and Projects Authority. (2016) 'National infrastructure delivery plan 2016–2021'. Available at: www.gov.uk/government/uploads/system/uploads/attachment_data/file/520086/2904569_nidp_deliveryplan.pdf (Accessed 14.02.18).

Hui, A. and Shove, E. (2013). 'All this talk about lights hides bigger energy challenges'. *The Conversation.* Available at: http://theconversation.com/all-this-talk-about-lights-hides-bigger-energy-challenges-1986 (Accessed 14.02.18).

Jalas, M., Rinkinen, J. and Silvast, A. (2016) 'The rhythms of infrastructure', *Anthropology Today*, 32(4): 17–20.

Johnson, C. (2018) 'District heating in Belgrade: the politics of provision', in Shove, E. and Trentmann, F. (eds.) *Infrastructures in Practices: the dynamics of demand in networked societies.* London: Routledge.

Lopez, F. (2018) 'Self-sufficiency in architectural and urban projects: towards small-pipe engineering', in Shove, E. and Trentmann, F. (eds.) *Infrastructures in Practices: the dynamics of demand in networked societies.* London: Routledge.

Rinkinen, J. (2018) 'Chopping, stacking and burning wood: Rhythms and variations across practice', in Shove, E. and Trentmann, F. (eds.) *Infrastructures in Practices: the dynamics of demand in networked societies.* London: Routledge.

Smits, M. (2018) 'Situating electrification: examples of infrastructure-practice dynamics from Thailand and Laos', in Shove, E. and Trentmann, F. (eds.) *Infrastructures in Practices: the dynamics of demand in networked societies.* London: Routledge.

Strbac, G., Konstantelos, I., Aunedi, M., Pollitt, M. and Green, R. (2016) 'Delivering future proof energy infrastructure'. Available at: www.gov.uk/government/uploads/system/uploads/attachment_data/file/507256/Future-proof_energy_infrastructure_Imp_Cam_Feb_2016.pdf (Accessed 22.9.16).

Sustainable Energy for All (2015), 'Clean energy mini-grids, annual report 2015'. Available at: www.se4all.org/sites/default/files/SE4All-HIO-CEMG-Annual-Report-2015-25-2-16.pdf (Accessed 22.09.16).

United Nations (2013) 'Decade of sustainable energy for all, report of the Secretary-General, sixty-eighth session', 6 Aug 2013'. Available at https://sustainabledevelopment.un.org/content/documents/2005 energysgrep.pdf (Accessed 22.09.16).

Urry, J. (2016). *What is the Future?* Cambridge: Polity Press.

Vannini, P. and Taggart, J. (2014). *Off the Grid: Re-assembling Domestic Life.* Routledge.

INDEX

Page numbers in **bold** denote tables, in *italic* denote figures